For Jeannie, Lynnit, Eileen and Helen.

THE RED DEVILS TRILOGY

The Red Devils Trilogy is comprised of *Red Devils, True Dare Kiss* and *Command or Promise*, three plays which can be read and enjoyed in isolation but which together offer a radical insight into the lives of four Manchester women. All the plays were premiered at the Liverpool Playhouse in 1983 and were then played in London: *Red Devils* at the Man in the Moon in 1984, and *True Dare Kiss* and *Command or Promise* at the National Theatre in 1985.

'Horsfield is reporting from the front line, where human nature is sharp in tooth and claw, where young people go rioting because it's a good night out, where shipyards close down and hairdressers open, and where small business is run on borrowed cash, plucky enterprise, and robbery with or without violence . . . the dialogue is a robust mixture of rough, go-getting romanticism and sardonic, whiplash northern humour: Horsfield's view of the world is unsentimental and streetwise.'   *Observer*

The photograph on the front cover is by Graham Fath.

THE RED DEVILS TRILOGY

Red Devils
True Dare Kiss
Command or Promise
by

DEBBIE HORSFIELD

A Methuen Paperback

A METHUEN PAPERBACK

This Trilogy first published in its entirety in Great Britain as a paperback original in the Methuen New Theatrescript series in 1986 by Methuen London Ltd, 11 New Fetter Lane, London EC4P 4EE and in the United States of America by Methuen Inc, 29 West 35th Street, New York, NY 10001.

Red Devils first published in 1984 by Methuen London Ltd, in *Plays by Women Volume Three*. Copyright © 1984, 1986 by Debbie Horsfield

True Dare Kiss and *Command or Promise* copyright © 1986 by Debbie Horsfield

Printed in Great Britain

British Library Cataloguing in Publication Data

Horsfield, Debbie
   Red devils trilogy. – (A Methuen new
   theatrescript)
   I. Title
   822'.914   PR6058.071/

   ISBN 0-413-41900-2

AUTHOR'S PREFACE

Red Devils was commissioned by Bill Morrison for the Liverpool Playhouse in 1982, subsequently submitted for, and awarded, a Thames Television Writer's Award, carrying with it a year's attachment to the Playhouse as Writer in Residence for 1983.

Following the final performances of *Red Devils* in May 1983, Bill Morrison floated the suggestion that Phil, Beth, Alice and Nita, on the threshold of adulthood, should not be consigned to oblivion in the backstreets of Manchester, but could each be the subject of four separate plays which would continue their lives up to the then present, 1983. Financial constraints inevitably intervened: four short plays became two longer plays, each half concentrating on one girl in the respective years from 1980 to 1983. As an added 'incentive', the plays were to commence rehearsal at the end of September, allowing the princely period of four and a half months in which to produce five hours of drama. For a companion-cum-supporter on this odyssey, I was assigned the Playhouse's new trainee director, Richard Brandon: my first works as a full-time professional writer were to be his first productions as a professional director. Bill Morrison is a great exponent of the 'in-at-the-deep-end' philosophy.

In retrospect it seems an act of near-lunacy to undertake such a mammoth enterprise in so short a period, but at the time we were obliged to call it 'daring'. Bill Morrison challenged us to take risks, experiment with form and content, above all to shrug off the temptation to re-cover old ground. It was always accepted that such risks might not pay off, but, in a spirit which owed more to naivity than fearlessness, the work commenced. *True Dare Kiss* had its first performance at the Playhouse on 19 October and *Command or Promise* followed on 17 November. Just.

Red Devils arrived in London in 1984, and *True Dare Kiss* and *Command or Promise* a year later in 1985 at the Cottesloe Theatre, to a response which was fairly indicative of the physical, cultural and social gulf between the north and south of England. In Liverpool the plays were a critical success, but broke no records at the box office. An oft-repeated response was 'Too close to home – too true for comfort'. In London, this was countered by shouts of 'improbable', 'far-fetched', 'I can't believe people like that still exist' on the one hand, and on the other a kind of reverent curiosity about the actual subject matter of the plays, coupled with the embracing of a writer who was 'determined' to take a strong stance' on Issues (with a capital 'I') like Inner City Unemployment, Poverty and Lack of Opportunity. In reality, neither assumption is accurate (though the first is the more easily repudiated). For the second, it was never my intention to turn Phil, Beth, Alice and Nita into political mouthpieces or agitprop caricatures. When Beth describes her experiences during the 1981 Moss Side riots, or Phil sums up her reasons for returning to Manchester in 1983, they are not mounting soap boxes, banging the table or making speeches. They are reporting and responding to what they see around them. If disillusion, despair and defeat (as well as the attendant loyalty, humour and tenacity) figure prominently in their stories, I am aware only of recording, without exaggeration, sentiment or sensationalism, what it was like for four young women growing up in the Manchester of the early 1980s. If the girls, as dramatic characters, are allowed simply to tell their own stories, the wider social and political implications arising from their narratives will make their own points, without the need for directorial underlining.

Note on Performance

Through my own involvement and experience of *The Red Devils Trilogy* in production, I have become aware of particular problems which arise from certain ambiguities in the way I have used dialogue to describe character, and my intentions regarding the roles those characters should have within the dramatic context of the plays.

In the latter stages of writing *True Dare Kiss* and *Command or Promise* (where Richard Brandon was instrumental in helping to define a clearer direction for both narrative and character) and during the rehearsal periods for all three plays, I worked in close conjunction with the directors (George Costigan for *Red Devils,* Richard Brandon for *True Dare Kiss* and *Command or Promise*). The decisions arrived at during those periods were therefore born out of fertile working relationships, and I took for granted that what (as a result of our close collaborations) seemed obvious to us, would inevitably seem so to others approaching the plays for the first time. I have since realised that this is not by any means the case, and I now succumb to the temptation of appending a Note on Performance in order to clarify my intentions regarding certain choices which must be made by anyone planning to stage the plays. Occasionally I have found it desirable to interpolate an additional stage direction, where the ambiguity of a line – if wrongly interpreted – could cause some strand of character or narrative to depart in an entirely inappropriate direction.

In his own Note on Performance for his play *Plenty,* David Hare urges the case for what he describes as a 'balance of sympathy' to be maintained in the actual playing of his characters (and in particular his central character Susan Traherne). I entirely endorse his views, and would go further, stating what must appear obvious (but which in practice is less so): for the trilogy to succeed dramatically it is imperative that the sympathies of an audience are engaged by *all* characters, however, superficially at least, there are indications to the contrary.

Of the four central characters it is Phil's which tends to create the most problems. In my experience it is not possible to resolve the apparent contradictions in her character and role unless it is taken as a fundamental premise that of the four girls she is the most naturally affectionate, the most passionate, has the strongest sense of humour and always acts with the best (if sometimes mistaken) intentions. If this is not established from the outset, it is possible for Phil to be played as an abrasive, charmless, self-opinionated young woman who alienates rather than engages – an interesting interpretation no doubt, but one which is ultimately fatal to a satisfactory resolution of the plays. The ending of *Red Devils,* the whole of Act Two of *Command or Promise,* and indeed the driving force and climax of the whole trilogy will count for nothing unless an audience can genuinely be made to care about what happens to Phil and the things she represents.

With the male characters there is an added complication: this is an oft-mistaken and damaging belief that a woman writing plays which contain powerful women characters must have a strong feminist axe to grind, and that consequently all her male characters are to be viewed (and played) unsympathetically. This is emphatically not my desire, and I cite two examples to illustrate my real intentions. The first is Kevin, a character who, if played without compassion, could be seen as little more than a loutish wife-beater. In fact he is as much a victim of circumstance and environment as Alice, but tragically, without the imagination, intelligence or outside support to cope with his inadequacies. The second is Nash, a character who can create even greater problems in the playing, and at worst, severely unbalance the central male/female relationship of the play. The fatal error here is to assume that Nash is in control simply because he appears to Phil to be in control. He will then seem patronising and complacent to an audience, when in fact what defines his character is his inner conflict between what he *wants* to say and what he will *allow* himself to say. Failure to recognise this distinction will result in a complete absence of emotional and physical tension, and the whole of his affair with Phil will degenerate into aimless banter and prolonged sparring.

I make particular mention of these three characters because they are the ones which seem to me to create the most difficulties and demand most generosity in the playing. But on the trilogy as a whole I would say that, whereas there is no drama without conflict, that conflict loses its power if one side is weighted with unfair advantage. There are no Heroes and Villains in the plays, only complex personalities.

Note on Staging

The trilogy was originally written for a small studio space, with a low budget which allowed for minimal settings and costume changes. It can be made to work equally well in a larger space, provided a fluidity of action is maintained, with set and costume changes being kept to a minimum. In many cases a lighting change will be sufficient to suggest a different location (which will in any case be made clear by the subsequent dialogue). I have dispensed with scene numberings, since these appear to encourage directors and actors to consider each scene as a seperate entity with a strictly defined beginning and end, instead of interlocking slices of dialogue and action. In some cases several 'scenes' or 'dialogues' are going on simultaneously, and it would be impracticable to distinguish numerically where one ends and another begins. As a general comment on the staging of these plays, the more complicated and fussy the design, the less fluent and engaging the narrative.

I am indebted to Bill Morrison and the Liverpool Playhouse for causing — indeed *forcing* — the trilogy to be written; to Richard Brandon, whose support and sense of perspective during the writing of *True Dare Kiss* and *Command or Promise* enabled a more or less coherent mass to be sifted out of chaos; and to my four sisters, who influenced and inspired many of the dramas here recounted.

RED DEVILS

Red Devils was first presented at the Liverpool Playhouse on 23 March 1983, with the following cast:

PHIL *(18)*   Anna Lindup
NITA *(18)*   Ishia Bennison
BETH *(18)*   Angela Catherall
ALICE *(18)*   Judy Holt

Directed by George Costigan
Designed by Charlotte Bird
Lighting by Steve Drummond
Sound by Richard Sharratt

The action of the play takes place in the Manchester area prior to Cup Final Saturday 1979, in and around Wembley Stadium on the day of the Final between Manchester United and Arsenal, and at a motorway services car park after the match.

Scene One

PHIL's *house*. BETH *is sizing up a huge Union Jack, taking various measurements and scribbling notes down on paper, ready for making a banner.* PHIL *reads the 'United Review' in silence.*

BETH: 'Joe Jordan lays on more balls than Britt Eckland.'

PHIL: No.

BETH: Why not?

PHIL: No.

BETH: 'Jesus Saves but Coppell puts in the rebounds.'

PHIL: Oh yeah, dead original –

BETH: Is it?

PHIL: Ten years old –

BETH: Yeah, well you think of something, then –

PHIL: Don't need one –

BETH: Yeah, we do need one –

PHIL: You carrying it, are yer?

BETH: All of us –

PHIL: Not me –

BETH: Yeah, the four of us.

PHIL: Three.

BETH: Miserable bitch.

PHIL: Better things to do than stood about waving flags.

BETH: Yeah, well don't come asking f'r'a lend when we start winnin' –

PHIL: Yeah, I come to see the match, Beth – not play semaphore with a bit of old curtain.

BETH: Be a work of art this. You wait.

PHIL: Obscene is art now, is it?

BETH: Balls is not obscene.

PHIL: Britt Eckland is.

BETH (*fussing with the banner again*): How about 'Bionic Reds Outshoot Gunners'?

PHIL: Shut up, Beth.

BETH: Look dead ace on the telly, this will –

PHIL (*jumping up suddenly*): Where is she?

BETH: She'll be here –

PHIL: What is she doing?

BETH: Well, maybe there's queues –

PHIL: 'Course there's bloody queues –

BETH: Dead long queues –

PHIL: Four o'clock this morning she was getting there. She should be at the front.

BETH: Yeah, I know, but . . .

PHIL: She should be back –

BETH: Well, give her a chance –

PHIL: She should be here – she's two hours late –

BETH: Sit down, Phil –

PHIL: I'm going –

BETH: What for?

PHIL: Get up, out – anything – go looking for her –

BETH: No, don't go . . .

PHIL: Jus' get some air –

BETH: Well, what if I see her?

PHIL: Jus' cop hold of the tickets –

BETH: Hey, Phil, jus' suppose we didn't . . .

PHIL: What?

BETH: Y'know . . . didn't . . . sort of . . . get anything . . .

PHIL: Get what?

BETH: Well . . . get . . . *anything* . . . like *tickets* . . .

PHIL: Beth –

BETH: I mean, we *will* get them . . . 'course we'll *get* them . . .

PHIL: Don't even *say* it, Beth –

BETH: No . . . right . . . I won't . . . I'm not – where y'going?

PHIL: Gonna phone her –

BETH: What for? – she won't be there –

PHIL: See where she is –

BETH: No, don't phone her –

PHIL: Why not?

BETH: She won't go straight home –

PHIL: Well, where is she, then? –

BETH: Will y'get us something? – bar of chocolate – down the off licence?

PHIL: If she turns up here . . .

BETH: Or nuts or something –

PHIL: Jus' get the tickets off her. Okay?

PHIL *goes out.* BETH *resumes banner preparations.*

BETH (*under her breath*): Gordon McQueen Eats Rix For Breakfast . . . '

NITA *comes in looking panic-stricken.*

Y'just missed her.

NITA: Was in the coal shed. Watching her go.

BETH: Coming back though –

NITA: What's she say?

BETH: Well . . . nothing . . .

NITA: Nothing?

BETH: Well, not exactly . . .

NITA: What?

BETH: Not exactly nothing –

NITA: What, then?

BETH: Well, not exactly anything –

NITA: Why not?

BETH: 'Cos I didn't tell her –

NITA: Y'didn't tell her –

BETH: I didn't dare –

NITA: Oh, Beth –

BETH: What could I say, Nita?

NITA: Y'told me y'would –

BETH: Yer dead, Nita – you are, honest –

NITA: Y'said you'd tell her –

BETH: Yeah, well, I didn't, did I?

NITA: What'm I gonna say to her? – what'm I supposed to . . ?

BETH: Just say, 'Oh by the way, Phil, y'know them tickets? – well there's just been this god-almighty jumbo-sized cock-up . . .'

NITA: Oh yeah, thanks a lot, Beth –

BETH: An' then kill yerself.

NITA: Where is she?

BETH: Now?

NITA: Where's she gone?

BETH: Phone you – You goin' after her?

NITA: I'll have to tell her –

BETH: Geez, Nita, an' the face on it –

NITA: What d'y'mean?

BETH: Launch you halfway up the M6 –

NITA: I in't even told her yet –

BETH: Nita, y'was late. Ten minutes overdue an' she's after knee-capping yer. Turning up late an' no tickets, she gonna wipe the walls with yer –

NITA (*looking through the window*): It's her. She's back –

BETH: Oh Christ –

NITA: Y'gotta tell her, Beth. I can't. Y'gotta tell her for me –

BETH: Saying what?

NITA: Just say . . . I don't know . . . say anything . . . say I got mugged –

BETH: Mugged?

NITA: Say I had them – an' I got robbed – an' stabbed – an' I'm in Hope Hospital dyin' –

BETH: Oh, Nita, can't you?

NITA: I daren't, Beth –

BETH: Neither do I –

NITA: Pernods – I'll give yer anything – just say . . . (*Trying to propel* BETH *towards the door.*)

PHIL *comes in.*

PHIL: Where y'been?

NITA: Phil, I bin . . .

PHIL: Where are they? – Gi's a look, then –

NITA: Phil, there's bin a sort of . . .

PHIL: Where are they, Nita?

NITA: I in't got them, Phil –

PHIL: You stop pissing about, Nita?

NITA: Phil, there *is* none. Something happened. I in't got them –

PHIL: You in't got them –

NITA: I slept in –

PHIL: Y'didn't go –

NITA: Yeah, I went – I did go – only so did half of Manchester an' all . . . so's when it gets to me . . .

BETH: There's fuck-all left on sale, is there?

PHIL: No, Nita –

NITA: I know what y'gonna say –

PHIL (to BETH): This is a joke, in't it? This is her kidding –

BETH: No, Phil –

PHIL: It's gotta be. Nita, you gotta be . . .

BETH: She's not –

PHIL: Nita –

NITA: Yeah, if I was kidding, I'd say, wouldn't I?

PHIL: I don't believe this –

NITA: Phil, 'cos what happened is . . .

BETH: Dozy get slept in –

NITA: What can I say, Phil?

PHIL: Slept in? Nita, you stupid, dozy, tit-brained . . .

NITA: I've said I'm sorry –

PHIL: Say it's a joke, Nita –

NITA: I couldn't help it. You ask me mum – it wasn't my fault – she never woke me –

BETH: I told yer she'd hit the roof –

PHIL: You knew about this, didn't yer?

NITA: I didn't do it on purpose –

PHIL: How could yer sleep through?

NITA: Alarm was off –

PHIL: What did you say? – to let you go, y'said. Do the market, Phil, she says. I'll go, she says. An' now what? –

NITA: I was in late – I had a job on –

PHIL: What about us? We woulda gone. I woulda gone. Sod the market. Midnight, woulda been there. Last night – twelve hours. You said you was going –

NITA: I thought I was –

PHIL: Nita, you bloody stupid get –

NITA: I don't know what happened –

PHIL: I do. I know what happened. Twenty thousand tickets on sale, ten o'clock this morning. You, meant to be there – four o'clock – waiting –

NITA: I had it all worked out –

PHIL: Make sure, we said. Get there early. Ten o'clock, queues halfway down the Mancunian Way. Where's Nita? –

NITA: I know what we said –

PHIL: Where's Nita? On her back, dreaming. Twenty thousand tickets, Nita – going, going, gone. An' what's the score with Nita? – absolute bloody nil.

BETH: Saved us a bit anyway – coach fare an' that . . .

PHIL: You? – don't you open your mouth neither. You didn't shout up, did yer? Didn't bother lettin' us in on the good news –

BETH: Oh yeah, an' get me teeth kicked in fer the sheer fun of it?

PHIL: I shoulda gone. I shoulda gone meself – let you lot go begging –

BETH: Yeah, well it's done now anyway –

PHIL: Y'what? –

BETH: Well, it is in't it? – fat lot of use moaning . . .

PHIL: Shut up, Beth – just shut up – Oh Christ, I could . . .

BETH: She only said she'd go as a favour . . .

PHIL: I don't believe this – this in't happening to me . . .

Enter ALICE.

ALICE: Hey, y'know what your Shameen's just said? –

NITA: Shut up, Alice –

ALICE: Oh it's not, is it?

PHIL (*pointing to* NITA): Ask her –

BETH: No, don't bother –

ALICE: Aw Nita, no . . .

NITA: Oh, don't you start an' all –

PHIL: Nice one, Nita –

ALICE: No, honest? I mean, straight?

BETH: Oh what d'you think, Al?

ALICE: Oh . . .

PHIL: Yeah. Right. Oh.

ALICE: Well . . . I dunno . . . y'know, p'raps we could . . .

PHIL: What?

ALICE: Y'know . . . like . . . ask round . . .

PHIL: *What*?

ALICE: Y'know . . . fer tickets. Ask round. See if there's any spares going . . .

PHIL: Ask round? Oh, great. Brilliant Al. Tesco's prob'ly got an offer on right now.

ALICE: Oh yeah, dead funny, Phil. I'm only saying . . .

PHIL: I don't wanna hear –

ALICE: Yeah, 'cos otherwise it means . . .

PHIL: Yeah, what?

ALICE: We can't go. Well, I mean, it does. Dun't it?

NITA: Yeah, well don't try an' make me feel like I just ran over someone's cat –

BETH: Your cock-up –

NITA: So y'needn't rub it in –

PHIL: Shut up, Nita –

NITA: I been saying sorry all morning –

PHIL: Shut it *now*, Nita –

NITA: There must be other ways of gettin' to Wembley –

PHIL: Oh yeah, there *is* other ways. None of which involve relying on you – an' all of which cost five times more than we can lay our mitts on.

NITA: Well, what we supposed to do, then – give up?

PHIL: Who says we're giving up?

NITA: Well are we?

PHIL: Okay, now listen –

BETH: We could get a few cans in . . .

PHIL: Said *listen*. Okay? Right. So think about it. First thing is, we stick an ad in the paper –

ALICE: An ad?

PHIL: In the *Evening News* –

ALICE: Oh, d'y'mean in Under a Fiver?

PHIL: *Under a fiver*?

BETH: Saying what?

PHIL: Saying we want tickets. What else, dickhead?

ALICE: How much'll that cost?

PHIL: Nita's paying –

NITA: Y'what? – Me?

PHIL: *You* are paying, Nita. All right?

NITA: Oh, ta very much.

PHIL: You arguing?

NITA: Yeah, okay – me – I'm paying. Right.

PHIL: Four tickets needed. An' the phone number . . . after six o'clock –

NITA: Whose number?

PHIL: Yours, Nita. That in every day –

BETH: How long?

PHIL: F'r as long as it takes. Right, get yer money out, Nita.

NITA: What money?

PHIL: Yeah, money, Nita – blue ones.

NITA (*reluctantly getting her purse out*): Yeah . . . well . . . how much d'y'want? . . .

PHIL: Gi's it here. Tenner – this'll do. Go on then –

NITA: Oh yeah, but that's from . . .

PHIL: What?

NITA: Me two perms – did last night –

PHIL: Tough.

NITA: All I made this week –

PHIL: Next time, wake up, Nita –

NITA: Saving up for new perm rods –

PHIL: Get yer old feller to cough up –

NITA: I can't –

PHIL: Oh yeah, not much –

BETH: So what d'y'reckon, then?

PHIL: Hey?

BETH: The chances?

PHIL: What chances?

BETH: Getting the tickets –

PHIL: There *is* no chances –

BETH: Y'what?

PHIL: We're getting them. Whatever.

NITA: Glad you're so sure –

PHIL: We're getting them. Else Nita is getting something. An' it won't be half as entertaining as a Cup Final.

ALICE: So we just carry on?

PHIL: So we plan it out, we book the coach – we just carry on –

BETH: As if nothing had happened –

ALICE: Yeah, well, nothing *has* happened – we didn't get tickets, did we?

PHIL: Yeah, but that makes no odds – we're going –

ALICE: Fingers crossed –

PHIL: No fingers crossed – nothing – we're going. We'll be there.

ALICE: Yeah, an' if we're not, we can always . . .

PHIL: An' if we're not, Nita will wish she got an alarm that worked – 'cos where she's going, they don't need alarms. Fair enough, Nita?

NITA: Yeah, thanks a lot, Phil –

BETH: Hey, I know – ace idea –

PHIL: What?

BETH: Brainwave –

PHIL: What is?

BETH (*holding up the banner*): 'Stevie Coppell Sells More Dummies Than Mothercare.'

Blackout.

Scene Two

NITA'*s house.* NITA *and* ALICE *are on all fours on the floor making a banner as the lights come up.*

NITA: What job?

ALICE: Yeah, there was.

NITA: Where?

ALICE: Seen it.

NITA: Go 'way.

ALICE: Last week.

NITA: I was in every day last week.

ALICE: Where was y'looking?

NITA: How much?

ALICE: Forty-two.

NITA: For what?

ALICE: Kitchens. Skivvying . . . I dunno – I couldn't get near the bloody counter –

NITA: Watch where y'sticking it –

ALICE: She won't like this, y'know – Phil . . .

NITA: Hard luck.

ALICE: I know what she'll say.

NITA: Let her say. Who's making it?

ALICE: She'll say it's a waste of time.

NITA: Y'shoulda asked.

ALICE: What?

NITA: About the job. Y'shoulda asked about it.

ALICE: Oh yeah, d'y'see the queue? Halfway round the . . .

NITA: Yeah, I seen the queue. There's always queues –

ALICE: Wouldn't fancy it anyway. Not scrubbing. Not on me hands an' knees.

NITA: Been talking to me dad.

ALICE: Oh yeah?

NITA: About money. About setting me up.

ALICE: Up where?

NITA: Me own shop. Hairdressing, y'know. Seen this little place round by here . . .

ALICE: Oh yeah?

NITA: He's thinking if he can afford it.

ALICE: He's raking it in.

NITA: People think that . . .

ALICE: What?

NITA: That doctors are raking it in. Well, they're not. They don't. Well, not all of them . . .

ALICE: No. Just your dad.

NITA: Anyway, he's thinking about it.

ALICE: All right fer you then, in't it? No point *you* hanging round Job Centre, is there? Nose stuck up against the windows. Looking at all the nice things inside.

NITA: Said y'wasn't fussed on getting a job –

ALICE: Oh yeah, I wasn't – till I met Kev. Till I sussed gettin' engaged.

NITA: Why, y'paying him, then, are yer?

ALICE: Yeah, it's steep though – gettin' engaged. Think it's all Babychams an' ruby clusters, don't yer –

NITA: No . . .

ALICE: Hen parties an' final flings? Yeah well, it's not. No way.

NITA: Oh . . .

ALICE: Ruby clusters cost, y'know. The earth. Well, depending if it's fake or real.

NITA: Yeah . . .

ALICE: I want real.

NITA: 'Course . . .

ALICE: No point getting engaged if all yer worth is fake. Know what I mean?

NITA: Oh yeah . . .

ALICE: Yeah, but guess how much. Go on, guess . . .

NITA: I can't –

ALICE: Hundred an' seventy-five quid.

NITA: Hundred an' seventy-five . . .

ALICE: Have to have it, though. Yer see it, y'set yer heart on it. Won't feel I'm engaged without. Not proper engaged.

NITA: Yeah, but Alice, think what y'could buy fer . . .

ALICE: Trouble is, he says *I* have to put towards it. Yeah, I don't think that's right, Nita. Should be the bloke buys the ring. Shouldn't have to put towards yerself, should yer? Dunno what sort of job I'm s'posed to get.

NITA: Shoulda listened more in class.

ALICE: Y'what?

NITA: Got CSEs.

ALICE: Don't need CSEs for what *I* want. Don't need certificates to have kids.

Don't need a degree to cook fish fingers.

NITA: Alice, there's more to living than frozen foods.

ALICE: Seen Phil breaking into the big time, then, is she? Eight 'O' Levels, what's she got? Saturday an' Sunday morning on the market, weighing out spuds. That's education.

NITA: That's just fer now.

ALICE: You an' all. Playing about with people's hair. Stick a bit of colour on, stuff a few rollers in – big deal.

NITA: An' I'm taking book-keeping. Do me own books. Run it all meself.

ALICE: Yeah, well, see me, two years time. Got me own house. Kev bringing in the money – couple of lovely kids – me knitting matinee coats . . .

NITA: If that's what yer after –

ALICE: Well, what else is there?

Enter PHIL *with a newspaper.*

PHIL: Seen it, then? Looks okay, dun't it?

NITA (*looking at the paper*): Four tickets . . . after six . . . telephone 707 . . . yeah, ace. That's us okay.

PHIL: Us an' about fifty others.

NITA (*looking down the column*): Oh God, yeah – there's millions of them . . .

PHIL: Yeah, well, we'll see . . .

ALICE: Tonight. They might ring tonight.

PHIL: Who?

ALICE: Somebody might.

PHIL: Where is she?

NITA: Beth?

PHIL: Meant to be here –

NITA: Said she'd be round. Feeling rough, she said. After last night.

PHIL: Oh yeah?

ALICE: Down the disco. Me an' her. Met these two lads –

PHIL: Never –

ALICE: Y'won't tell Kevin, will yer? –

PHIL: What lads?

ALICE: Beth had a fiver off her dad. Putting away a bit – doubles an' all –

PHIL: Getaway –

ALICE: Sick in the toilets – twice –

Enter BETH *looking fragile.*

BETH: Nobody mention Riccadonna – (*Nobody does.*)

Had this whole bottle of Riccadonna last night. God, I am never gonna look at that stuff again . . . I am never . . . oh God, me head's killing – I shoulda stopped in bed.

PHIL: You're supposed to be *here*. Somebody might phone.

BETH: Somebody might phone? – Somebody better bloody phone, after me getting dragged up half-dead at all hours of the day.

NITA: Six o'clock?

BETH: Well, there's sod-all else to get up for round here, is there?

PHIL: Well, are you stopping or what?

BETH (*taking her coat off*): Threw up over the peonies when I got in. Me dad's gonna go wild. He's training them for a show.

PHIL: He'll get first prize.

BETH *looks as if she's going to be sick.*

PHIL: Y'sure it's the Riccadonna?

BETH: No, don't!

ALICE: What d'y'mean?

PHIL (*tapping her head*): Use it, Al.

NITA: Y'don't see many pregnant Stretford Enders, do you?

ALICE: Oh . . . d'y'mean? . . . hey, y'not, are yer, Beth?

PHIL: Who is it this time?

BETH: Don't know.

PHIL: Should try doing the pools. Perm any one from twelve.

ALICE: You'll have to start goin' in the seats –

NITA: Hey, we could have a whip-round among the likely suspects an' buy her a season ticket –

PHIL: Yeah, if the likely suspects clubbed together we could buy a new centre forward –

BETH: Get lost, Phil –

PHIL: So what if it's not the Riccadonna? So what then?

BETH: How should I know?

PHIL: Hadn't yer better start?

BETH: Y'never give it much thought, do you?

PHIL: Well, no – *you* don't –

BETH: Never think it's gonna happen, do you? Like getting run over by a bus. Y'always think it happens to someone else.

PHIL: Except if y'walk in the road all the time, y'stand a good chance of getting knocked over.

BETH: Pardon?

PHIL: Never mind.

NITA: So where d'y'get to last night? You was seen . . .

BETH: What d'y'mean?

NITA: Edging off with Gaz Jones –

BETH: Oh ta for that, Al – why don't you broadcast it next time?

NITA: Our Shameen saw you an' all –

BETH: Yeah, well actually it's got nothing to do with you lot –

PHIL: Y'mean you can't remember what happened –

BETH: I mean I prefer not to discuss my private concerns –

PHIL: Private? – that's a good one. Everyone else knows what y'was up to –

BETH: Oh, I bet they don't –

PHIL: Down behind the multi-storey, next to the trolley check-out –

BETH: Your mouth, Al –

PHIL: Not just Al – we could hear yer the other side of Salford –

NITA: So in other words –

PHIL: She scored.

NITA: Y'make her sound like Joe Jordan.

PHIL: Joe Jordan? Hey, I wish he could keep up with her. That's what I'd call a decent striker.

BETH: Calling me a slag?

PHIL: Did I say slag?

BETH: Is that what y'calling me?

PHIL: Is that what I said?

BETH: Oh yeah, well, nobody says nothing about *you*, do they? You an' Ged Stewart.

PHIL: What's me an' Ged Stewart?

BETH: Yeah, well, we all know about that little episode, don't we?

PHIL: Oh, do we?

BETH: Oh yeah, well it's obvious, in't it. Y'*must've* –

PHIL: Pardon?

BETH: No messing, Phil. Y'*must*. Y'was going together three weeks.

PHIL: So?

BETH: So, he has anyone within three days.

PHIL: Y'mean *you* lasted three days –

BETH: Three an' a half.

PHIL: Oh, beg yer pardon – is this a record?

BETH: Hey, tell yer though – it's not up to much, is it? I mean, it's not as good . . .

PHIL: What?

BETH: As they say.

NITA: As who says?

BETH: Oh, y'know, people say, don't they – an' magazines an' that – say it's a beautiful experience –

NITA: Who says?

BETH: But it's not.

PHIL: What y'been reading, Beth?

BETH: Yeah well, strictly speaking, of course, it's all meant to be all furry duvets an' candlelights – Demis Roussos givin' it hell on the stereo. I know that. I'm not daft. I don't expect the works. I'm not asking fer Barry Manilow.

NITA (*to* PHIL): What is she talkin' about?

BETH: But on the other hand, if yer stuck on the front-room sofa with half the springs poking through yer backside – his gran next door taking her teeth out an' liable to burst in any minute with a fresh brew . . . well it's not the same, is it? It's not yer love-is-a-many-splendoured-thing set-up, is it?

PHIL: Ged Stewart's front-room sofa? No, I wouldn't've said so.

BETH: Yeah, well – so yer 'magical moments' is all out the window, in't it?

NITA: Magical moments?

PHIL: Magical what?

BETH: Oh yeah, was yours 'magical' then? Was yours all 'beautiful'?

PHIL: Was what?

BETH: You know . . . the first . . .

PHIL: Oh yeah, fantastic.

BETH: No, I mean, straight . . .

PHIL: Amazing.

BETH: Oh, come on, Phil – I'm only asking yer –

PHIL: What's it to do with you?

BETH: Yeah, she's right, y'know – Janice Blake is – y'never know with you –

PHIL: Janice Blake says what?

BETH: Well, that's what she says. She says – 'Phil's dead cocky, in't he?' – like she knows it all. But I wouldn't be surprised if she never had' –

PHIL: Y'what?

BETH: In fact she said – 'I wouldn't be surprised if she was a bit . . . '

NITA: What's she talking about? –

BETH: Well, y'know what it's like – people say things, an' y'start thinking . . . I dunno . . .

PHIL: Who says? – who says what?

BETH: Y'know, 'cos people starting to say yer never have . . .

PHIL: Oh, I don't believe it. Great, Beth. Y'don't go round like a slag, y'get accused of still being a virgin. Brilliant.

BETH: Hey, no – hang on – *I* never said – *I* wouldn't go spreading things like that, would I?

PHIL: Yeah, well, stuff the lot of them –

NITA: Except fer Stevie Coppell.

BETH: That Garry Yates fancies you –

PHIL: Great.

BETH: You like him an' all, don't yer?

PHIL: Oh yeah, Beth – is this joke time or what?

ALICE: Yeah, go on Phil – I seen you an' him – eyeing each other –

BETH: Love at first sight –

PHIL: Guess what Beth – Love is not having to have your name blasted across his windscreen in blue psychedelic tape –

ALICE: Bet you'd go with him. If he asked yer. Bet yer would.

PHIL: Oh yeah, I would –

BETH: Dead right –

PHIL: If I really fancied getting brained by a pair of giant furry dice, yeah.

ALICE: I've been in his car. Dead smart it is. 'Cept he forgot to take Sharon's name off the windscreen when they finished. Felt a bit of a dick, sat there, looking like I was someone else.

BETH: Great car, though –

PHIL: Bloody deathtrap. Y'could suffocate in all that tiger-fur. Should make it an endorsable offence, having a red furry dashboard.

BETH: One of these days, lads is gonna stop asking you into their motors altogether.

PHIL: Oh my God – no, really . . . ?

BETH: You hang on to it much longer, no one's gonna want to know –

PHIL: Yeah, tragic –

BETH: Yeah, well, y'should have fun while y're young – I think.

PHIL: Yeah, the maternity wards is stacks of fun, Beth – it's one big laugh.

BETH: Don't ask for your advice, Phil. Don't need it.

PHIL: Good. Don't ask. Don't care.

ALICE: Hey, what if they don't phone? What if no one phones? What if there is no tickets?

PHIL: What if you kept it shut, Al? What if y'give us a chance to hear the phone if it does ring?

ALICE (offended, to NITA): Y'coming to town, Sat'day morning?

NITA: What y'getting?

ALICE: Looking at rings –

NITA: Might do –

BETH: Yeah, well don't ask her — (meaning PHIL)

ALICE: Why not?

BETH: Working, in't she? Gotta work, dun't she?

PHIL: Should be bloody glad you don't need to –

BETH: Sick of hearing you moaning about it –

PHIL: Got no choice, do I?

BETH: Pack it in – if it's so terrible –

PHIL: Goin' a bit dense, are you?

BETH: Yeah, well, if y'need the money –

PHIL: If I need the money? – oh yeah, well, it comes in, y'know, Beth. Bit extra, y'know – helps out – stops me goin' begging to me dad to keep me in Pernods –

BETH: If it's that bad, leave it –

PHIL: Hey, our house in't like your house, y'know. We don't get paid to keep out the way like you do.

BETH: Yeah, I make it worth his while, don't I? Keep out when he's got his posh-get mates round. Don't show him up. Worth a fiver any time.

PHIL: Could do without all the crap, Sat'day mornings. Do without all the ear-ache.

NITA: Yeah, Sat'day mornings, get yerself all geared up fer the game. One-track-minds –

PHIL: Right, 'cos yer thinking . . . two points today or forget the title. Half the team's got groin strains or ears missing. Y'tryna weigh up the odds an' some burk's screaming at you for two ton of King Edwards an' a packet of dried peas. Piggot's winking at me, tryna get me to flog marmalade oranges half-price before they go off. Yer up to yer eyes in onion skins an' bits of rotting cabbage. An' all the time y'thinking, is it worth it fer the bloody fiver yer come out with? Skin off yer hands, five quid an' a bag of bruised plums. That what y'get 'O' Level maths for?

BETH: An' you're all set to fork out fifty quid to watch a football match? – want yer head testing –

PHIL: Y'what?

BETH: So short of money, give up the Reds –

PHIL: Give up the Reds?

BETH: If it's that desperate –

PHIL: It's not –

BETH: Well, then –

The phone rings. They all freeze.

ALICE: It's the phone . . .

PHIL: Here y'are – get it – *get it* –

BETH: *You* get it –

NITA: Go on, will you?

BETH: What'm I gonna say?

PHIL: What d'y'mean *say*?

BETH: Oh God . . . what shall I . . . ?

NITA: Go on . . . someone . . . one of yer . . .

PHIL: Oh, fer Christ's sake –

NITA: Just say . . .

PHIL: Here – gi's the bloody thing –

She picks up the phone. Takes a deep breath.

Hello? . . . hello? . . . yes. Yeah, that's right. What? Nita? . . .

NITA: *Me?*

PHIL: Yeah? . . . who wants her? . . . *Who* . . . (*To* NITA:) Nita, it's someone wanting a cut and blow an' green bloody highlights . . .

NITA: What?

PHIL: Just get hold of it, will yer?

NITA picks up the phone.

NITA: Hello? . . . yes. Oh yeah, fine . . . yeah, great. Seven o'clock. Fine, yeah . . . ta very much . . . yeah . . . ta-ra then . . . (*NITA puts the phone down. She looks shame-faced.*) Yeah . . . it was someone wanting . . .

PHIL: Yeah, we heard.

NITA: Well, *I* couldn't help it, could I?

PHIL: Coulda been someone tryna get through while you was on there. Coulda been stacks of offers missed while you're gassing on about cut-and-blow-jobs. Coulda been . . .

The phone rings again. They all make a grab for it. PHIL *gets to it.*

Hello? . . . Yeah . . . yeah, s'right. Yeah, yeah . . . four. That's it . . . er . . . yeah . . . er . . . fine. Okay, yeah. Right – Old Pack Horse – Irlam Street . . . what? – nine? – yeah, okay . . . got it. Green. Green chevette. Great . . . yeah . . . great . . .

She puts the phone down.

NITA: That was enlightening –

PHIL: That was him –

ALICE: That was who?

NITA: How much?

PHIL: Not cheap.

NITA: What's 'not cheap'?

PHIL: Thirty –

BETH: Quid?

ALICE: Each?

BETH: Jesus –

PHIL: Well, what d'y'expect? – s'a Cup Final, in't it?

NITA: It's okay –

PHIL: Yeah, think about it, Nita – thirty quid –

NITA: Worth it.

PHIL: Is it? Better be. Thanks to you we're shelling out this much –

NITA: I've said I was sorry . . .

PHIL: Yeah, well . . . let's get shifted, shall we? Let's go and round up the pennies. We gotta be there by nine.

ALICE: Where?

PHIL: Y'deaf, are you? Old Pack Horse – didn't y'hear me say?

NITA: All of us?

PHIL: Yeah, all of us –

BETH: Yeah, in case there's any . . .

NITA: What?

BETH: Any . . . y'know . . . aggro –

NITA: What aggro?

PHIL: We're all going –

NITA: Yeah, all right then – only I was gonna . . .

PHIL: What?

NITA: Mix up some green tint . . . yeah, but I got a seven o'clock –

PHIL: Don't try it, Nita, hey? – just don't – all right?

Blackout.

Scene Three

The car park of the Old Pack Horse. PHIL, BETH, NITA *and* ALICE *are waiting around – they look as if they have been there for some time.*

ALICE: Whose idea's this anyway?

BETH: He might've come early.

ALICE: Well, he might, but he's not – has he?

NITA: Five minutes.

BETH: What?

NITA: Got five minutes. Till he's due.

PHIL: He'll be here.

BETH: He better be.

PHIL: He said nine.

BETH: Yeah. Well, then . . .

Pause.

P'raps he meant the Hare and Hounds . . .

Pause.

I mean, have y'thought?

PHIL: What?

BETH: Yeah well, just think – what dicks we're gonna look . . . if he meant the Hare and Hounds . . .

PHIL: He said the Old Pack Horse.

BETH: Yeah . . . but just suppose . . .

PHIL: Shut up, Beth.

Pause.

ALICE: Hey . . . look . . .

PHIL: What?

ALICE: Look who it is –

PHIL: Where?

ALICE: Stood over there –

BETH (*diving for cover*): Oh Christ –

NITA: What is it?

BETH: Get me out of it –

PHIL: Where y'going?

BETH: Kaz Johnson –

NITA: Is it?

PHIL: Who's he?

ALICE: Oh, y'know he's the one that . . .

BETH: Don't wanna see him – don't wanna be seen . . .

ALICE: Oh, he's got someone with him –

BETH: Oh God, this is just . . .

PHIL: What?

BETH: Dead embarrassing –

PHIL: Who is he?

BETH: Tryin' to avoid him all week –

ALICE: I think it's Maxine –

BETH: His dad, y'see –

PHIL: Pardon?

BETH: Last Friday – come in – without knocking –

PHIL: Come in where?

BETH: An' me an' him there on the settee –

PHIL: Whose dad?

ALICE: Jesus, what's he say?

BETH: He says to get some clothes on –

ALICE: Oh God, I woulda died . . .

BETH: Dirty old bugger, just stood there – smirk all down his face. Me, half-stark, groping about under the stereo, hunting for me tights –

ALICE: An' what's Kaz doing?

BETH: Kaz? He's doing nothing, is he? – puttin' his own house in order, not stirring a foot to help me get decent. Then he leaves us at the bus-stop – all stood there with ripped tights an' tits all over the place . . .

NITA: Yeah, I heard he was good like that –

BETH: Then halfway home – realise it's getting a bit draughty –

ALICE: Not another pair?

BETH: Left behind the cushions on the settee . . .

NITA: P'raps he's come to return them –

BETH: Honest, if I'm not dead pissed off with lads. I am. Tell yer, if Joe Jordan come here – now – begging me . . . I'd make him wait at least three minutes.

PHIL: Oh yeah, he's that short of something to do, in't he?

NITA: Hey, who's this?

PHIL: What, y'mean him?

NITA: What d'y'think?

ALICE: *He* looks like a spiv – he looks like a really mean bastard –

PHIL: Nita, that's Father Flaherty –

NITA: Is it?

PHIL: He's got a wooden leg –

NITA: Does that mean he can't be a tout?

PHIL: Cunning old bugger – where's he get his mitts on four Cup Final tickets?

BETH: Confession – that's his game – bet yer – some poor sod's penance – ten Hail Marys and four Cup Final tickets –

ALICE: He should be reported – he should have his frocks taken off –

PHIL: It's not him –

BETH: Why not?

PHIL: He's not coming here – he's away into the pub –

BETH: Bloody disgrace –

NITA: What if he dun't come – the man?

PHIL: You better hope he comes, Nita –

ALICE: Hey, here y'are –

BETH: Is it?

ALICE: Over there –

PHIL: Is that green, y'tit?

ALICE: Did he say green?

PHIL: He said green –

NITA: Chevette.

PHIL: Green Chevette.

ALICE: Oh –

PHIL: That's a Datsun.

ALICE: Oh, yeah . . .

NITA: It's a blue Datsun.

ALICE: Yeah. Right. Here . . . no . . .

BETH: Where?

ALICE: Gone past –

PHIL: He said nine.

NITA: Any minute then –

ALICE: What if he asks for more?

PHIL: He said thirty.

ALICE: But what if he asks?

PHIL: He won't.

ALICE: He might've got a better offer.

PHIL: How much y'got?

BETH: I'm not paying more than thirty –

PHIL: How much – give it here –

BETH: Hey, no chance –

PHIL: Beth –

BETH: This is to last me two weeks –

PHIL: Y'don't wanna go?

BETH: Thirty quid's a lot of money –

PHIL: The Final, Beth –

BETH: Yeah, I know, but . . .

PHIL: Yeah, but . . . what? Yeah, but it's the Final. If it costs fifty, hundred – y'gotta be there –

BETH: Me dad's got a fiver on Arsenal –

PHIL: He's what?

BETH: Old wanker –

NITA: Who's gonna give him the money?

BETH: What money?

NITA: To the bloke. When he gets here –

PHIL: Does it matter?

NITA: In case it's someone . . .

PHIL: Who?

NITA: That we know . . .

PHIL: Who's bothered?

NITA: 'Cos me dad, see – go mad if he knew what I was spending, getting to this game –

PHIL: You an 'all now?

NITA: He dun't understand –

PHIL: I'll give it him –

BETH: Hundred and twenty quid.

PHIL: Hundred and twenty. I'll give it him.

NITA: God, it *is* a . . .

PHIL: What?

NITA: Lot. Of money. Isn't it?

PHIL: Yeah, Nita. Would try not to mention money if I was you, Nita. On account of we might remember . . .

ALICE: Yeah, Nita – just think . . . know what this is from? – deposit on me ring, this is – been saving since Christmas.

PHIL: On account of just think, Nita – how we could be paying three quid face value – if it weren't for *you*, engineering the biggest cock-up this side of Malcolm Allison –

NITA: Gonna be dark soon anyway. Not gonna know *what* colour the bloody car is.

BETH: Know what we *could* do? – duff him up a bit –

PHIL: Duff *who* up a bit?

BETH: The bloke. Whoever he is. Sort of negotiate fer the tickets . . .

PHIL: Yeah, and find y'self negotiating the inside of Stretford Police Station?

BETH: Y'scared, are yer?

PHIL: What of?

BETH: Yer bloody are – aren't yer?

PHIL: Try acting yer age, Beth –

BETH: Oh yeah, we're not all soft, y'know – we're not all like you –

PHIL: What y'tryna prove, Beth – prove y'can hit hard? – prove y'can hurt – just like a bloke?

BETH: Yeah, why not? – they don't corner the market, y'know.

PHIL: Hey Beth, who's arguin' with yer? *I* believe in bein' equal. I think you're just as capable of making an arse of yerself as

any of them dick-heads who rip up trains an' rob old ladies –

BETH: Stuff it, Phil –

PHIL: Yeah, I do. In fact, I'm quite prepared to swear on Matt Busby's big toe that I think Beth is a real dick, an' if she continues to make such astonishin' progress she could soon find herself supporting Stockport County.

BETH: Oh yeah, like to see *you* carrying a knife around with yer –

NITA: Oh God, not the knife again –

BETH: Yeah well, think on – (*She pats her inside pocket.*)

ALICE: Yeah, but yer never use it, do yer? –

BETH: Do me for carrying offensive weapons then, wouldn't they?

ALICE: You *do* carry them –

BETH: Yeah, but I don't use them –

NITA: Dun't matter if y'*use* them – y'still get done for carrying them.

BETH: Well, that's a bloody cheat.

PHIL: Soft get –

BETH: Might as well use them if y'gonna get done fer carrying them –

NITA: Well, at the Final . . .

BETH: At the Final – oh Christ, they've bloody had it – just let them bloody try it . . . 'We Are The Stretford Enders' . . . (*She starts to dance around waving her scarf.*)

PHIL: At the Final – listen, you – at the Final y'bloody watch y'self, right?

BETH: What?

PHIL: Cup Final, right? No messing, okay? No way I'm paying thirty quid to view the inside of a police cell, right? So you wanna start – you see it through. On yer own, okay? Don't come wingeing to me. I'm not gonna be there.

NITA: Me neither.

BETH: Hey, I got two feet, y'know. Got two fists. I can look after meself.

PHIL: Good.

BETH: Don't need your help.

PHIL: Glad to hear it. Pleased for yer. Three of us here witness to that.

BETH: 'Course, if there's any real bother –

PHIL: No –

BETH: Any trouble –

PHIL: Nothing, Beth. Keep it shut, okay?

BETH: That's assuming we get there –

PHIL: Shut up –

BETH: That's if we ever *get* to Wembley –

PHIL: Y'never learn, do yer? – y'never listen –

BETH: Could end up watching it in our front room –

NITA: Was you born dense, Beth – or did y'just pick it up as y'went along?

BETH: Just being realistic – about the chances –

PHIL: What would y'give for *your* chances, Beth? Against the three of us, here?

ALICE: Here y'are. This is it . . .

PHIL: Where?

ALICE: Green Chevette –

NITA: Christ, yeah it is –

PHIL: Right – that's it – gi's the money –

BETH: All of it?

PHIL: Gi's the money –

She collects the money – she steps forward.

BETH: Try an' look hard, Phil – y'll get ripped off if he thinks yer a girl . . .

Blackout.

Scene Four

Cup Final morning. Downstairs at NITA's *house.* PHIL *and* NITA *sit waiting.* PHIL *suddenly jumps up and starts pacing about.*

PHIL: Eight o'clock, Nita. We said eight.

NITA: Yeah, an' he was called out, wasn't he? If y'called out, y'have to go.

PHIL: Don't you have clocks in your house, Nita? Don't you have alarms?

NITA: He's allowed, isn't he? – some rest?

PHIL: No way, Nita. Not Cup Final morning, he in't. Not with us here – all sat an' waiting since seven o'clock.

NITA: Half the night he's been up –

PHIL: That's what he's paid for –

NITA: What if he drops dead at the wheel? – of exhaustion. What if he carves up a lamp-post?

PHIL: Imagine he's called out now. Imagine there's people, now at their last gasp – waiting on your dad condescending to drop in. He'd *have* to get up then, wouldn't he? – he'd *have* to stir hisself.

NITA: Not just been sat on his backside all night, y'know –

PHIL: What then? – you'll have me crying in a minute –

NITA: Every Friday night, Phil, someone drops dead –

PHIL: Pardon?

NITA: Three o'clock, in the car, gets there, not dead at all. Dead drunk more like. Someone's idea of a good time. What about his idea of a good time? Not dragged up at three in the morning, treating heart attacks that end up as indigestion. So now he's ten minutes late taking us to get the coach. So what?

PHIL: He better bloody move it –

NITA: Coach dun't leave till nine o'clock. Takes ten minutes getting there.

PHIL: We wanna get good seats, don't we? – we don't wanna get shoved off somewhere naff –

NITA: Phil, we're queuing for a coach – not the bloody Cup Final –

PHIL: Enough kip to last him till Christmas –

NITA: Phil, yer bloody pathetic sometimes, you are –

PHIL: Well, if he dun't shift hisself, I'm out an' catching the bus –

NITA: Alice isn't done yet, is she –

PHIL: Yeah, an' where's she playing about?

NITA: Upstairs. Ironing her jeans.

PHIL: Oh God, Nita –

NITA: She got new jeans, just for the Final – an' now she's putting creases in them –

PHIL: She always gotta look like she just stepped out the front window of Top Shop, dun't she?

NITA: Yeah, *and* the face –

PHIL: She's not getting her eyes on –

NITA: The works – red mascara –

PHIL: Oh God, Nita – don't let on she's with us –

Enter BETH.

BETH: We all ready then?

NITA: Since seven o'clock.

PHIL: What's all this lot? (*Pointing to bags* BETH *is carrying.*)

BETH: It's provisions.

PHIL: What? –

BETH: Y'know, scran –

PHIL: What for?

BETH: In case we get bit peckish –

PHIL: Peckish? – what y'talking about? – telling me yer even gonna *think* about eating today?

BETH: I can always think about eating –

PHIL: I don't believe it. I couldn't eat a crumb. Inside here feels like being on Belle Vue Big Dipper. (*She points to her stomach.*)

BETH: Me mum made these f'r'us. I nearly died. She must have another feller. She gets dead generous when she's feeling guilty.

PHIL: Or maybe she just sobered up –

BETH: Nah, no chance. Took her six port an' lemons to start de-frosting the dinner last night. Then *I* get stick fer smelling of half a cider.

PHIL: Yeah, Beth, but throwing up on the dahlias –

BETH: Peonies –

PHIL: Not a nice gesture –

BETH: Should stop breeding flowers, shouldn't he? – else plant them well away from the front gate –

Enter ALICE *hardly able to move in skin-tight jeans.*

NITA: Very nice, Alice –

PHIL: This what the fuss is all about? –

ALICE: I hope I'm not gonna be doing too much bending –

PHIL: Where's the creases?

BETH: Why d'y'have to buy jeans a size too small, Al?

ALICE: D'y'think they look daft?

PHIL: They will with a great split up the backside.

ALICE: It's to incent me to slim.

PHIL: Get yer jaws wired up.

ALICE: Can't see meself being dead active with these on.

NITA: You'll have to stay stood up all the way to Wembley.

PHIL: Are we right, then?

ALICE: D'y'think y'could pass us that bag . . . I don't wanna move about too much . . . (PHIL *hands bag to her.*) Just let me get this sorted . . . (*She gets out a small radio.*)

PHIL: What's that for?

ALICE: It's for the match, in't it?

PHIL: The match? –

ALICE: What d'y'think it's for?

PHIL: Yeah . . . I had this idea we was *going* to the match –

ALICE: Yeah – but so I know what's going on.

PHIL: What d'y'think these are for? (*Indicates eyes.*)

ALICE: Oh, watching it, yeah – but *I* mean, knowing what it's all about.

PHIL: What it's all about?

ALICE: The significance. Y'know, like appreciate –

BETH: The what?

ALICE: Yeah, like Shakespeare — like modern art –

PHIL: What is?

ALICE: Understanding –

PHIL: Alice –

ALICE: No, 'cos y'there, right? – goin' cross-eyed lookin' at it – an' it's all wiggly lines, in't it? It's all funny words an' things that don't rhyme till someone comes an' *explains* it all to yer –

NITA: Explaining what?

ALICE: 'Cos what *I* reckon is – this dun't come cheap, right? Just forked out thirty quid a ticket. Well, I'm not paying thirty quid a ticket an' not understand what sort of Final it is.

PHIL: What sort of Finals is there?

ALICE: Just watching it, don't get much idea, do yer? Y'need Bob Wilson to analyse it for yer. He knows what to look for. Y'*need* him 'cos he tells yer if it's good or not –

PHIL: If you think I'm stood up there with that thing racketing on . . .

ALICE: An' Kevin'll want to know all about it –

PHIL: Why, dun't he believe Bob Wilson?

ALICE: No, from *my* point of view –

PHIL: You don't *have* a point of view –

ALICE: Not that Kevin's much into football. He prob'ly won't even watch the match. He'll be at karate –

PHIL: Rippin' up phone books –

ALICE: Oh no, they don't do that yet. That's fer advanced. He done an A–Z last week, though –

PHIL: He's practising backhanders for when y'get married –

ALICE: Hey, y'know, I hope we win today –

PHIL: Never. *Do* yer?

ALICE: Yeah, 'cos this might be the last one there'll be –

NITA: Great supporter *you* are – great faith in them –

ALICE: For *me*, I mean.

PHIL: Copping out, are yer?

ALICE: Yeah, but when me an' Kev's married, he won't want me to keep coming.

PHIL: Tell him to sod off.

ALICE: Yeah, but y'can't, can yer?

PHIL: Y'bloody can.

ALICE: I'll have other things to do then.

NITA: Like what?

ALICE: I dunno. Sat'days there's lots to do when y'married. Shopping, an' tidying. Cleaning up –

PHIL: Sounds a barrel of fun –

ALICE: Shifting the furniture round – stuff like that –

NITA: Alice, getting married doesn't mean acting like an old woman –

ALICE: What d'y'mean?

NITA: There's other things going besides polishing furniture an' peeling spuds –

ALICE: What y'talking about?

PHIL: She's talking about not turning into a *bore* –

ALICE: *I* don't think it's boring – I *like* peeling potatoes –

PHIL: She means not letting y'world close in on you –

ALICE: Pardon?

PHIL: She means still being able to *choose* –

ALICE: I don't know what y'talking about. I *choose* to get married –

NITA: But being married doesn't have to *change* anything –

ALICE: Oh *I* think it does. I think it changes lots. It means y'don't have to bother sticking make-up on every time he comes round. It means daring to be seen in face packs an' wearing slippers. It means y'can relax.

PHIL: Let y'self go.

ALICE: Not have to put on a parade.

PHIL: Act like a tramp.

ALICE: Oh yeah, Phil – I don't see anyone rushing to get engaged to *you* –

PHIL: I don't see a stack of lads I'd exactly like to get engaged to –

ALICE: Yeah, well y'can't spend the rest of yer life drooling round after Stevie Coppell –

PHIL: Yeah, well – not seen anyone else comes close yet –

ALICE: Should try going after something y'can get hold of – 'stead of something miles out of reach –

PHIL: Not interested in something to get hold of, Al. Not interested in jerks y'can pick up on any street corner –

ALICE: Y'should be so lucky –

PHIL: Yeah, pick up a lot in this dead end dump –

ALICE: Dead end dump, yeah – what's wrong with it?

PHIL: Depends what yer after –

ALICE: Got big ideas all of a sudden, have yer?

NITA: Yeah, what's wrong with that?

ALICE: Big ideas, yeah. Where's it get yer? Same place, Nita. Same place as the rest of us. They don't have special dole queues for people with big ideas.

PHIL: Not aiming to make a career out of bein' on the dole, Al –

ALICE: Oh, listen to her – get a few good marks, few right answers. Think yer something special now, don't yer? Bloody secretarial college –

PHIL: Yeah, Al – bloody learning to make a living an' not banking on some poor bastard bloke to give me housekeeping –

ALICE: Training to be a typist – big deal –

PHIL: Secretary –

NITA: What's the difference?

PHIL: Don't you start –

NITA: Dogsbody –

PHIL: We've had all this before, Nita –

NITA: Yeah, Phil – fifty words a minute, eternal tea-maker – paint yer nails, file the odd letter – Big deal.

PHIL: Big deal. So what? S'a job, in't it? S'a career. Better than stuck at home washing baby's nappies.

NITA: Career? Oh yeah – career in getting nowhere. Training to be a what, Phil? Somebody's toe-rag?

ALICE: Yeah, right. Only difference is, *you* get paid for it.

PHIL: Nita, you know as well as I do . . .

NITA: What you sat exams for, Phil? – end up being dictated to? – Most highest qualified dish-washer?

BETH: Good career, being a secretary – me dad says – says *his* secretary got herself a dead cushy number – got all the perks –

NITA: Yeah, I bet –

PHIL: I can't go to college –

NITA: Why not?

PHIL: Because I can't –

NITA: Scared –

PHIL: No –

NITA: What then?

PHIL: What for?

NITA: Get out. Do something decent. Not some pissing little shorthand school where they teach you to dress like prison wardens an' not answer back. Come top in three languages just so you can lick envelopes –

PHIL: Come top here, yeah – out there, where am I? Get to college an' find out I'm the only thick-head on the course –

NITA: You might, yeah –

PHIL: Right, then –

NITA: Chance y'gotta take –

PHIL: No chance –

NITA: Oh no, 'cos that's not what you want, is it, Phil? 'Cos basically yer just mouth, Phil. Y'shout about it, but deep down yer play safe. Yer a bloody coward, you are, Phil –

PHIL: Oh yeah, you reckon?

NITA: Yeah, I *do* reckon, Phil. I reckon you're all mouth an' nothin' else. Saving it all for Sat'day afternoons an' the rest of the week can go stuff itself, right?

PHIL: Dead easy for you, Nita. Bloody talk's cheap. Landed nicely in it, you. All set up, daddy with the readies. Don't talk to me about copping out. You sat on yer backside all yer life an' let it come to you.

NITA: Yeah, well it won't come to *you*, Phil – so bloody get up off yer arse an' get after it –

PHIL: I'm going, Nita. I'm going to tech' – learning to type letters –

NITA: Get yer head seen to sometime, Phil –

BETH: Hey, are we going or what?

PHIL: We're waiting, aren't we? Till the man of leisure gets hisself stirred up –

BETH: Or are we gonna be stood about screaming all morning?

NITA (*to* PHIL): Yeah, an' don't bother listening to her fer advice. She's not gonna starve neither.

BETH: Hey, don't drag me in an' all –

NITA: Old feller's not short of money there neither – she won't be on the streets –

BETH: Who's on the streets?

The sound of a car horn from outside.

PHIL: 'Bout bloody time.

BETH: Are we taking all this stuff?

PHIL: Leave the radio –

NITA: Who's got the tickets?

ALICE: I want it –

PHIL: Leave it –

NITA: Ask Phil – she got more brains than Bob Wilson –

ALICE: Y'better tell me, Phil . . .

BETH *and* ALICE *go out.*

PHIL (*getting ready to go*): Don't start, Nita – 'cos I'm not going –

NITA: Cop-out –

PHIL: I know what I'm doing here, Nita. Know where I am.

NITA: Playing safe –

PHIL: Don't notice *you* going off training to be an engineer –

NITA: Don't have it up here, Phil. (*She points to her head.*) Don't have the right equipment.

PHIL: Just want a decent job, Nita – me own place – an' watching the Reds every Sat'day.

NITA: The Reds is not the end of the world, Phil.

PHIL: Well, *mine* it is, Nita –

NITA (*as they go out*): Yeah, well . . . bet yer Stevie Coppell dun't marry a typist . . .

Blackout.

Scene Five

Outside Wembley Stadium. PHIL *stands, as if looking down Wembley Way.*

PHIL: Oh, God, let me be here – please God, let me be here . . .

NITA (*running on*): Phil, is there a fire?

PHIL: Don't let me wake up –

NITA: You on speed or something?

PHIL: Oh God, jus' look at it Nita – jus' look . . .

NITA: Phil, will y'stand still –

PHIL: Say it's for real, Nita – tell me it's happening –

NITA (*hits her hard*): Y'feel that? –

PHIL: I'm awake – thank Christ fer that – (*She throws her arms round* NITA.)

NITA: Phil, will yer get off me scarf –

PHIL: Nita, I forgive . . . everything . . .

NITA: For what?

PHIL: For the thirty quid – for the cock-ups – it's nothing –

NITA: Oh yeah?

PHIL: Nita, y'could double it – three times it –

NITA: Could you repeat that?

PHIL: Anything, Nita – don't care –

NITA: See the result first –

PHIL: Don't let anyone wake me up –

NITA: Twenty to five, y'll be awake –

PHIL: Nita, we gonna piss on them, aren't we?

NITA: Exterminate –

PHIL: Yeah, like rats –

NITA: Brady first –

PHIL: Best day of my life this, Nita.

NITA: Better than Liverpool? – '77?

PHIL: Oh yeah, Liverpool was good – but not best – 'cos we weren't here for Liverpool. I had to sit squashed between me old Auntie Fanny who's out there shouting fer Bolton Wanderers . . . yeah, well, I couldn't get it through to her they weren't playing . . . her, an' that deaf old bugger from across the way who's too tight to rent his own telly. An' I didn't much feel like kissing *either* of them when we scored –

NITA: Brilliant game, that –

PHIL: Today, though – be better – be 3-1 today, no messing – nothing piddling – we want a big score –

NITA: Four at least –

PHIL: *Five* – too bloody moderate, you are –

NITA: Six then –

PHIL: Stevie get a hat-trick –

NITA: Brady sent off –

PHIL: Bob Wilson lynched –

NITA: But poor Alice –

PHIL: Best day of my life this . . .

The sound of fans chanting:

QUE SERA SERA
WHATEVER WILL BE WILL BE
WE'RE ALL GOING TO
    WEM-BER-LEE
QUE SERA SERA

PHIL *and* NITA *join in.*

PHIL (*top of her voice*): Yeah, an' the next – an' the year after – an' the year after . . .

NITA: I hope I'll still be here then –

PHIL: Why, where y'going?

NITA: I mean *there* . . . I mean, with the Reds –

PHIL: Why, what else is there?

NITA: Things happen –

PHIL: What things?

NITA: People stop coming –

PHIL: Part-time supporters –

NITA: Get older – get grown up –

PHIL: 'We'll support you evermore,' Nita –

NITA: Que sera sera –

PHIL: Yeah – evermore – whatever –

NITA: Some of us missing, come next Cup Final –

PHIL: Like Al, y'mean

NITA: Next season – you wait – Sat'day afternoons, out with his mother, sizing up

baby buggies an' spit roast ovens –

PHIL: Please herself. Dun't deserve it, anyway –

NITA: What?

PHIL: Coming here. She's bloody ignorant, Nita. She is, honest. Last week – y'won't believe this – can't even name '68 Cup Winning team. Forgets who Shay Brennan is –

NITA: No –

PHIL: Straight. Asks if Kiddo's playing. Can yer imagine – calls herself a supporter, can't even tell yer who got the goals.

NITA: I can believe it –

PHIL: Gormless get. I reckon she's a bit light up here . . .

NITA: Me dad reckons that –

PHIL: What, Alice?

NITA: 'Bout me. Calls us a bit tapped –

PHIL: Good of him –

NITA: For keep coming, he says –

PHIL: Watching the Reds? – that's common sense, that is? That's IQ miles above the average –

NITA: Sees me going out – all weathers – no money – blizzard, gales – earache, backache, frozen feet – calls it insanity. Says I want seeing to.

PHIL: Oh yeah, well it *is*, in't it –

NITA: What?

PHIL: Sometimes. 'Cos y'gotta admit, Nita – what's sane seeing them go down two nil to a bunch of 3rd Division wankers? – Midweek cup-ties, stood there, getting hammered – nails chewed off . . .

NITA: Sleet down yer neck –

PHIL: Some bastard's pissed in yer pocket – half time scores is up an' how's it happened? City's in front – the tea's got lumps in – some drunk's thrown up on yer foot . . .

NITA: An' there's you screaming down me ear – Nita, I'm not coming again –

PHIL: When did I ever . . .

NITA: Spurs game last season, yeah? – half time getting hammered – second half, out the tunnel, animated as a bunch of wet rags –

PHIL: Don't remember –

NITA: Yeah, an' you going, 'God, give us a goal – give us two an' I'll give up biting me nails – make it three an' I'll give 50p to the donkey sanctuary' –

PHIL: Oh yeah – I remember that – I remember saying about the donkeys. An' I says to you, didn't I, Nita, how the air's gone nippy – y'can see your breath in front of you – an' the floodlights, dead bright –

NITA: Frost on the rails –

PHIL: Hush on the terraces – getting restless –

NITA: Then that corner –

PHIL: Played short – an' the cross in from Macari –

NITA: It was McIlroy –

PHIL: Wham! In the net like a bloody 125 –

NITA: Second goal in – forty yards out –

PHIL: Five minutes to go an' no voice left. Me, kissing anything that moves – an' thinking . . . just one . . . just one more an' I promise I'll sponsor a whole knackers yard fer just one more goal – an' it's there, back of the net – an' there's me, dead in a heap at the foot of the terraces, going 'that's it, that's it' – ever an' ever – world without end –

NITA: Amen.

They both laugh.

PHIL (*after a pause*): So he's got a point, right – your dad –

NITA: Sort of –

PHIL: 'Cos what is it, Nita? – it's a game, right? It's twenty-two fellers hoofing a pig's bladder between two sticks. Okay, this is your old man talking now . . .

NITA: I've had it all before –

PHIL: 'Cos here's us, right – this is what he reckons – not dim, not stupid –

NITA: Quite rational, even –

PHIL: Yeah, quite rational, even. So what's rational about this, he says – what is the sanity of it? Okay, so y'tell him, Nita – so I'm rational, so what? Sod that.

Analysing it. Y'don't analyse. In't mental arithmetic, is it? Y'don't try an' make it add up.

NITA: What I told him. You're a doctor, I says. Should be able to find reasons for it. It's irrational, he says –

PHIL: Bloody disgrace that. Money spent on education – fortunes spent teaching your dad the right answers – doesn't understand football.

NITA: What I tell him – he's a great embarrassment to me, Phil – doesn't even know who Dave Sexton is –

PHIL: Hey, those two – what they playing at?

NITA: Al's probably sticking her face back on –

PHIL: Hey, Beth, y'know – she's asking fer trouble –

NITA: Why d'y'let her bring that bottle?

PHIL: Didn't know she had it, did I?

NITA: She had some cans an' all –

PHIL: Alice coulda said something –

NITA: Oh yeah, as if –

PHIL: She's half pissed already –

NITA: You better keep an eye on her –

PHIL: I'll bloody have her if she starts something – or if we have to carry her – or if she gets sick –

NITA: Dead cert – one of the three – bet yer she tries something –

PHIL: Yeah, she gonna feel the back of my hand if she does –

Enter BETH.

Speed on yer –

BETH: There's queues a mile long –

PHIL: Where is she?

BETH: Zip got stuck –

NITA: I don't believe it –

BETH: Ten minutes to get them peeled off f'r a piss – now can't get them up again –

NITA: We should leave her –

BETH: We can't leave her –

PHIL: She deserves leaving –

BETH: I said where we'd be –

PHIL: She better bloody move it.

BETH (*looking down Wembley Way*): How many, d'y'reckon?

PHIL: Who?

BETH: Come up from Manchester?

PHIL: I dunno . . . conservative estimate, I'd say . . . millions –

BETH: Wouldn't believe it, would yer? Getting this far.

PHIL: Me, I would. I said, didn't I? Third round tie, I said – get through this one, go all the way.

BETH: Don't see none of their lot. Where are they all? Too bloody scared, aren't they? Fuckin' petrified. Stretford End on the rampage – all run for cover.

PHIL: They'll be in already –

BETH: That's if they *got* any –

NITA: There's one . . . no, two . . . I do believe it's two –

BETH: Oh yeah – mebbe go down an' fettle them up a bit –

PHIL: Maybe you won't –

BETH: Kidding, Phil – *joke*, Phil –

PHIL: Killer, Beth –

BETH: Hey, what's the odds, then? – favourites?

PHIL: You askin' us, Beth – straight face?

BETH: Nah – don't need – got a winner either way –

PHIL: Pardon?

BETH: Fiver on Arsenal – so's if the Reds blow it, I won't be too disappointed –

PHIL: Beth, I'm touched –

BETH: What?

PHIL: Great faith y'got – great supporter –

BETH: Y'well, gotta cover y'self, don't yer?

PHIL: Backed a loser, Beth –

BETH: Oh yeah – but if Liam Brady . . .

PHIL: Stuff Brady –

BETH: Oh yeah, stuff him –

PHIL: Not gonna even *see* Brady –

BETH: Nah – Macari's all right – stuff him right out the game.

PHIL: Joe Jordan – I hope he bites the lot of them. I hope he has a feast –

BETH: Hey, d'y'think anyone's gonna . . .

PHIL: What?

BETH: Start. Y'know, *start* something –

PHIL: *Start* something?

BETH: Yeah, y'know . . . bit of . . .

PHIL: What?

BETH: Aggro –

PHIL: What?

BETH: Stick the boot in –

PHIL: *Aggro*?

BETH: Bit of . . . y'know . . . (*Shows fists.*) . . . well it's the Final, in't it? There's bound to be *somebody* . . .

PHIL: Don't you dare –

BETH: Y'know, 'cos everyone's gonna be . . . bit niggly an' that. Bit of needle. An' y'know what it's like – when we're on telly – get a bit of attention . . .

PHIL: Pardon?

BETH: Well, *somebody*'s bound to . . .

PHIL: Somebody might, yeah. That somebody best not be you, Beth. 'Cos this (*She grabs her round the neck and shoves her fist into* BETH's *mouth.*) will be clearing space between your front teeth, an' no help needed from visiting supporters. All right?

BETH: Yeah, well, if somebody hits me, I'm not just gonna be stood around –

PHIL: Who's gonna hit you?

BETH: Twenty thousand Arsenal fans out there –

PHIL: All of them profoundly *un*-interested in you –

BETH: Not just gonna be stood around, Phil –

PHIL: Depending on you getting hit, depending on who hits first, y'might just find yerself entitled to some assistance. But then again . . .

Enter ALICE, *hardly able to walk.*

PHIL: Thanks fer turning up, Alice –

ALICE: Zip was jammed –

PHIL: Twenty minutes you bin in there –

ALICE: I've had to put a pin in it . . .

PHIL: Let's just get in there, shall we?

NITA: Beth, you coming with us?

BETH: Who says I am?

NITA: Stay together –

BETH: Go off on me own, can't I?

NITA: Best if we don't split up –

BETH: Who's asking you? – want your guidance, I'll ask fer it, won't I? –

NITA: I'm only saying –

BETH: Don't start instructin' me, Nita – too handy at that sorta thing, you are –

PHIL: Leave her, Nita –

BETH: Don't need lookin' after –

NITA: Good –

PHIL: Let's get in there –

ALICE: Yeah, come on – I wanna see the doggies goin' through the hoops –

NITA: Get a drink first –

PHIL: *You* are?

NITA: Tea –

BETH: What a surprise –

NITA: Yeah, I'd rather know what's goin' on round me. Rather not be seein' *two* of everything –

PHIL: Specially not two of *her* –

BETH: Someone is gonna get their head kicked in this afternoon . . .

PHIL, NITA *and* ALICE *go out, followed by* BETH *trailing behind. The crowd sounds and chanting rise to a crescendo.*
Blackout.

Scene Six

Half-time – the back of the terraces. BETH *sits on the floor, head in hands.* ALICE *kneels beside her, dabbing at a gash in the back of her head with a scarf.*

BETH: An' who's Gary fuckin' Bailey anyway? – where's he dug up from? –

second goal coulda saved it meself, eyes shut – Sexton's out, that's a dead cert – he should be fuckin' shot –

ALICE: Say if it hurts –

BETH: An' Jordan's playin' like a geriatric – only slower –

ALICE: Hold still a minute –

BETH: Bloody crap – bloody disgrace it is –

ALICE: Will y'keep still –

BETH: Thirty quid pissed down the drain – thanks to that dozy bitch –

ALICE: It's quite deep, y'know –

BETH: Bloody starve before they get *me* there again – thirty quid to see a bunch of stiffs get ripped to rags –

ALICE: Should get it cleaned up really –

BETH: Bin more entertained queuing f'r a bus – an' them lot out there call themselves . . . Hey, watch where yer poking it –

ALICE: Prob'ly looks worse –

BETH: Than what?

ALICE: Worse than it is. Prob'ly just nicked it.

BETH: Oh, ta fer that consolation, Al. Where I'm sat, it dun't feel to me like just nicked. Feels like some bastard's took half me head away with him –

ALICE: Just a bit of a gash –

BETH: Want stitching?

ALICE: Doubt it – maybe just half a dozen . . .

BETH: Feels ripped up enough –

ALICE: Dead lucky, you was –

BETH: Blood all down me neck –

ALICE: Kid next to yer took a dart – through here. (*Points to head.*)

BETH: Bloody animals –

ALICE: Aimed fer you, bet yer –

BETH: Black bastard –

ALICE: Yeah, c'mon, you was spoiling for it –

BETH: They want locking up –

ALICE: Shoulda kept yer mouth out –

BETH: Stick 'em in cages –

ALICE: Still bleeding this, y'know –

BETH: Have her bloody neck –

ALICE: Oh yeah, an' that bunch of lads?

BETH: I'll have the lot of them –

ALICE: Y'want this seeing to –

BETH: Stick them in a gang – hard as nails. Get them on their own – shit scared. Bloody petrified. Hang around in packs, don't they –

ALICE: Y'shoulda kept out – not get involved –

BETH: Black bitch –

ALICE: You went f'r'it – you first –

BETH: Look on her face – fuckin' insolent –

ALICE: Shoulda bin watching the game –

BETH: Not looking at *me* like that – Bloody wogs –

ALICE: She's all right. Just leave it. Don't get involved –

BETH: Hey, don't *you* start – getting to sound like her – bloody Nita – I'll have her before the end of the day an' all –

ALICE: Nita's gone fer some tea for yer –

BETH: Big of her – see them two pissed off pretty sharp, didn't they? Somebody gets a bottle out, they dive fer cover –

ALICE: Watch yerself, maybe – second-half. Coppers getting edgy. Took out them lads along from us –

BETH: Not getting *me* out.

ALICE: Maybe should settle down a bit –

Enter PHIL.

PHIL: You stupid bitch.

BETH: Me? Oh yeah, I thought it'd be *me*. Don't mention *her*, will yer? – don't mention her that half split me head open.

PHIL: Stupid cow.

BETH: You ask her – go on, ask her – was it my fault, Al?

PHIL: You have to open yer mouth, don't yer? Bloody trap always on the go –

BETH: Y'don't ask who started it, do yer? don't bother asking that –

PHIL: Don't care who started it, Beth. Who bloody finished it? Who finished it with a spanner through her skull?

BETH: Y'shoulda seen *her* face, then.

PHIL: Yeah, yer proud of that, are yer? Chalked yerself up a couple of points?

BETH: 'Bout the only two points we *are* gonna chalk up today.

ALICE: If we hadn't stuck with them lads . . .

BETH: Oh yeah, well *you* was keen enough to get palled up with them –

ALICE: Yeah, an' don't no one breathe one word to Kevin –

PHIL: Stuff Kevin – I'm talking to this bitch here –

BETH: Yeah, well ta fer the sympathy.

PHIL: You got a bloody cheek –

BETH: I never said nothing –

PHIL: You never said nothing? – What she say, Al?

ALICE: She never said nothing – not till she got called . . .

PHIL: What? – what she get called?

ALICE: Fascist bitch –

PHIL: Who called her that?

BETH: Yeah, well, like to see *you* stood by an' get called things like that –

PHIL: You? – y'don't even know what it means –

BETH: Yeah, well I do, Phil – I do know an' I don't fuckin' care –

PHIL (*to* ALICE): What did she say?

ALICE: When?

PHIL: What did she say to her?

ALICE: To this girl?

BETH: Nothing.

PHIL: Nothing?

BETH: Nothing . . . only . . . where to stuff herself –

PHIL: Sounds more like it –

BETH: Yeah, I told her to piss off back to the jungle, if y'must know –

PHIL: That what you said?

BETH: Bloody wogs, yeah – all of them – fuckin' parasites –

PHIL: You stupid bitch –

BETH: Bloody animals they are. Seen this?

PHIL: That all you can say?

BETH: Need stitching, that will –

PHIL: Beth, y'bloody sick, you are –

BETH: Bloody sub-cultures –

PHIL: Pardon?

BETH: My dad was in South Africa. My dad says they live like pigs. Live in hovels –

PHIL: Yeah, Beth – that's all they're fuckin' given, in't it?

BETH: Act like pigs, he says –

PHIL: Treated like pigs –

BETH: Same over here now. Turn yer back ten seconds – knife between yer shoulder blades – streets not fit to walk out in –

PHIL: Just thank Christ you're pissed, Beth –

BETH: Who's pissed? – I've had half a bottle –

PHIL: Oh, who had the other half?

BETH: I don't get pissed on half a bottle –

PHIL: You're pathetic –

BETH: I started nothing. That one – she's the one started it –

PHIL: Yer a bloody liar. You started it. You were first. An' if Al had more gumption to her, she'd bloody admit it –

BETH: I was just stood there – wasn't I, Al? – watching the game . . .

PHIL: Stood there. Stirring it. 'Cos you was bored. 'Cos we was losing – 'cos you had nothing better to do –

BETH: Bored? – yeah, wouldn't *you* be? Bailey an' McQueen – wanna stick them in the ground an' drive a tank over them –

PHIL: Oh yeah, well, let's face it, Beth – you don't give two shits what goes on out on the field, do you? You come here to make an exhibition of yerself. To talk through yer arse an' give yer mouth a work-out –

BETH: Last time I'm paying to see this shit-heap –

PHIL: Tell yer this fer now – fer nothing – you keep it tight shut, second half. Else y'll be hearing the final whistle from the back of an ambulance –

BETH: Oh yeah, who's gonna put me there? – not you, f'r'a kick-off.

PHIL: I wouldn't chance it –

BETH: Oh yeah, don't make me laugh –

PHIL: Promise you, Beth – you keep it shut – else I'll knock you to the middle of next week an' back again.

Enter NITA *with tea.*

NITA: Got yer some tea –

BETH: Piss –

PHIL: Drink it.

BETH: Get off me –

NITA: C'mon, drink it –

BETH: Get away from me –

ALICE: Shall I get someone?

NITA: Ambulance?

PHIL: She's all right –

NITA: It's bleeding –

BETH: Mind yer own bloody business, you –

PHIL: She's pissed, that's all –

BETH: Not your charity, Nita –

NITA: Only offering, wasn't I?

BETH: Don't need favours from pakis –

PHIL *suddenly leaps up and smashes* BETH *in the face.*

NITA: What y'doing? – get off her –

PHIL: Bitch –

NITA: Phil, don't touch her –

BETH (*sitting up*): I'll have you fer that –

NITA: Just leave her, will you?

BETH: I'll bloody have you –

PHIL: Don't fuckin' talk to me –

PHIL *gets up and walks about.*

ALICE: Tea here, Beth –

BETH: Vodka –

ALICE: What?

BETH: Coat pocket – bottle stashed –

ALICE: Where?

BETH: Gi's it here –

NITA: Al, I don't think she should have any more . . .

BETH: You – don't you try it, Nita –

NITA: Y'tryna kill yerself?

BETH: Oh yeah, love that, wouldn't yer? – get in there, couldn't yer? – another job taken over –

ALICE: You haven't got a job . . .

BETH: Al, just get me cleaned up, will yer?

ALICE: Cleaned up? – what with?

BETH: Hankie – wet it – clean it up –

NITA: Should get her to First Aid –

ALICE: Give her her own way –

BETH: Jus' 'cos your dad's a bleedin' doctor – dun't give you the right to start prescribing *me* what I'm s'posed to be doing –

NITA (*to* ALICE): She's stupid –

BETH: Call me stupid once too often, you will. Not all got dads pinching a living, writing out pills, can't speak six words of English –

NITA (*ignoring her*): Go septic, that will – needs proper cleaning –

ALICE: I'll see to her –

NITA: Tetanus or something –

ALICE: Y'coming, Beth?

BETH (*being helped up*): Getting back in there –

ALICE: Get it seen to first –

BETH: Getting back. See them get hammered. Be some fun tonight. C'mon, what you gawping at now?

BETH *goes back into the ground.* ALICE *looks blank, then follows.*

NITA (*to* PHIL): You coming?

PHIL: Y'okay?

NITA: She's only pissed –

PHIL: Dun't make it okay, does it?

NITA: Two goals we gotta get now –

PHIL: No chance –

NITA: All we need. Two goals. Extra time, murder them –

PHIL: Y'never gonna see two goals out there –

NITA: Forty-five minutes yet –

PHIL: Play all night, they're never gonna score –

NITA: Two goals, Phil – easy –

PHIL: That's what I hate about you, Nita – yer such a fuckin' optimist . . .

They go out.
Blackout.

Scene Seven

On the terraces, as if at a crash barrier. Sound of the crowd shouting. PHIL *looks completely dejected,* ALICE *is looking bored and miles away,* NITA *eagerly watching every move on the field.* BETH *is fidgeting up and down, taking no notice of the game, trying to aggravate anyone who will notice her. No one does. She then tries to rile* NITA *by flicking cigarette ash on her.*

BETH: Oh, sorry 'bout that, Nita . . .

NITA: What?

BETH: Ash all over yer . . . (*Ferociously starts to flick ash off her coat.*)

NITA (*intent on the game*): S'okay . . .

BETH (*seeing no one is taking any notice*): I want me head testing. (*Pause.*) I do. I want me bloody head testing.

NITA: No one's arguing with yer.

BETH: I mean, what *is* all that? – must be short of something to do, stood here watching that. In't yer got no homework to do, Phil? In't yer got no dissecting of rats to be getting on with? Give yer a hand if yer like – better than stood here gettin' rigor mortis –

PHIL: Give it a rest, will yer?

BETH: Oh, look at that, will yer – Jesus Christ – could do better meself blindfold with one leg tied behind me back –

PHIL: Yeah well get out there then – could bloody use yer –

BETH: Is it a bird? Is it a plane? No, it's a Stevie Coppell shot at goal.

PHIL: Beth, I'll bloody leather you –

BETH: Hey, hey, steady on – this is getting daring – another twenty yards an' we could be out of our own half. Christ, in't it a shame the goal's not on the halfway line – we'd really be looking dangerous then, wouldn't we? – (*Pause. Everyone ignores her.*) Hey Phil, is that a shot or a cross?

PHIL: Shut up.

BETH: I'm only asking 'cos it didn't look like neither – but being as it was Stevie, I felt sure there must be some logical, strategical reason why he hoofed it twenty yards over the fuckin' crossbar.

PHIL: Okay, so he's having an off-day –

BETH: No. Is he? You'd never think it, would yer? Y'mean every time he goes fer goal an' it just skims the corner flag, it's all a big cock-up?

PHIL: You leave it out, Beth – three shots on target he's had today –

BETH: Shots on target? Is that what he's getting paid for? I thought it was to give the ball boys a bit of exercise.

PHIL: Yeah, okay – he's playing pretty naff.

BETH: Pretty naff . . .

PHIL: Shut up.

BETH: Yer a bit of a wizz at understatement, aren't yer, Phil. S'pose that comes of being more intelligenter than the rest of us, hey? With the benefit of her education she calls him pretty naff – when the rest of us poor mortals would call him absolutely fuckin' rubbish.

ALICE: Which is Brady?

BETH: Talk about pinching a living –

ALICE: Who's that number seven?

BETH: I don't know what the fuck I'm stood here for –

NITA: Makes two of us.

BETH: Beg yer pardon?

NITA: Two of us, I said.

BETH: Oh, don't you start an' all, madam –

PHIL: Watch the bloody game, will yer?

BETH (*to* NITA): Left up to me, wouldn't have you here – tell yer that fer nothing –

PHIL: Ignore her –

BETH: Tagging along with us, can't get shot of yer –

NITA: Not arguing with yer –

BETH: Dun't mean yer in, y'know. Wear the colours, fly the bleedin' flag – dun't

mean yer belong. You wanna start reminding yerself of a few things, Nita – few facts, maybe –

NITA: Like what, Beth?

BETH: Like I'm out of work, Nita –

NITA: Three of us out of work, Beth –

BETH: No jobs, Nita. So what's going, Nita? Watching the Reds. An' you have to come along an' cock that up an' all, don't yer?

NITA: What is up with you today, Beth?

BETH: Just you, Nita, start reminding yerself. Fact One, I in't got a job. Fact Two, there is no jobs. Fact Three, so how come you's all lined up with a job?

NITA: Beth . . .

BETH: Yeah, 'cos like, seven people in your family, Nita. That's seven people, no rights to be here – taking seven people's jobs an' seven people's homes that does have rights to be here –

NITA: What's 'rights to be here' when it's at home, Beth?

BETH: Belonging here.

NITA: Who decides that?

BETH: Brought up – lived here –

NITA: When?

BETH: Hundreds of years –

NITA: I was born here.

BETH: You in't lived here hundreds of years –

NITA: Not getting involved, Beth –

BETH: Tag along as much as y'want, Nita – dun't mean yer belong –

NITA: Y'wann see me passport? –

BETH: Pardon?

PHIL: British citizen, Beth – now watch the bloody game.

BETH: Oh yeah, so bloody clever, in't she? So bleedin' smug –

NITA (*to* PHIL): What's the matter with her?

PHIL: Pissed up an' pissed off. Ignore her.

BETH: Oh, so reasonable, Nita, in't she?

NITA: What?

BETH: Nita so fair, so bloody smart. Can't lay nothing on Nita, can't point the finger – always so nice –

NITA (*to* PHIL): What've I done?

PHIL: Nothing. She gets like this.

BETH: Knows what she's doing, dun't she? Got it all sussed. Bloody racial discrimination, that is.

NITA: Pardon?

BETH: Against whites –

NITA: What?

BETH: That's what it is. Look down on us 'cos we in't got rings through our noses, don't eat with our fingers . . .

PHIL: Oh, here y'are, this is a good one. This is the 'anti-whites-racists-bit' –

NITA: What is?

PHIL: Her dad, y'know – got a soft spot for this one. One of his favourite pieces –

NITA: Her dad?

PHIL: Hey, y'didn't think it was all *her*, did yer? Thought it all come from up there! (*She indicates* BETH's *head*.) I love this one, y'know. Professes to hate the bloke's guts. He's there, churning out all this crap – she's there, taking it all in, storing it up. What happens? – gets a few drinks inside her – out it all comes – passing it off as her own work. Don't you believe it, Nita – she in't got an original idea in her skull.

BETH: *She* knows what she's doing –

PHIL: What *is* she doing, Beth?

BETH: Undermining –

PHIL: Oh yeah?

BETH: Slow needle — quiet nag-nag-nagging away –

PHIL: Don't know what the hell you're on about –

BETH: *She* does. She bloody does, though. Pushing it – further an' further. Stood back, all wide eyes, innocent –

PHIL (*to* NITA, *deciding to ignore* BETH): Got any chewy left?

BETH: Setting people at each other's throats –

PHIL (*to* NITA): I am gonna bottle her in a minute –

BETH: That how they go about it in the jungle?

NITA: What is she talking about?

BETH: My best mate before you come along –

NITA: What?

BETH: Me an' her – just us two – then you come an' stick yer nose in –

PHIL: Don't be so bloody soft –

BETH: What's bloody soft? – notice you're not saying much, are yer?

PHIL: I'm tryna watch this, Beth, okay? – so will yer just put a fist in it, before I do it for yer?

BETH: Oh, watch the game, is it? Game, is it called? Not a lot of fun where I'm stood –

PHIL: How long, Nita?

NITA: Not sure. Ten minutes?

ALICE: 'Bout eight.

BETH: What a bunch of wankers –

PHIL: Christ, if you don't fuckin' shut up –

BETH: What? you'll fuckin' what? – yeah, go on then – go on . . .

PHIL: What you doing here? C'mon, what you here for? –

BETH: Christ knows –

PHIL: Does he? – he knows, does he? – I wish *I* did –

BETH: Bloody ask him, then –

PHIL: Stood next to you, Beth – five seasons, every week – heard the mouth on yer, seen you looking round, grinning like a dick – see who's watching yer, thinking yer bloody great –

BETH: I am bloody great –

PHIL: All mouth, arsing around with some kid's penknife in yer back pocket – great in a crowd, aren't yer – so fuckin' tough.

BETH: Scared the shit out of you enough times –

PHIL: Oh yeah? Get yer on yer own, then what? Bloody shaking, aren't yer? Couple of twelve-year-olds, shaved heads, Doc Martens – bloody petrified.

BETH: Fuckin' do you any time –

PHIL: I wouldn't try it.

BETH: Any time –

PHIL: Don't bank on it –

BETH: Hey Al, y'still awake – surprised you in't dropped off –

ALICE: Fat chance, you lot gobbing it like that –

BETH: See, Alice appreciates the finer points of the game – 'cos Al knows a thing or two about class, dun't she? – Riveting stuff, in't it, Al?

ALICE: Was thinking about what to do fer Kevin's mum an' dad when they come round next week –

BETH: There y'are – told yer –

ALICE: Was thinking about doin' a beef curry, but what's the point? – might as well give them a couple of quid an' send them down the Takeaway –

PHIL (*under her breath*): I don't believe this –

BETH: So who's Man of the Match, then, Al? – go on, nominate someone –

ALICE: I dunno . . . who's that number seven? –

BETH: Stevie? – are you kidding? –

ALICE: I mean theirs –

BETH: Not them, y'daft get – nominate us –

ALICE: Oh . . . I dunno . . . Sammy maybe . . .

BETH: Oh, is he still playing? – thought he'd retired years ago –

NITA: He's having a good game –

BETH: Oh is he? Good game? – made my day, that has, Nita.

NITA: He's doing all right –

BETH: Oh yeah, not exactly scintillating, is it? – I mean, to be honest, can't see I'm gonna be cherishing any part of this little balls-up in years to come.

PHIL: Shouldn't get so pissed then, should yer? Might enjoy yerself a bit then.

BETH: Wanna be paralytic to enjoy that spectacle – need to be arseholed –

PHIL: I wouldn't worry, Beth – got some battle scars, don't you? Plenty of laughs showing them off when we get home –

BETH: Should try it some time –

PHIL: Fighting's not my idea of laughs –

BETH: Yeah, what *is* your idea of laughs, Phil?

PHIL: Bit over your head, Beth –

BETH: Bit over my head? Yeah, all of three inches over my head to be exact, Phil. That, out there? – five foot eight nothing? – that's your lot, is it?

PHIL: Better than what *you're* knocking off every week –

BETH: Bit old for that, aren't yer? Bit old for crushes, wall papered in pictures of something y'can't get hold of. Y'wanna try pulling yer own lads, Phil.

PHIL: Not interested.

BETH: Well, bloody get interested – 'cos no way you're ever gonna be on the receiving end of anything *he's* giving away –

PHIL: Don't need it, Beth –

BETH: What d'y'go with Ged Stewart for, hey? 'Cos in a bad light an' all dressed up he got half a look of Stevie Coppell? –

PHIL: Y'must be joking –

BETH: Oh yeah? Three weeks an' he's getting restless. Three weeks an' not even a bit of tit. Then he gets the red card, dun't he? – 'cos the virgin Mary dun't go for physical contact, does she? But up here she's getting laid every night the week (*She points to her head.*) – provided it wears a red shirt an' plays outside fuckin' right.

PHIL: Y'finished, have yer?

BETH: Got any answers, have yer?

PHIL: Paid to watch this game, y'know – not get earache from you –

BETH: Oh, bit near the knuckle, Phil? Bit too much like true? Is it Phil? Is it, Philippa?

PHIL: Talking to me?

BETH: That your name, in't it?

PHIL: Phil.

BETH: Y's christened Philippa.

PHIL: I'm called Phil –

BETH: Nothing wrong being a girl, Phil. Dun't hurt, Phil. Play yer cards right, it's a good laugh –

PHIL: Good laugh? – yeah, play yer cards right, that's how y'get treated.

BETH: Calling yerself a boy dun't change it –

PHIL: Beth, are you watching this or not? –

BETH: Oh, we still playing, are we? – thought we'd packed it in –

NITA: S'a good game –

BETH: Should pack it in – should face up to it. No one gives a monkey's now anyway. All dropped dead of boredom.

NITA: Still got time left –

BETH: Look at that, Nita –

NITA: Unlucky –

BETH: See that pass? – seen better balls on the beach at Blackpool –

ALICE: Their number seven's having a good game –

PHIL: Wish I could put a brick through him –

BETH: Had more fun cleaning me toe-nails out than watching this lot perform. Oh Christ, what is that meant to be? (*Shouting.*) Who's that for? Jerk.

PHIL: Greenhoff's too slow –

NITA: Been injured –

PHIL: Shouldn't be playing then –

BETH: I'd have Coppell off f'r'a start –

PHIL: What's left?

NITA: Five minutes – at the most –

PHIL: That's it then, in't it?

BETH: Y'do wake up sometimes, then, do yer? – we're getting leathered an' she still thinks we're in with a chance?

NITA: Seen them pull back before –

BETH: Bit old for fairy stories, aren't yer?

PHIL: I'm going.

NITA: What y'doing?

PHIL: Not stopping here, watch them get walked on –

NITA: Stop to the end, Phil – y'never know –

PHIL: Bloody do –

BETH: Still arsing about in our own half, y'notice –

PHIL: They're not gonna do it, Nita –

NITA (*ignores her, shouting*): Get it down – all the way –

PHIL: There's nobody there –

NITA: Buchan . . . give it Buchan . . . here y'are – free kick –

PHIL: Oh yeah, well we all know what happens to *our* free kicks, don't we?

NITA: Here – Stevie's taking it –

BETH: Straight over the stand –

NITA: Give it McQueen – on his head –

BETH: No chance – don't let him near it –

PHIL (*suddenly animated*): Yeah, Jordan's there – get up there, Joe –

NITA: McQueen – take it through – give it McQueen –

BETH: No way. There is no way they are gonna . . .

The crowd suddenly erupts. NITA and PHIL leap into the air. BETH follows suit. Even ALICE is dancing about on the spot.

NITA: Oh God, it's there . . .

PHIL: I don't believe it . . . I don't believe it . . .

BETH: Bloody ace. Bloody great. Told yer, didn't I?

More hugs, kisses, cheers.

PHIL: I can't believe it –

NITA: What'd I say, Phil? – what'd I say?

ALICE: McQueen – he's Man of the Match – that's who it is –

NITA: I said no giving up –

PHIL: It's only two-one, Nita –

ALICE: Yeah, two-one – I mean, they're never gonna get two –

PHIL: Chance'd be a fine thing –

NITA: Yeah they could. We got . . . three minutes?

PHIL: Less –

BETH: Nah, no chance. Flash in the pan, Nita. One off.

NITA: Due for some luck –

BETH: That was it.

PHIL: Oh well, it was good. Great while it lasted. Least they can't call it a massacre. Least we didn't get pissed on.

NITA: Still a bit left –

PHIL: Not a chance –

NITA: Yeah, go on Reds – double it –

BETH: Bloody play for time now, won't they – you wait –

PHIL: Yeah, just play possession –

BETH: See? Seen that? – smack it over the stand – anywhere'll do – (*Even louder.*) Bloody timewasting, ref – get him off –

NITA: Just take it right down – take it slow –

PHIL: Can't take it any slower, can they? – they're knackered –

NITA: If we make it evens – extra time – we'll kill them –

BETH: What extra time?

NITA (*shouting*): Hang on to it now –

PHIL: Out on the right – use it . . .

NITA: Get it across – over here, over here – give it Jordan –

BETH: Go on, Joe, bite his balls off –

PHIL: Move it about – come on – get it down here –

NITA: That's it – go on, go on – down this end –

PHIL: Give it Sammy – give it him –

NITA: Go on, Sammy – get it, get it –

BETH: Have his knee-caps, Sammy –

PHIL: All the way Sammy, take it through the . . .

An even louder roar. They all leap into the air.

PHIL: Oh my God . . .

NITA: They did it, they did it, they did it . . .

They all leap on top of each other, hugging and kissing. The noise is deafening. PHIL extricates herself, wipes away tears.

PHIL: Oh God . . .

NITA: We'll hammer them, Phil. Dead on their feet – two minutes left – we done it now –

PHIL: Oh God, we *are* gonna do it, aren't we, Nita? We *are* gonna make it?

NITA: It's ours. We are. We done it.

PHIL: Just let them do it – I'll give anything . . . I'll give *anything* . . .

NITA (*bracing herself*): Right, now – just gotta stay calm –

PHIL: Yeah, right – keep it cool – slow it right down –

BETH (*loud*): Possession, Reds – waste all the fuckin' time you want . . .

ALICE: That number seven – should have him off – who is he?

NITA: Right, now get it back – keep it away from them –

PHIL: Oh God, now look at that – (*Loud:*) Who was that to?

BETH: Keep it away from that Irish bastard –

PHIL: Look at it – who gives him all that space?

BETH: Bastard Brady – cripple him someone –

ALICE: Is that Brady?

PHIL (*loud*): On him, somebody . . .

NITA: All that space – who's meant to be there – where are they all?

PHIL: Yer giving him too much room –

BETH: Kill him, f'Christ's sake – have him down –

PHIL: Oh Jesus, get him stopped –

NITA: Where is everyone?

PHIL: Stop the cross – watch Sunderland – McQueen, where is he? – someone stop the bloody . . .

NITA: No . . . oh no . . . no . . . no . . . no . . .

Another deafening roar from the crowd. They stand horror-struck. PHIL, head in hands, leans on the crash barrier.

BETH: Fuck.

NITA: Oh no, Phil . . . they couldn't have . . .

PHIL: It isn't fair – oh Christ, it isn't fair –

BETH: Bastards –

PHIL: It isn't fair, Nita –

BETH: The bastards –

NITA: I can't believe it –

PHIL: Oh Nita . . . (*She cries on* NITA's *shoulder.*)

BETH (*dancing up and down with rage*): They've had it now – bastards –

PHIL: Nita, I can't stand it –

NITA (*half-heartedly*): Still a minute left –

PHIL: No, don't Nita – don't say it – I couldn't stand it all over again —

BETH: That's it now – they've had it – we'll have their fuckin' necks for that –

PHIL: If we got another, Nita – I couldn't take it – I would just . . . drop dead . . .

NITA: We won't get another.

PHIL: I can't watch it, Nita.

BETH (*dancing about, chanting*): You're gonna get your fuckin' heads kicked in – You're goin' home in a fuckin' ambulance –

NITA: Beth, will y'stop waving that thing about?

BETH: Don't you speak to me, paki —

NITA: Put it away, Beth –

BETH: Have the whole bloody pack of them –

NITA: Get it off her, will yer –

BETH: Starting with you, Nita –

PHIL: Alice, get it –

ALICE: What? – what'm I supposed to . . . ?

NITA *backs off*. ALICE *behind makes a pathetic attempt to grab the knife*. BETH *rounds on her. She backs off*. BETH *lunges towards* NITA.

BETH: This is for you, Nita –

BETH *topples forward, trips and collapses, dead drunk on the terrace.*

PHIL (*picking up the penknife*): Get these free with Weetabix –

ALICE: Oh Christ, what's she . . . ?

PHIL: Pissed. Leave her . . .

ALICE: Yeah, but she might've . . .

PHIL: Leave her . . .

NITA: She okay?

PHIL: Rat-legged. Don't touch her.

PHIL *prods* BETH *with her foot.* BETH *snores.*

PHIL: Flat out – (*She kicks her.*) – absolutely fuckin' flat . . .

The final whistle. There is a roar from the crowd. NITA *stares dejectedly ahead.* ALICE *looks annoyed.* PHIL, *head in hands, leans on the barrier.*

ALICE: Well, I'm not watching this – I'm not seeing them go up for the medals –

NITA: Don't be daft, Al – we best stay together – not get lost –

ALICE: Have to cart her out an' all, I suppose?

NITA: Got plenty of time –

ALICE: Dead pissed off now – wish I'd stayed at home an' watched it with Kevin –

NITA: Alice –

ALICE: Yeah, well, we got colour now y'know – dead life-like – what's the use coming all this way? – y'can see them lose on telly an' costs yer nothing –

NITA: That is not the point, Alice –

ALICE: What *is* the point, Nita?

NITA: Being here —

ALICE: Coulda stayed at home – Kevin woulda made me tea an' all –

PHIL *looks up.*

PHIL: Nita, I'm getting out –

NITA: Y'can't go yet –

PHIL: Not watching them go up fer the Cup –

NITA: See us collect our medals –

PHIL: Loser's medals –

NITA: Least we got here –

PHIL: Big deal –

NITA: Phil, the world doesn't end, y'know – just 'cos the Reds lost the Cup —

PHIL: Doesn't it?

Blackout.

Scene Eight

A few hours later. The coach park of the Watford Gap Motorway Services. PHIL, NITA, BETH *and* ALICE *are drinking coffee.* BETH *appears quite recovered,* PHIL *almost still in shock.*

PHIL: There isn't a God –

ALICE: Y'shouldn't say that –

PHIL: I can. I am doing. There is none.

ALICE: Well, there might be –

BETH: Yeah, an' he's on loan to fuckin' Arsenal –

PHIL: I wanted that so much. Every Sunday, goin' begging for it. Oh He's had it now. There is no way do I set foot inside St Peter an' Paul's again. Not ever.

ALICE: That's blasphemy, that is – y'won't go to Heaven –

PHIL: There is no Heaven. It doesn't exist.

ALICE: She shouldn't say that. What if He hears yer?

PHIL: What do'you know about Heaven, Al? Heaven is what you want. Not arsing about in wings an' white dresses. Heaven is Old Trafford on European Cup night.

BETH: An' purgatory is blowing the fuckin' Cup in the final thirty seconds –

ALICE: No, don't, Beth – you'll get done – He listens to all this, y'know –

PHIL: What else can He do? – what is there, worse than this, what happened today?

NITA: Well, yer still breathing aren't yer?

PHIL: Probably not. Probably dead an' don't know the difference. Feel like the socks must feel goin' through the spin-drier –

BETH: Y'been asleep two hours –

PHIL: That all? Feels years away. Feels like a dream.

ALICE: Hey, I in't got no pulse. Should I be clinically dead?

NITA: Well, we're all still here. I mean, we blew the Cup – an' nothing went bang, did it? Nothing fell apart –

BETH: Bar the fuckin' defence –

PHIL: That's easy for you to say, Nita –

NITA: That's not easy for me to say, Phil –

PHIL: How long we got?

ALICE: Ten minutes, the bloke says –

BETH: An' anyone late back gets left –

PHIL (looking round): The Blue Boar –

BETH: The Boar's Arse more like.

ALICE: D'y'get boars that colour?

PHIL: Y'coulda saved us some vodka, Beth –

BETH: Medicinal reasons, Phil – sup all or nothing. So I opted for . . .

PHIL: Yeah, we know.

BETH: Hey, y'know what I have got, though – all that scran – not touched it yet.

PHIL: Brilliant. Get it out.

BETH gets out food, hands it round.

NITA: Needed that.

BETH: Pure nectar.

PHIL: What is?

BETH: Food of the gods.

NITA: That's ambrosia, y'dick.

BETH: Oh, I thought that was . . .

NITA: No, it isn't pudding. How's yer head?

BETH: Still ticking. Gonna go off any minute.

PHIL (getting up): Oh, look at that – just look at it. All them coaches. Thousands of us – still going home.

NITA: Be some drowning of sorrows tonight. Buckets of tears. Pillows wet –

ALICE: Hey, I hope Kevin remembers to come an' meet me.

PHIL: Least we didn't make arses of ourselves –

BETH: When?

PHIL: Least we was dignified –

BETH: Dignified?

PHIL: Yeah, in defeat. No fighting – no gettin' disgraced –

BETH: Yeah, I know – what a let-down. I had this spanner saved (She gets it out.) – I had it all geared up –

ALICE: That what your skull copped for?

BETH: That's a trophy, that is – that's spoils of war –

PHIL: Yeah, well done, Beth – now y'can hang it on the wall an' stuff it –

ALICE: Hey, look at that – falling star . . .

PHIL: Where?

BETH: S'an aeroplane –

ALICE: S'gone –

PHIL: Not dark enough for falling stars –

ALICE: Something fell –

PHIL: Musta been eighty thousand today –

BETH: What?

PHIL: Reds. This afternoon.

BETH: Yeah, easily –

PHIL: An' all the bridges – over the motorway – all the way home. Never forget that. Strewn with red scarves. All the fans that never got there – watching us all come home.

BETH: Walking wounded –

PHIL: The Red Army – in retreat.

NITA: No – strategic withdrawal – till next year.

PHIL: Yeah, be back next year –

BETH: Yeah, no fuckin' messing.

NITA: Might win something then – if we get a new team –

ALICE: I did think their number seven was quite good –

PHIL: Yeah, but they were magic, though, weren't they, Nita. They played bloody magic.

NITA: No, Phil, they played crap.

PHIL: Nita –

NITA: They played useless.

PHIL: They played brilliant –

NITA: Well, it dun't matter anymore, does it?

PHIL: What d'y'mean, it dun't matter? Matters to me, Nita –

NITA: Yeah, but they were crap, Phil –

PHIL: Not all the time –

NITA: Most of the time. 'Cept the last five minutes –

PHIL: More than that –

NITA: Last five minutes, magic. Rest of the game, embarrassing. Shots on target,

two. We were rubbish, Phil. They ran rings round us.

PHIL: Don't believe you saying this, Nita. We shoulda won it –

NITA: Shoulda won it, yeah – but we cocked it up, didn't we?

PHIL: In extra time we coulda nailed them –

NITA: Could of. Should of. Might have. Yeah, but we didn't, did we?

PHIL: Best day of my life this, Nita – shoulda been –

BETH: Next year, Phil –

PHIL: Sod next year. I want it this year. I want it now. I want us bringing back the Cup, Albert Square half a million people. Into Europe, back at the top –

BETH: Next year, dead easy – sweep the board –

PHIL: Make a pact – shall we? – all of us next year, same place. Only next year . . .

NITA: Might be started in me shop next year –

ALICE: Hey, what if I get married? I could have commitments –

BETH: Yeah, well I'll be there. I'll have fuck-all else to do –

PHIL: She'll give yer a job. Hey, Nita, give her a job, will yer?

NITA: What doing? Puttin' out the rubbish?

PHIL: Cut hair, can't yer?

BETH: No.

PHIL: She'll teach yer –

BETH: Seen me hands? Seen the size of them? Would you let that loose on your head?

ALICE: Wish I could cut hair –

PHIL: Anyone can cut hair –

ALICE: Kevin says he dun't want me working –

PHIL: Go 'way –

ALICE: Kevin says no wife of his is going out to work. Says the day a wife of his goes out to work is the day he stops bein' a man. Y'don't like to argue, do yer?

PHIL: Depends. If y'like getting used to wipe feet on –

NITA: Yeah, an' who's talking? This time next year, where you gonna be?

PHIL: Back here.

NITA: The Blue Boar? That about your level, in't it? Taste of this tea, just about as stunning as your head at the moment –

BETH: Is she startin' again?

PHIL: Y'givin' me earache, Nita –

NITA: Getting bored talking to you, Phil –

PHIL: That's good news anyway –

NITA: Getting bored hearing you find excuses for bein' a dosser –

PHIL: Nita, there is no money . . .

NITA: It's not the money, Phil –

PHIL: I can't afford it –

NITA: They give yer grants, Phil. They give yer all that. All y'gotta do is *be* there. What else d'y'want? – Someone to go an' do it all for yer?

PHIL: Can't afford United on a grant. What about away games?

NITA: Well, give something up –

PHIL: Like what?

NITA: I dunno – like eating –

PHIL: Oh ta, Nita. Down the market, least y'get the left-over Granny Smiths – least y'get the dog-ends from the apple carts.

NITA: Yeah, great, Phil – left-overs. If that's what you want. If it suits you being somebody's dog-end –

BETH: Y'get dead offensive, you, don't yer?

PHIL: Don't you get sick, Nita – don't you never get tired telling people what to do? – sorting other people's business for them?

NITA: Just 'cos we lost, Phil –

PHIL: Just 'cos we lost, Nita, dun't mean you got free hand organising the rest of my career –

NITA: What career, Phil? – who else is gonna sort it out for yer?

PHIL: Well, not you fer starters –

NITA: S'only a game, Phil –

PHIL: What is?

NITA: What we just lost. It's no great tragedy –

PHIL: If it was, would you know it? Who's gonna teach you that, Nita? What d'you know about anything not the most cushy, the most dead smooth, the most laid out on a plate for yer? Got a dad who gives yer all the answers, runs your life, tells yer what to do, what to think, who to talk to, who to screw . . .

BETH: Who not to screw –

PHIL: Who's asking you?

BETH: Miss Dead Respectable, Miss Untouchable, Miss Virgo Intacta –

PHIL: I don't want you running my life, Nita. I don't want leading by the nose. Don't you get bored, always being right, always got smart answers, Nita? D'y'never fancy *being wrong* jus' f'r'a change –

NITA: Not really, no –

PHIL: I get sick listening to yer. I get worn out bein' on the receiving end of your advice –

NITA: Do something, then –

PHIL: Do what, then?

NITA: Give us a break, Phil –

PHIL: Love to, Nita –

BETH: Shall we go, then?

PHIL: Don't need telling what to do. I know all those things. I know what's here for me. I can get out. If I want. If I choose.

ALICE: Let's go. He's waving us –

BETH: Y'coming, you two?

ALICE *and* BETH *begin to gather their stuff together and move off.*

PHIL: I can go all the way. If I wanted.

NITA: Yeah, like the Reds?

PHIL: I don't need pushing. You, shoving me in the back –

NITA: Oh, is that right, Phil?

PHIL: Yeah, that's right, Nita –

NITA: You won't go, Phil. Head down,
   play it safe, take no chances. You in't
   going anywhere, Phil. You don't have the
   guts.

BETH (*as she follows* ALICE *out*):
   Y'gonna miss the bus, you two –

PHIL: You think that, then, Nita.

NITA: You are going nowhere, Phil . . .
   (*Collecting stuff and following the others
   out.*)

PHIL (*calling after her*): Oh yeah, Nita –
   d'y'wanna bet on it?

   PHIL *is left holding the banner. Chants up
   loud. Lights down.*

TRUE DARE KISS

True Dare Kiss was first performed at the Liverpool Playhouse on Wednesday October 19 1983, with the following cast:

ALICE (*19*)	Sally-Jane Jackson
NITA (*19*)	Tara Shaw
PHIL (*19*)	Julia North
BETH (*19*)	Angela Catherall
KEVIN (*22*)/REUBEN (*35*)	John Wild
JOEY (*25*)/JAY (*20*)/FIRST MAN/ DOCTOR/DANNY (*34*)	Roger Hyams
NASH (*23*)/NIDGE (*23*)/SECOND MAN/ MISS BANKS' FRIEND/POLICEMAN/ SHEIK/COMPERE'S VOICE	Martin Wenner
JANINE (*17*)/LINDY (*20*)/MISS BANKS/ CARLY (*23*)/CANDY (*28*)/CARMEN (*25*)/ MRS WILSON	Kate Lynne-Evans

Directed by Richard Brandon
Designed by Phil Cutts
Lighting by Steve Drummond
Sound by Jimmy Simmons

The play was subsequently seen at the Cottesloe Theatre from 3 October 1985, with the following cast:

ALICE	Sally-Jane Jackson
NITA	Tara Shaw
PHIL	Stella Gonet
BETH	Lesley Sharp
KEVIN/POLICEMAN	Adam Kotz
JOEY/SHEIK/COMPERE'S VOICE	Stephen Petcher
NIDGE/JAY/FIRST MAN/ MISS BANKS' FRIEND/REUBEN	Roderick Smith
NASH/SECOND MAN	David Fielder
JANINE/LINDY/CANDY	Katrin Cartlidge
MISS BANKS/MRS WILSON	Caroline Goodall
CARLY/CARMEN	Cheryl Prime
DOCTOR/DANNY	David Cardy

Directed by John Burgess
Designed by Alison Chitty
Lighting by Stephen Wentworth
Sound by Nic Jones

The play is set in Manchester, Salford, Bristol and Tyneside in 1980 and 1981. Characters' ages given above are for 1980.

ACT ONE

February-April 1980

*As the audience arrive the sounds of
Manchester United fans singing football
chants can be heard. As the lights go
down the chants mingle with and are
finally drowned out by the sound of
church bells ringing.*
   *Outside a church in Salford. An
afternoon in late February. A wedding
party begins to assemble.*
   KEVIN *(the groom) enters with*
JOEY *(the best man)* and NIDGE.
BETH *and* NITA *walk on together.*
ALICE *(the bride) arrives with her
sister* JANINE. *Finally* PHIL *walks on.
She makes no attempt to speak to any
of the group.*
   *As she comes forward the wedding
bells stop and the lights focus on her and
the figures of* ALICE, NITA *and* BETH.

PHIL: Thanks a lot, Alice. Are y'satisfied
   now? Y'coulda kept yer invitation. I
   don't *wanna* come back. I put two
   hundred miles between me an' this
   dive – an' times like this it's like
   livin' on the doorstep.
   Yeah. Okay. Once.
   We divvied up. Shared things. God
   knows how.
   Classrooms . . . ciggies . . . Sat'days . . .
   spots . . .
   Alice gets skint, so Nita coughs up.
   Beth's gettin' pasted so in weighs
   Phil. 'You hit my mate – c'mere an'
   say that.'
   Home for tea with two black eyes an'
   front teeth hangin' out. 'Where y'bin,
   Phil? Them three again? Upstairs, you.'
   Thanks Beth. Thanks pal.
   And four years – every week – stood
   with you three on the Stretford End.

   (*She chants*:) 'Que sera sera . . .
   whatever will be will be . . .
   We're goin' to Wem-ber-lee . . . que
   sera sera . . .'
   United? Now? Joke, innit?
   Look, I don't wanna argue. Give over,
   will yer? It's not the same, Nita. Beth,

it isn't like that now.
We're not still coming back from
Wembley. An' we didn't win the Cup.

*The wedding bells start to ring again.
From inside the church come the
opening strains of the Wedding March.*
KEVIN, JOEY *and* NIDGE *go off
into church.* ALICE, *attended by*
JANINE *and* BETH, *follows.*
NITA *is about to follow when she
notices* PHIL *is lagging behind. She
goes over to her.*

NITA: Y'goin' in?

PHIL: I don't know.

NITA: What y'doin' here, then?

PHIL (*without malice*): God knows.

NITA: Y'come two hundred miles, get
   all togged up, just so y'can stand
   outside?

PHIL: I don't like funerals.

NITA: Phil, it's a wedding.

PHIL: Is it?

   NITA *giving up already, walks away.*

PHIL (*calling after her*): Believe it or not,
   Nita, I would love to be wrong.

NITA: Oh, is that right, Phil? You would
   love to be wrong? Well that's a new
   one, Phil.

   NITA *walks off into church.* PHIL
   *hesitates for a moment then follows
   her in.*

The wedding reception.
   *The stage is empty. Suddenly the
doors fly open and in burst* NIDGE, *with
no shirt on, his tie round his head, leading*
KEVIN, JOEY, ALICE, JANINE *and*
BETH *in a conga.* NITA *follows.* PHIL
brings up the rear.
   ALICE *captures* NITA *and takes off
for a chat.* PHIL *is about to join* BETH
when KEVIN *calls her. He has been
drinking all afternoon and is very
unsteady.*

KEVIN: Hey, Phil! (*She turns round.*)

Gi's a smile, Phil? Y'gonna say congratulations?

PHIL (*determined not to be provoked*): Yeah, well done, Kevin. (*She starts to walk off.*)

KEVIN: Aw, don't be like that. (*He goes over to her.*) Y'not want us to get married, then?

PHIL: What give yer that idea?

KEVIN (*putting his arm round her*): I think yer dead fit, you, y'know.

PHIL: Do yer?

KEVIN: I do, yeah. I've always fancied you.

PHIL (*gently removing his arm*): Good for you, Kevin.

KEVIN: Hey, y'know where I live, don't yer?

PHIL: Oh, don't worry, Kevin — I've had it for some time. (*She starts to walk off.*)

JOEY. Hey, Phil — (*She turns back. JOEY grabs her wrist.*) Y'not gonna give the groom a good luck kiss?

NIDGE: Oh yeah, go on, Phil — give yerself a treat.

PHIL *considers for a moment then goes up to* KEVIN, *puts her arms round him and starts to kiss him. JOEY and NIDGE cheer encouragement. The kiss becomes more and more involved. Suddenly KEVIN starts to struggle and squeal. Finally PHIL releases him.*

PHIL: Now piss off, Kevin. (*She walks over to join BETH.*)

JOEY *goes over to where KEVIN is still clutching his mouth.*

JOEY: Aw Kevin . . . bit yer tongue off, did she? She must fancy yer, Kev.

JOEY, KEVIN *and* NIDGE *sit down and break out a pack of cards.*

ALICE *brings* NITA *forward to look at her wedding presents.*

NITA: Seven butter dishes? (*Looking at them.*) What d'y'want seven butter dishes for?

ALICE: I don't. I only asked for one. We don't even have butter. Kev's a Flora man. (*Counting them.*) Two plastic, two Pyrex, two stainless steel, and one Fabulous Unbreakable Melamine. (*Then, in great disgust.*) An' what d'y'think of this, then?

NITA (*pleasantly surprised*): It's a wok.

ALICE: Yeah. Exactly. A wok. *What* y'supposed to do with a wok? I asked for a chip pan, Nita. What's Kev gonna have for his tea now? How'm I gonna feed him?

NITA: How d'y'mean?

ALICE: Without a chip-pan? What'll he eat? Y'can't always be dining out down the chippy, can yer? What do *I* look like then? (*Anticipating a response.*) Yeah, exactly — failed housewife. An' have y'seen this? Look at that. Five bathmats, fifteen towels . . . nothing goes, of course . . . not one Tangerine Dream like the bathroom suite. I could scream. Oh yeah, could always repaint the bathroom, I s'pose — get a new suite put in. Trouble is, I like this one, but the towels don't go . . .

NITA: Alice, is everything . . . all right?

ALICE: Pardon?

NITA: You have done the right thing?

ALICE: Right thing?

NITA: Getting married.

ALICE: I don't know what y'mean.

NITA: To Kevin.

ALICE: Well who else would I get married to?

NITA: Look, Alice — if you ever need anything . . . y'know . . . anyone . . .?

ALICE: What d'y'mean? I've got Kevin. Why would I need anyone?

NITA: Y'never know . . .

ALICE: See Phil's not speaking to me. (*They both look round at* PHIL.) You tell her, Nita – bein' married's great. Y'get new clothes, y'get yer picture took – An' all them prezzies . . . see all that? That's my home, that is, perched up there, top of the piano. Tell Phil she dun't know what she's missing.

NITA *is on the verge of tears and pretends to have something in her eye to hide it.*

Hey, did I show yer me ring? It's not the one I asked for, but Kevin says it's got more class. I don't know where he got the money . . .

ALICE *is about to circulate when sounds of cheering and shouting break out. Attempts are being made to make* JOEY *give a speech.* ALICE *rejoins* KEVIN.

NIDGE (*standing up*): Okay . . . okay now . . . quiet please . . . *quiet* will yer? . . . speech . . . speech . . . best man . . . speech . . . (*Other shouts of encouragement.*)

JOEY: Y'what? Me? Y'can frig that.

KEVIN: Yeah, go on, Joey . . . speech . . . speech . . .

JOEY: Well *I* in't got nothin' to say. I think he's married the wrong bit . . .

KEVIN *and* NIDGE *simultaneously.*

KEVIN } Joey, f'Christ's sake . . .
NIDGE } Joey, can it, will yer –

JOEY (*finally persuaded*): All right . . . well . . . I'd just like to say . . . Alice is a very lucky girl . . . (*Shouts of 'Hear, Hear', 'Dead right' etc.*) . . . an' if Kevin's still on the loose in two years time, she'll be even luckier . . . (*Shrieks of laughter from* KEVIN*'s party.*) . . . hey, c'mon now – Alice has landed herself a real prize there – (*More laughter.*) . . . I mean it – straight now. Our Alice says, give us the moon, Kevin . . . know what he'd do? I'll tell yer what – on with the

gloves . . . straight up there . . . no fingerprints, no messing . . . (*More laughter.*) . . . assuming he could flog it over the odds when he got it down again . . . (*Laughter and applause.*) Okay, okay . . . I would like to propose a toast . . . I would like to raise a glass. (*He smashes an empty bottle and holds up the broken end.*) To Alice and Kevin . . . (*They all raise glasses.*) Kevin and Alice, may they rest in peace . . .

Toasts and cheers from KEVIN*'s side.* ALICE*'s side look faintly disgusted. Shouts from* KEVIN*'s table of 'Speech, speech'.* KEVIN *finally gets up.*

KEVIN: I'd just like to say . . . to all me mates an' that . . . ta for coming . . . an' for all the prezzies . . . wherever they come from . . . whatever much they didn't cost . . . an' to me newly-acquired sister-in-law, Janine, for bein' a smashin' bridesmaid . . .

JOEY: Even though she slapped his hands coming home in the car . . .

KEVIN: An' to Alice's mam an' dad – no doubt thinking, Christ what's our Al got herself landed with? . . . look at it this way . . . yer not so much gaining a son as losing a daughter . . .

KEVIN *gets down amid cheers and shouts.* KEVIN *and* JOEY *settle down for some serious drinking at their table.* JANINE *has joined* NITA, BETH *and* PHIL *at their table.*

JANINE: Well, what are we now? February? I'll be an auntie by Christmas.

PHIL: A what?

JANINE: Well, y'know what it's like, Phil. Kev wants her at home . . .

PHIL: So?

JANINE: Well, she'll soon get bored ironing his socks. If she's gonna stop in, might as well keep fit fending off nappy rash.

PHIL: I don't believe this.

NIDGE (*coming over*): Hey Phil, how y'doing? Courting yet, are yer?

PHIL (*now beset on all sides*): Y'what?

NIDGE, *very drunk, tries to man-handle* PHIL.

NIDGE: Anyone special, hey? Nice lad? Do I know him?

PHIL: What sort of a word is 'courting'?

NITA: Are y'seeing anyone he means?

PHIL: I see lots of people.

NITA: Phil . . .

PHIL: I see people who know what they're on about. Who got something worth listening to. Who think there's more to life than giving birth and getting buried.

PHIL *gets up and walks out.*

NIDGE: Seen that? Education for yer. University. Ignorant bitch.

KEVIN (*shouting across*): Hey Nidge, get us a taxi, will yer?

NIDGE: What, y'mean rob yer one . . .

NIDGE *goes out laughing to himself.* ALICE *and* KEVIN *are making a move to go.*

NITA (*eager to find an excuse to go*): Is it that late already . . .

ALICE (*seeing her preparing to leave*): Oh, y'not leaving? They're all goin' into town.

NITA: Alice, I gotta get up. Getting the work done on me shop tomorrow.

BETH: Oh, me an' all. Got six hours solid kip to get in before tea time.

ALICE: Oh, are y'sure y'won't . . .

JOEY (*shouting over*): Hey, Alice – time to go – get yer clothes off.

ALICE (*trying to ignore him*): Listen . . . can I just say? . . . thanks for coming . . .

BETH *and* ALICE *kiss each other.*

BETH: I'll give yer a ring . . .

ALICE *kisses* NITA.

ALICE: I *am* dead happy, y'know.

NITA: Are you?

ALICE: It's what I wanted, Nita.

JOEY (*shouting*): Hey, Alice – get yer arse across here for the old man . . .

ALICE: I'll have to go . . . (*She goes over to* KEVIN.)

JOEY (*springing across*): Sneaking off, are yer? Nobody fancy a quick poke behind the car park wall?

ALICE: Joey . . .

JOEY: Oh, hey, I forgot, didn't I? Y'got yer posh mates round. Did I show yer up, Alice? Did I disgust yer?

ALICE: You always disgust me, Joey.

NIDGE (*off, shouting*): Taxi's here.

ALICE: Are we going?

JOEY: Is she startin' already?

KEVIN: C'mon you – let's get going . . . (*He puts his arm round* ALICE *and starts to take her out.*)

JOEY: Hey, where's yer manners, Kevin? (*He grabs* ALICE *violently and kisses her.*) Best man, aren't I?

KEVIN *sticks up a finger to* JOEY *and takes* ALICE *out.*

(*To* BETH *and* NITA:) Well, what can I do for you, girls? Any offers? Any requests?

BETH: Just one, Joey.

JOEY (*grabbing* JANINE): Looks like it's gonna be you, then.

JANINE (*as she is being led out*): I wouldn't bank on it. (*To* BETH *and* NITA:) I'll see yer, then.

JOEY: 'Night, girls.

JOEY *and* JANINE *go out.*

BETH: Y'walking?

NITA: Might as well. (*They are about to leave.*) Oh look . . .

BETH: What?

NITA: Look what she left behind . . .

She goes and picks up ALICE's *wedding bouquet.* BETH *makes a face.* NITA *throws it at her.* BETH *dives out of the way.*
They go off together.

As the lights fade the sound of a train announcement can be heard saying: 'This is Bristol Temple Meads . . . This is Bristol Temple Meads . . . British Rail apologise for the late arrival of the 19.55. from Manchester Piccadilly, due to arrive at 23.05 . . .'

The lights come up on NASH, *at home, stretched out in a chair, reading.*
From offstage, the sound of a door closing and PHIL's *voice saying 'Is he in?' Someone replies 'Yeah, his light's on.'*
NASH *turns in his chair so that he has his back to the door.* PHIL *comes in, carrying a hold-all, and stands in the doorway.* NASH *affects not to notice her. She stands unsure of what to do. Finally he turns round.*

PHIL: Well don't ask us in, Nash.

NASH (*going back to his book*): Yer back early.

PHIL: I didn't stay.

NASH: Never.

PHIL (*coming into the room*): Well what did *you* think?

NASH: Thought it might be good for yer.

PHIL: Well it wasn't. It was a shambles. I felt sick.

NASH: Y'shouldn't eat so much.

PHIL: Nash, it isn't funny.

NASH (*putting his book down*): Sick of what, Phil?

PHIL: Oh, I dunno. Everything. I hate it. I hate goin' back. The narrowness, the back-chat, the stupid jokes, the bitching in corners — 'Oh she *must* be

queer, she got A Levels' — 'Oh, is that 'cos she can't get a feller?' — 'When y'gettin' married, Phil?' — 'What *she* needs is a good screw' — 'Or a good hiding'. Ha ha ha.

NASH: Ignore it.

PHIL: I can't. I hate it. All that 'salt-of-the-earth' solidarity makes me sick. Yer working-class, y'live in a dump — they think that's clever. Think it's a virtue in its own right. Well it's not. It doesn't excuse. It doesn't make it okay to be a narrow-minded, intolerant, foul-mouthed dickhead.

NASH: Like you, y'mean?

PHIL: Y'could at least sympathise. Or is it too close to World's End?

NASH: Wallsend, Phil. Though the distinction is minimal.

PHIL: Nash . . . don't you ever go home an' think, Christ, there but for the grace of God?

NASH: Yeah, I do go home.

PHIL: And what d'y'think?

NASH: There but for the grace of God?

PHIL (*picking up her bag and heading for the door*): It's not funny.

NASH: Y'not staying?

PHIL: I'm goin' back to Hall.

NASH: Well I'm not walkin' yer.

PHIL: So?

NASH: So y'might as well stay.

PHIL *looks at him for a moment. His face gives nothing away. Finally she puts her bag down.*
The lights go down.

The lights come up on NITA's *salon.*
ALICE *rushes on excitedly.* BETH *saunters on behind her and looks round, coolly appraising.*

BETH: Bit much, innit?

ALICE: God, Beth, wish *I* had a dad like that.

BETH: Not bad, is it? Come over here, can't write six words of English. Scrawl the odd presciption an' here he is settin' up shop for her.

ALICE (*picking up one of* NITA's *cards*): 'Nita Sharman welcomes you to Nita's Headlines Hairdressing Salon. Tinted mirrors . . . streamlined back-wash . . .'

BETH: Wall-to-wall fitted ferns . . .

ALICE: God, Beth, it's brill, though.

BETH (*acting it out*): 'Oh, come this way, madam . . . what can we do for you? You may be a dog . . . you may have a face like a bag of bruised plums, but we can transform you. Sheena Easton? Kate Bush? For the price of a cut, blow an' decent tip, even you can be Pamela Ewing. Now, how d'you like your music, madam? Loud? Deafening? Or sonic? What, goin' already? Not before a restyle, manicure, pedicure, sunbed, face lift? Oh, an' there's your bill, madam. That'll give you something to read on the way home.'

ALICE: S'all right for some.

BETH: Makes yer sick, dun't it?

She saunters off out. ALICE *continues to gaze wistfully around her.* NITA *comes on and announces her presence with a fanfare.*

NITA: Well? What d'y'reckon?

ALICE: Is it yours? Is it really all yours?

NITA: Mine an' no one else's!

ALICE: God, Nita, yer dead lucky, you are, having all this.

NITA: What d'y'mean 'lucky'? It's not a birthday present, y'know. It's my neck on the line.

ALICE: Oh yeah, but at least yer dad . . .

NITA: What d'y'mean, me dad?

ALICE: Settin' yer up.

NITA: Oh, here we go again. 'It's all right for Nita. Her dad's a doctor, he's rakin' it in. Oh well, they all are, aren't they — these pakis.'

ALICE: Oh, hang on, Nita — I never said that.

NITA: Well forget about me dad. Me an' the bank manager, this is. No one else.

ALICE (*sudden thought*): Oh God . . . but s'pose nobody comes in . . . s'posing you have to close . . . s'posing it doesn't work . . . ?

NITA: It will.

The phone rings. NITA *answers it.*

NITA (*as the lights go down*): Hello . . . Nita's Headlines . . .

The lights come up again on the salon. NITA *is on the phone.*

NITA: Thank you . . . that'll be ten o'clock Wednesday for a cut and blow . . .

BETH *marches on, salutes and stands to attention.*

BETH: I did it.

NITA (*putting the phone down*): Did what?

BETH: Volunteered. (NITA *looks blank.*) The army.

NITA (*as if she's heard it all before*): Really.

BETH (*performing it*): Information? Yeah, I come for information. I come on a recce.

Committed? What's it look like? I'm here, aren't I?

Know what *I* done last week? — I'll show yer 'committed' — y'know what? Seen *The Wild Geese* six times. Oh yeah, well there in't much *I* don't know about blowing people's balls off.

Question Number Two: Physical — right? Well cop this f'r'a specimen.

(*She assumes a muscle-man pose.*) Rock hard, this is. (*Tapping her stomach.*) Solid rock.

I done two press-ups last week. Well not on the same day, obviously. Oh yeah, but ask us about marksmanship. Go on. Marksmanship? Now yer talking. I bin having a crack at me dad's air rifle . . . an' I'm getting pretty nifty. Oh yeah. Brought down — yesterday this is — brought down two japonicas an' an hanging basket. With one eye shut.

Yeah, right, okay — in traditional fields of armed warfare, what is the call — I know what yer saying — for gunning down a fuchsia? Okay, okay, fair question. Let me finish. It's not the fuchsias, is it? It's the principle.

Have y'seen *The Wild Geese*? Y'should, honest. It's invaluable. The tactics . . . the manoevres . . . the right attitude . . . the right face. Like . . . what's this? (*She assumes a horrible face. Then as if it's obvious.*) Roger Moore. (*She does another face, accompanied by a growl.*) Richard Burton. Yeah. You *have* seen it, haven't yer?

Oh no, I'm not daft — I do know — *The Wild Geese* is mercenaries, right? — which is not *strictly* the same as army. Yeah, but it's all the same in the long run, in't it? Join the army, learn to be a bastard — then go out there an' put all that skill into practice. Get a few wars goin' . . . stage the odd coup. Y'could retire on yer winnings by the time yer forty. Also . . . and this is a point worth thinking about . . . mercenaries don't pay income tax. Well . . . yeah . . . that *is* usually 'cos they're dead . . . but what a way to go, eh?

NITA: Beth . . . I don't know if you'd really be suited for the army.

BETH: What d'y'mean?

NITA: Bigoted . . . bad-tempered . . . loud-mouthed . . . aggressive . . . d'you

want me to go on?

BETH: Yeah, right, I know. I'm over-qualified. So I'll just have to go in as a general.

ALICE *and* KEVIN*'s house.*
ALICE *and* KEVIN *are sitting watching TV.* KEVIN *sits in a chair with* ALICE *at his feet. He is watching the TV intently but absent-mindedly stroking* ALICE*'s hair as he does.*

KEVIN (*suddenly*): Aw watch this now — just watch — that's brilliant, that is.

ALICE: Could we have four?

KEVIN: Have what yer like.

ALICE (*slight pause*): When could I start? (*No reply.*) No, 'cos, what I mean is . . . once I know we're goin in f'r'it . . .

KEVIN (*still glued to the TV*): Sssssssssssshhhhhh . . .

ALICE: I could put me mind to it. I could start trying harder.

KEVIN: Well get yer skates on then.

ALICE (*delighted*): Can I?

KEVIN: What y'askin' us for? Y'don't *think* about it, do yer? Y'just get on with it.

ALICE: Oh no, but y'*should* think about it, Kevin. Y'should.

KEVIN: Oh, where d'y'read that crap, Al? Having kids is easy. It's a piece of piss. (*Suddenly transfixed by the TV.*) Oh, look at that, Al — that's bloody great acting, that is.

ALICE: What is?

KEVIN: Bloke there with the pint in his hand. (*Seeing she's unconvinced.*) Yer bloody ignorant, you are, Al. I'm talking about genius.

ALICE (*snuggling up to him*): Kevin . . .

KEVIN: Alice, d'y'mind? The adverts is on.

ALICE: I love you, Kevin.

KEVIN: Shut up, Al.

ALICE: I do.

KEVIN: Yeah, all right.

ALICE: D'you love me?

KEVIN: I married yer, didn't I?

ALICE: Oh . . . just say it, Kevin . . .

KEVIN: You're all right. (*He pushes her away, then absent-mindedly strokes her hair, still intent on the TV. Suddenly, the sound of the door. JOEY comes in.*)

JOEY: All right newly weds? All right Kevin? (*To* ALICE:) What you doin' layin' on yer backside. Y'got no ironing to do? Hey, y'wanna watch that Kev, y'know — two weeks time, she'll have yer making yer own dinner.

KEVIN (*to* ALICE): Go on, then — up you get.

ALICE: What d'y'mean?

KEVIN: Let's have some tea on. (JOEY *smiles in encouragement.*)

ALICE (*getting up, annoyed*): Is he stopping?

JOEY: In't yer pleased to see me, Al?

KEVIN (*reproachfully*): Alice . . . (ALICE *stalks off into the kitchen.*)

JOEY: Well?

KEVIN: No.

JOEY: No what?

KEVIN: I in't told her.

JOEY: What y'bin doin' Kev? Y've had a week.

KEVIN: Oh, what can I say, Joey? You wanna try tellin' her?

JOEY: Hey, *I'll* tell her — y'want me to tell her? Hey, Alice . . .

KEVIN: No. Don't. I'll do it.

JOEY: All right then. We moving this week?

KEVIN: Cross Lane Warehouse?

JOEY: I'm skint, Kevin. An' Carly's got a

stack of orders this high for Sonys.

KEVIN: Yeah, I'm easy. Thursday?

JOEY: Tomorrow.

KEVIN: Nah, s'no good, I'm out.

JOEY: Where?

KEVIN: Round her mam's.

JOEY: Yer joking, aren't yer? Eight, nine hundred, two-way split — Are we in this game, or aren't we, Kevin?

KEVIN: I said I'd go, Joey. Okay? An' if we're gonna keep this hush, I can't go breaking arrangements two weeks into me marriage. I'll do Thursday.

JOEY: Oh yeah — we get there, find half of Salford's beat us to it? (KEVIN *refuses to argue.*) I know what, Kev — I think yer goin' soft.

KEVIN: I didn't get married for a joke, y'know.

JOEY: Oh, what, Kev? — Y'love her, do yer?

KEVIN (*sheepishly*): Yeah, I do as a matter of fact.

JOEY (*sentimental*): Aaaah, Kevin . . .

KEVIN: What?

JOEY: You soft bastard.

LINDY *and* JAY's *flat in Bristol. NASH, LINDY, PHIL and JAY sit round a table. NASH and JAY are engaged in a game of chess. NASH, looking very relaxed, is sitting next to LINDY who is gazing at him enraptured and eagerly watching every move he makes. JAY is trying to play cool but is really tense. PHIL is earnestly attentive, but conscious of being a real outsider. It is JAY's turn to make a move in the game. He studies the chess board intently.*

LINDY (*suddenly*): Don't you think . . .

JAY (*furious*): Sssssssssssshhhhhhhh!

LINDY (*to* NASH, *gazing into his eyes*): Don't you think . . . that this music . . . is really *expressive*? . . . I mean, *really eloquent* . . . Don't you find it makes you think of . . . running water?

NASH *stifles a giggle.*

JAY: A mountain stream.

LINDY: No, no, no . . . more like . . . a waterfall.

NASH: Or a soda syphon.

LINDY (*taking him seriously*): D'you know what I mean? Like . . . Pacific Ocean . . . Like . . . really knowing what being the Gulf Stream is all about. (*To* PHIL:) D'*you* feel that, Phil?

PHIL, *who is smoking for the first time, starts to choke on the joint which* JAY *has passed to her.*

PHIL (*choking, but trying to look cool*): Oh yes . . . definitely.

LINDY: Hey, Phil – good stuff, this, hey? Jay knows this guy . . .

JAY: Right.

LINDY: This really amazing guy. I mean it, this guy is just . . .

JAY: Amazing.

LINDY: Right. Amazing deals. Some really unbelievable stuff. Nash, I promise you . . . (*Offering the joint.*) . . . you do not know what you're missing.

NASH: I can't. I'm a Catholic.

JAY *suddenly, with a shriek of delight, moves his chess piece.* NASH *ponders a few seconds, then moves.*

JAY (*tearing at his nails*): Shit!

LINDY: I don't believe it! (*They all turn to her.*) I seriously don't believe it! This reminds me *so much* of that time at Lindos. No, seriously. It's like . . . *being there*. D'you know what I mean? . . . It's like . . . this is really weird . . . this is something right out of Proust.

PHIL: Sounds amazing.

LINDY: Shit – you've never been? Phil, you *must*. You have seriously got to go.

JAY: I'm not kidding, Phil – the acropolis . . .

LINDY: And we know this guy, right? This guy with . . . oh shit, what's it like, Jay? he has got . . . the most *amazing* . . . you wouldn't believe it . . . this absolutely *huge* . . .

JAY: Villa. Right. Yeah, I say *villa* – actually it's more like a palace.

LINDY: Seriously.

JAY: Very boring. (*He yawns.*)

LINDY: Right.

JAY: They had that Roman guy staying there last time, right? (*To* PHIL, *as if it's obvious:*) Y'know . . . Polanski?

LINDY: Right.

Suddenly, without thinking, JAY *makes his next move.* NASH *immediately makes his.*

Fuck!

LINDY: Jay! – sssssssshhhhhhhh! – listen. I must just listen to this bit now. It reminds me of . . .

JAY *and* LINDY *simultaneously*

JAY } That little taverna.
LINDY } That little taverna!

JAY: Right.

LINDY: With that cracked-up dinky little waiter! Who fought for the Resistance during the war!

JAY: Bor-ing . . . (*He yawns.*)

LINDY: And had all the scars to prove it! Oh shit, and I don't know *what* happened – we just went *completely mad* . . . the walls . . . they just got *plastered* . . . in *food* . . . and *booze* . . . and . . .

JAY (*suddenly*): Sssssssshhhhhhhh! (*He concentrates his attention on the game.*)

LINDY (*whispering, to* NASH): Things not quite so repeatable!

JAY (*suddenly*): Ah! (*He delightedly makes his move.*)

NASH (*making his move*): Checkmate.

JAY: Aaaaaaaaagh! Shit!

LINDY: Bor-ing, Jay . . . (*She yawns.*)

NASH (*getting up*): Well . . . all good things . . .

LINDY: Oh, you're not going? We were going to watch the sun rise. (*Sidling closer.*)

NASH: Sorry, Lind — got a nine o'clock tomorrow.

LINDY: Oh, deadly . . .

JAY: You mean you actually *go* to nine o'clock lectures?

NASH: Comes of bein' backward. Y'need a lot of help.

PHIL (*kissing JAY*): It's been lovely . . .

JAY: Sure you won't stay for just another blast?

LINDY: Next time, hey? (*Standing up.*) Oh God . . . I feel . . . I think I'm going to be . . . (*She rushes out.*)

JAY (*rushing after her*): Deep breaths, Lind . . . take deep breaths . . .

Out in the street, PHIL *and* NASH *are walking home in silence.*

PHIL (*suddenly*): Funny? And what's funny about it? You were just . . . I don't believe you tonight, Nash. We get asked round — you go through two bottles of wine, three packets of twiglets . . . Jay cooks us this most amazing moussaka . . .

NASH: It was not amazing, Phil. It was all right. It was edible.

PHIL: This most amazing moussaka. You sit there — you don't even *attempt* to look interested in Jay's slides of Tunisian rabies victims. Then, after the wine's run out . . . okay, Nash, so

you don't smoke . . .

NASH: Neither do you.

PHIL: Well, I tell you, Nash — y'don't know what yer missing.

NASH: Well, what I *do* know, Phil — what I *do* know is the bloke who sold them the stuff.

PHIL: Oh, so what?

NASH: He's a mate of mine.

PHIL: Big deal.

NASH: And for your information, Phil — that dope was not dope at all. It was privet leaves.

PHIL: What? —

NASH: Dried privet leaves. Far out, hey Phil?

He strolls off.

ALICE's *house.*
    ALICE *sits with* NITA *doing a jigsaw.* NITA *is bored and quickly gives up.*

NITA: Alice, I can't do this.

ALICE: Oh Nita, I give yer the Ptarmigan 'cos he's dead easy. Look, yer only missing his beak an' a bit of his groin . . .

NITA: Where's yer telly gone?

ALICE: Oh, it just went. We're gettin' another next week though. Oh no, Nita — that's the Snowy Owl's foot . . . We sometimes get stuff, y'know, 'at the right price' — y'know, like, something off?

NITA: Off what, Alice? The back of a lorry?

ALICE: Nita . . . y've put its beak where its tail should go.

NITA: Alice, d'y'want a job?

ALICE: A what?

NITA: Y'know, like *work*? Hairdressing.

ALICE: I can't do hair.

NITA: I'll teach yer.

ALICE: No, I couldn't.

NITA: Why not?

ALICE: Well . . . see . . . Kev . . .

NITA: What?

ALICE: He wants us at home. He likes to know where I am.

NITA: But it's a *job,* Alice.

ALICE: Oh, I couldn't, Nita. He'd get upset. He'd say I wasn't satisfied.

NITA: Well *are* yer?

ALICE (*looking at the jigsaw*): I think there's a piece missing somewhere . . .

NITA: What's up with yer face?

ALICE: Look, I think we ought to see this off now, Nita. I have to get the tea on. (*Seeing she's about to argue.*) If I do the Red Grouse will you finish the Snipe?

Suddenly a figure disguised in a stocking mask, brandishing a gun, bursts into the room.

MAN: Okay, hit the deck – hit the deck – get down on yer fuckin' knees!

NITA *and* ALICE *dive to the ground in terror.*

Okay, where is he?

ALICE: Who?

MAN: Gilmore. Where is he?

ALICE: He's gone out.

MAN: Well I'll just have to sit here and wait f'r'him, won't I? (*He sits down.*) And while I'm here . . . (*He takes the mask off: it is* JOEY.) Can yer brew us a cup of tea, Alice? (ALICE *and* NITA *look up.*) Aw, can't y'take a joke, Alice?

ALICE: He's not coming back till after.

JOEY: Oh, is he not, Alice?

ALICE: He's doin' a job. (*Deliberately.*) A building job.

JOEY (*amused*): Oh a *building* job. Well let's just see if he doesn't show his lovely little face round here within the next fifteen minutes?

ALICE: How d'you get in?

JOEY: American Express.

ALICE: Pardon?

JOEY (*patiently*): An' how do people usually get in round here, Alice? (*Demonstrating with his American Express Card.*) They force the bleedin' lock. (*Suddenly very pleasant.*) Shall we have tea, Alice? (*Seeing her continued look of terror.*) What? . . . Oh yeah, I nearly forgot . . . (*He point his gun at* ALICE *and fires caps. His glee is almost child-like.*) Good, innit? (*He puts the gun away.*) Got any cake, Alice? Any biscuits?

ALICE: I've got some wedding cake.

JOEY: Oh yeah, that'll do. Three sugars for me, Alice. (*Seeing* NITA *about to sidle off into the kitchen.*) Oh no, don't go. You stay here an' talk to me, eh? Alice knows what she's doin'.

He pats the sofa invitingly next to him. NITA *nervously sits down.*

So . . . what is it you do, then, Nita?

NITA: I'm a hairdresser.

JOEY: Oh, hairdresser, eh? Very nice. Y'take bookings, Nita?

NITA: Yes . . .

JOEY: I could do with a cut. Where is it, this place of yours?

NITA (*reluctantly*): It's . . . on the way to town.

JOEY: Well y'can give us the number, can't yer? I'm not gonna rob yer. I don't do mates. (NITA *reluctantly hands over a card.*) *That* often. (*Looking at it.*) Oh yeah, very smart. I'll look forward to that, Nita.

NITA: And what is it you do?

JOEY: What do *I* do? Well that's a good question. Manual jobs mostly. Lot of shop work – bit of roofing. I'm very versatile.

ALICE *comes in with tea and cake.*

Well this is nice, isn't it? Cake for you, Nita? (*Politely passing the cake.*) Alice? (ALICE *declines.*) Ah, that's a nice reminder of a very pleasant day we all shared not long ago. So . . . how's married life treating you, Alice?

ALICE: Joey . . .

JOEY (*still very pleasant*): Mind, Kev's a different person since he took the pledge — know what I mean, Nita? Oh, no doubt about it — a changed man. Well, has he struck oil yet, Al?

ALICE: Pardon?

JOEY: Or has all that hammer he's bin givin' the bed springs come to nought?

NITA (*getting up*): I think I ought to be going . . .

JOEY: Oh, Nita, surely not? An' just when the conversation was beginning to get personal.

NITA (*hurrying on with her coat*): I'll give you a ring, Alice.

JOEY: An' I'll give *you* a ring, Nita. Oh, it's all right — I do have your card. D'y'do streaks, Nita? Or is that all a bit avant garde?

NITA: Yes, we do . . . do streaks.

JOEY: Streaks it is, then. Nice seein' yer, Nita.

NITA *heads for the door.* ALICE *is about to show her out.*

JOEY: Er . . . Alice? (ALICE *stops.*) I think Nita can see herself out? (NITA *goes out alone.* ALICE *sits down again.*) More tea, Alice?

ALICE: No.

JOEY: No thank you.

ALICE *goes on with the jigsaw.*

Bit quiet here, in't it, Alice?

ALICE: What d'y'mean?

JOEY: Not much happening? (*He studies her.*) Nice dress that, Alice. (*She doesn't reply. Suddenly animated.*) The kestrel! Not a nice piece of work.

Hey, y've missed its beak haven't yer? S'all right, I've got it. (*Fitting in the beak.*) An' a kestrel, as you are probably aware, Alice . . . is a bird of prey.

Suddenly he turns and pounces on ALICE. *For a second she acquiesces, then she starts to struggle. The sound of the door is heard offstage.* JOEY *leaps away.* KEVIN *comes in.*

KEVIN: All right?

JOEY: Safe enough.

KEVIN: D'y'wanna get goin'?

JOEY: Yeah, let's move.

KEVIN (*to* ALICE): Here y'are. (*He throws her a small box.*)

ALICE: What is it?

KEVIN: Something for yer. Y'can open it after.

ALICE: Is it for me? Honest?

KEVIN: Well who else would it be for, y'soft get? (*He ruffles her hair. To* JOEY:) You right?

KEVIN *goes out.* ALICE *begins to unwrap the present.* JOEY *grabs her round the neck and kisses her violently.*

JOEY (*releasing her*): I'll be seein' yer, Alice. (*He goes out.*)

ALICE *opens the box and discovers an obviously expensive watch, realises it must be stolen. In terror bundles it back into the box and puts it away, as the lights fade on her.*

Bristol University: the English Department common room. NASH *sits working.* PHIL, *opposite him, looks distracted.*

PHIL (*suddenly*): Look, there's no such place as Coronation Street.

NASH *looks up, then goes back to his work.*

They don't believe yer, do they? Where y'from, Phil? Manchester?

Never.
Beer an' bingo? Tripe an' onions?
Rovers Return?
That's right. Friday nights down the
dog track — blow yer wages — batter
the wife. Education? What's the point,
love? Yer only gonna get married.
Oh, we're all dead ignorant up North,
aren't we?
(*Pause.*) I am though, aren't I?
It's dead embarrassing. How d'y'admit
y've never been wind-surfing — never
read *Gormenghast* — never heard of
David Hockney? I've missed out.
I'm not a Feminist, Friend-of-the-
Earth, Ban-the-Bomber, Real Ale
Freak. What am I? I don't know
anything. Y'go to school, y'sit exams
— nobody tells yer about Jean-Luc
Godard or reading the *Guardian*.
Football? Oh but you don't actually
go? Oh no, not me.
Not much.
What d'y'do if y'can't stand yoga,
despise *The Hobbit* — an' thought
that Donizetti was a cheap martini?
How can y'be taken seriously if yer
favourite film's *The Jungle Book*?

NASH: Good film, *The Jungle Book*.

PHIL: It's not art, though, is it?

NASH: What's art, Phil?

PHIL: Four A Levels, eight O Levels — I
come here an' I know sod-all. Okay,
okay, *you* say it doesn't matter. You
say 'so what?'

NASH: Yeah. So what?

PHIL: Did *you* think Eugene O'Neill
played on the right wing for Northern
Ireland?

A street in Salford
    ALICE *walks on.* JANINE *suddenly
runs after her.*

JANINE: Oh, it IS you, is it? Forget
where we lived, did yer?

ALICE: Oh . . . I bin dead busy . . .

JANINE: What's up with yer eye?

ALICE: Oh . . . I bin tryin' out new
make-up. What d'y'think?

JANINE (*casually*): Cross Lane Mill got
robbed last night.

ALICE: It never.

JANINE: Two thousand quid's-worth
done a runner.

ALICE: Really?

JANINE: Where was he last night? 'Out
with the lads'?

ALICE: You know what they're like.

JANINE: Yer eye looks sore.

ALICE: It's a new shade.

JANINE: Tell us another, Alice.

ALICE: Look, don't interfere.

JANINE: Oh, 'don't interfere'?

ALICE: Y'don't understand, Jan. Y'don't
know anything about it.

JANINE: Well, what I *do* know, Al — is
what you got over your eye — is a
bruise.

    JANINE *walks off.*

ALICE *and* KEVIN's *house.*
    Saturday afternoon. ALICE *comes on
ready to do some housework.* KEVIN
gets up.

KEVIN (*studiedly casual*): Y'goin' out?

ALICE: No.

KEVIN: You are.

ALICE: Y'what?

KEVIN: I need the place to meself this
afternoon.

ALICE: What d'y'mean?

KEVIN: Alice, I got people coming
round. I got things to discuss. An' I
can't have you earwigging on me
conversations. (*He comes over and
puts his arms round her.*) So I'm askin'
yer — nicely — to please go an' piss off

f'r'a bit. Okay? (ALICE *starts to go.*)
That's a good girl. Hey, Al . . . (*She
turns round.*) There's a fiver f'yer —
go an' buy yerself a new coat.

ALICE *goes out. On the way she
meets* BETH *who hands her a
Manchester United scarf. They run off
together.*

JOEY *and* NIDGE *come on.* NIDGE
sits nervously in a chair flanked by
JOEY *and* KEVIN.

JOEY: Hey, I need to know, all right?
Does he want it — or doesn't he?

NIDGE: Joey, y'know me — I don't
make decisions — I just pass them on.

KEVIN (*taking his lead from* JOEY):
What's he playin' at, Nidge?

JOEY: You just tell him — say *I* told
yer this — when he orders something,
he pays for it, okay? I got better
things to do than risk me neck for
him. Twice last week — you listenin'?
— twice, we missed it by this much.
Right, Kevin?

KEVIN: This much, Nidge.

JOEY: An' no way me an' him's ending
up back in Strangeways on the fuckin'
money *he's* payin' us.

NIDGE: Couldn't yer . . . y'know . . .
like . . . 'keep it in stock' as it were?

JOEY: Nidge, there in't a lot of places
y'can stuff a bleedin' Space Invaders
machine — but if he dun't come up
with the cash, I can think of at least
one.

BETH *and* ALICE *run on.
They are on the terraces at Old
Trafford watching Manchester United.*

BETH (*shouting*): Y'want shooting. Y'do.
Y'should be bloody shot.

ALICE (*after a pause*): So anyway . . . he
missed.

BETH: Oh, he never. Oh, tough shit,
Kevin. (*As if addressing someone*

next to her.) Her Kevin's dead kind,
y'know. He likes her to feel involved.
When they play darts he uses her head
to practise for treble twenty.

ALICE (*trying to quieten her*): Beth —

BETH (*loud*): I didn't do it, Yer
Honour. I missed the board. (*Shouting:*)
Oh, move yer arse McQueen — yer not
on holiday . . . Oh, have y'seen that?
Get off, Coppell — y'couldn't score
in a brothel.

ALICE (*sympathetically applauding*): Oh,
hard luck, Stevie . . .

BETH (*addressing her neighbour*): Dead
careless with knives, he is . . . leaves
them lying about all over the place . . .
Like the back of her neck.

ALICE: I never said he used it. I said he
threatened to use it.

BETH (*shouting*): Shift y'self, Nicholl —
if yer still awake.

ALICE: Anyway, it was a pick-axe.

BETH: How to lose weight without giving
up food. Marry Kevin — lose a limb.
(*Shouting:*) Oh go on, Joe — bite his
leg off . . .

ALICE (*suddenly getting carried away by
the game*): Yeah, go on, Joe — show
'em who's boss!

BETH: Hey, I should watch yerself there,
Al.

ALICE: What d'y'mean?

BETH: Enjoying yerself. Y'might get a
taste for it.

ALICE *suddenly becomes silent. The
sounds of the football crowd subside
as* BETH *takes her leave and goes off.*

ALICE *and* KEVIN's *house.* ALICE,
*subdued now, furtively puts her scarf
away and stands nervously outside the
door. Inside* KEVIN *and* JOEY *sit
surrounded by cans and cigarette ends.*
ALICE *braces herself and goes in.*

KEVIN: Where y'been?

ALICE: Kevin, I been . . .

JOEY: Where y'been? He's waiting for yer.

ALICE: I bin out.

KEVIN: Quarter to six, Alice. My tea's at half past five.

JOEY: What y'playing at, Alice?

ALICE: I'm sorry Kevin − I'll get it started now. What d'y'want?

JOEY: Oh, use yer imagination, Alice. He didn't get married just so's he could get his own tea together.

KEVIN: Didn't yer mam give yer nothing this afternoon?

ALICE: Didn't go to me mam's.

KEVIN: Where y'been, then?

JOEY: What y'bin doing?

ALICE: I went with Beth.

KEVIN: With who?

ALICE: To United.

JOEY: Jesus Christ.

KEVIN (*taking his lead from* JOEY): Y'went where?

JOEY: What y'doin' Kevin?

KEVIN: C'mere, you − *now.* You went to the football? You stayed out all day with that slag while I'm sat here waiting for me tea?

JOEY: Y'tryna make him look an arsehole, Alice?

KEVIN: Y'tryna make me look an arsehole, Alice?

JOEY: Bloody football −

KEVIN: Bloody football? − I've had it up to here. D'y'never think about nothing else? D'y'know there's jobs need doin' round this house?

JOEY: She's bloody obsessed with it.

KEVIN: Yer bloody obsessed, you are. It's either bloody football or yer bloody dickhead mates. You get in there an' get some scran sorted, or I'll sort yer bleedin' face for yer. An' I'll sort it so you'll look like the 68 bus just reversed over yer. All right? Now get out.

ALICE *goes out.*

JOEY: Hey Kev − great conversationalist, your wife, in't she?

KEVIN: Joey − I talk, she listens. Know any better way to hold a conversation?

Outside KEVIN's *house. Night time.* KEVIN *nervously leaves the house, starts to walk. Suddenly a figure steps in front of him. He turns round − there is another behind him.*

1ST MAN: Hey, Kevin −

2ND MAN: Y'goin' out, Kevin? −

1ST MAN: Got anything for us, Kevin? −

KEVIN: Look, I in't got it −

2ND MAN: Oh dear −

KEVIN: I'll have it −

1ST MAN: It's Tuesday, Kevin −

KEVIN: I know. I'll get it −

2ND MAN: Two hundred quid, Kevin −

KEVIN: Tomorrow night −

2ND MAN: You better −

KEVIN: I'll have it − I will − I'll get it −

1ST MAN: I would, if I were you . . .

The two MEN *disappear.* KEVIN *walks off nervously.*

KEVIN *and* ALICE's *house.* KEVIN *paces up and down nervously.* ALICE *comes in.* KEVIN *looks gleeful with anticipation and relief.* ALICE *seems nervous.*

KEVIN (*encouraging*): Come on, then. (*He holds out his hand.*) Where is it? Gi's it here, then.

ALICE: Kevin . . . I didn't get it.

KEVIN: Nah, don't mess about, Al.

ALICE: I'm not. She wouldn't give it me.

KEVIN: Why? (*She doesn't reply. He is baffled.*) But why, Alice? (*She still doesn't reply.*) You told her, didn't yer. *I* know what you did. Mam, Kevin needs the money. Kevin needs it now — tonight — or he's gonna get his head kicked in. And my dear so-called mother-in-law — what's she say? Good? Let him? Then we'll get shot of him? Right, Alice. (*She doesn't reply.*) Is that right, Alice?

ALICE (*almost in tears*): No . . .

KEVIN (*now getting desperate*): I was counting on you, Alice.

ALICE: What can I do, Kevin?

KEVIN: I think y'can do a lot when y'want. When you really try. But y'didn't, did yer. You couldn't put yerself out. (*Now starting to panic.*) Who am I, Alice? I'm yer fuckin' husband. Yer supposed to do as I say. Now get over here.

ALICE: What?

KEVIN: Over here. (ALICE *reluctantly comes over.*) We need two hundred quid, Alice. *I* need two hundred quid. You . . . let me down. An' I *need* that money — by tonight — or I'm gonna get me neck broke. An' if they don't feel *I'm* worth enough, they might just come after you an' all.

ALICE: Oh no . . .

KEVIN: Oh, they would. They in't particular. They bin practising equality for years. (*Suddenly dead serious.*) Hey, it's no joke this, Al. I think we're gonna have to come up with two hundred quid now, else book us a room in Salford Royal Infirmary.

ALICE: But where we gonna get the money? Who's gonna give us . . . (*Noticing him looking at her.*) What? . . . what y'lookin' at, Kevin?

KEVIN (*quietly*): C'mere, Alice.

ALICE: What y'looking at?

KEVIN: C'mere, Alice. Give me your hand.

ALICE: What?

KEVIN: Yer hand.

ALICE: What for? (ALICE *gingerly puts her hand forward.* KEVIN *grabs it, turns it over to look at the rings.*)

KEVIN (*looking at her engagement ring*): Hundred an' seventy-five quid, right? (*Then at the wedding ring.*) Sixty quid, give or take, yeah?

ALICE: Oh no, Kevin . . . no, please, Kevin . . .

KEVIN: That'll do us.

ALICE: No, Kevin — I can't — not the rings — I can't . . . (*She wrenches herself free and runs to the other side of the room.*) Please, Kevin . . .

KEVIN: Get over here, Alice.

ALICE: No.

KEVIN: Get over here.

ALICE: Kevin, I'm not losing my rings.

KEVIN: Alice, you better get over here now. (*She tries to back off.*) Oh yes . . . oh yes you will, Alice . . . (*He moves towards her; she is too scared to move.*) Give me the rings, that's a good girl . . . (ALICE *takes off the rings and hands them to him at arm's length. He takes them from her and puts them in his pocket. Then suddenly turns on her and swipes her across the face with such force that she hits the floor. Then, realising he's really hurt her:*) Alice, I'm sorry . . . I'm sorry, Al . . . (*She still lies on the floor.*) Y'shouldn't do it, Al — why d'yer ask for it? Y'know what I'm like. (*She still doesn't move.*) Look . . . there's a fiver for yer . . . go an' get yerself a bottle of something . . . Listen, Al, I've said sorry, haven't I? . . . I can get yer another ring. I'll get yer ten. (*Unable to cope any longer.*) Look, I'll have to go . . . I'll see yer later . . . y'can do us a meat pie for me tea. (ALICE

looks up, horrified.) Oh, look
Alice . . . it's only a wedding ring . . .

KEVIN *goes out.*

ALICE*'s house. The middle of the*
afternoon. NITA *has come back to see*
ALICE, *who is now sitting with a cup*
of tea, nursing a bruised eye.

NITA: Great stuff. Brilliant. I drop
everything. I cancel seeing people. I
come tearing back here halfway
through a perm – an' what happens?
Keep out – it's none of my business.

ALICE: I know but . . .

NITA: Fine. Okay. I can go now, can I?
I got two tints an' a demi-wave waiting
back there . . . (*She is about to leave.*)
Look, Alice, you called me – and you
were bloody petrified. So don't you
sit there an' tell me it doesn't matter.

ALICE: It does matter. Yeah, it matters.
But what can y'do? It happens. Me
mam hits me dad. I'm used to things
gettin' settled on a knock-out.

NITA: Have y'seen your face, Al? Have
y'seen the state? Y'could have him
locked up for that.

ALICE: Yeah, but I love him, Nita.

NITA: What's that got to do with it?

ALICE: I'll just have to try a bit harder.

NITA (*unable to believe her ears*): What?

ALICE: I must be doing something
wrong, Nita. I must. People don't just
hit yer for no reason. I musta done
something.

NITA: I don't believe this. Alice, y'gonna
have to get out.

ALICE: No, I can't. We're goin' in for
a baby.

NITA: Yer joking.

ALICE: Oh, I'm not. I got it all worked
out. See, Kevin gets narked at me –
but Kevin gets narked 'cos I get on his
nerves an' what is there to take his

mind off it? If we had a baby, it'd all
be all right.

NITA (*suddenly*): Alice, are you
superstitious?

ALICE: Nita, don't say that word – it's
bad luck.

NITA: I want you to do something for
me. I want you to promise . . .

ALICE (*immediately suspicious*):
What? –

NITA (*trying to sound reasonable*): I
want yer to wait four weeks . . .
before y'try for a baby.

ALICE: Four weeks? What for?

NITA: 'Cos if you don't . . . well you'll
be sorry, that's all.

ALICE: Well how d'you know I will?

NITA: Well . . . because . . . (*A sudden
brainwave.*) I read tea-leaves.

ALICE: Tea-leaves?

NITA: That's right. (*Unable to believe
her luck that* ALICE *has fallen for it.*)

ALICE: Since when?

NITA: I bin goin' to classes.

ALICE: What? –

NITA (*following up her advantage*): And
believe me . . . (*Trying to sound
ominous.*) . . . if you start a kid in the
next four weeks, y'won't know what's
hit yer.

ALICE (*unconvinced*): Where's it say
that?

NITA: All over the bottom of that cup.

ALICE: But that's *your* cup, Nita.

NITA: Oh yeah . . . (*Hurriedly swapping
cups.*) Well *yours* is even worse.

ALICE (*starting to panic*): Oh God . . .

NITA: And that's only the first cup.

ALICE: What'm I gonna do?

NITA: Get yer coat on.

ALICE: Where we goin'?

NITA: You'll see.

> ALICE *reluctantly puts her coat on and follows* NITA.

ALICE: Nita . . . ?

NITA: What?

ALICE: Could we have tea bags next time?

The Family Planning Clinic. NITA *comes on followed by* ALICE. ALICE *sees a* MAN *and a* WOMAN *sitting together and does an about-turn.*

> NITA *pushes her back in again.*

ALICE: It's embarrassing.

NITA: What's embarrassing about contraceptives?

ALICE: Sssshhh, no don't, Nita — I don't like that word. It's disgusting.

NITA: Sit down, Alice.

ALICE (*sits down and hides behind a magazine; then emerging*): What is it you ask for?

NITA: You *discuss,* don't you? That's what yer here for.

ALICE (*in panic*): I don't wanna *discuss.* Why can't y'do it by mail order?

NITA: Alice, you have to be examined.

ALICE (*horror-struck*): What!

NITA: It's just a simple procedure . . .

ALICE: Physical?

NITA: Physical, yes. What would be the point of testing yer general knowledge?

ALICE: No, Nita, I can't. It isn't dignified.

NITA: Alice, you have had sex before haven't you?

ALICE: Sssssssshhh . . .

NITA: So the sensation won't be entirely new to you.

ALICE (*wailing*): Oh Nita . . .

NITA: Shut up and read this.

ALICE (*having studied the magazine for a few seconds*): Nita . . .

NITA: What?

ALICE: What d'y'think *she's* here for? (*Indicating the* WOMAN.)

NITA (*whispering back*): Well why don't you ask?

MAN (*having overheard previous conversation*): We're here for an IUD. (*He beams and pats the* WOMAN's *hand.*)

ALICE: Oh . . . (*She whispers to* NITA:) A what? (NITA *whispers back.*) Oh . . . (*She smiles to the* MAN *and* WOMAN.) That's nice . . .

A DOCTOR *enters.*

DOCTOR (*calls*): Miss Banks, would you like to come this way, please?

> *The* MAN *assists the* WOMAN *to rise as if she's an invalid, and helps her out.*

NITA (*scornfully*): What a performance.

> BETH *suddenly bursts in singing at the top of her voice.*

BETH: Gettin' topped up, are we? They don't last, do they? D'y'know what *I* got through last month?

NITA: Beth —

BETH: What *you* doin' here, Al? Bit of a fling?

ALICE (*whispering*): I've come to get some . . . y'know . . .

BETH: Y'what?

ALICE: Some . . . you-know-whats . . . y'know . . . some (*She whispers.*) precautions.

BETH (*loud*): Oh, what'y'havin'? — balloons?

ALICE: Sssssshhhh . . .

BETH: Know what *I* reckon? They should do gift packs for beginners. Y'know, sling a bit of everything in?

NITA: Beth . . .

BETH: That way, if y'get bored with the sex, y'can always vary the contraceptive.

ALICE *hides behind her magazine in embarrassment.*

NITA (*by now annoyed*): Beth, will you shut up?

ALICE (*wailing*): An' why's it always us?

NITA: What?

ALICE: Why can't lads see to their own . . . y'know . . .

NITA: Well some of them do.

BETH: Oh yeah? Y'must introduce us sometime.

The DOCTOR *enters.*

DOCTOR (*calls*): Mrs Gilmore, would you like to come through, please?

ALICE (*in terror*): Nita . . .

NITA *pushes her out of the seat.*

DOCTOR: Mrs Gilmore?

ALICE (*following him out*): Nita, there is no way I'm having anything that involves taking me clothes off . . .

DOCTOR (*coming out again*): Miss Sharman? Dr Cardwell will see you now.

NITA (*getting up*): See yer later.

BETH: Nita, are you screwing someone? (NITA *goes out.*) I wish *I* was.

A pub in Bristol.
   PHIL *sits at the bar biting her nails and looking miserable. She has a letter in her hand.*
   Eventually NASH *walks in. She jumps up to meet him. Almost imperceptibly he avoids her attempt at an embrace.*

NASH (*casually*): Waiting long?

PHIL: Twenty minutes.

NASH: Y'not drinking?

PHIL: Nash . . . I can't . . . go to London with yer this weekend.

NASH: Why's that, then?

PHIL (*handing him the letter*): I have to go home.

NASH (*reading the card*): 'To celebrate the opening of Nita's Headlines Hairdressing Salon . . . a Fancy Dress Party.' Sounds right up your street.

PHIL: I don't wanna go.

NASH: I think y'should.

PHIL: Why?

NASH: I have to go home too.

PHIL: What d'y'mean?

NASH: See me dad.

PHIL: What for?

NASH: Ship yards is shutting down.

PHIL: Yeah?

NASH: He's gettin' laid off.

PHIL (*suddenly*): *I* know. Don't *you* go – an' *I* won't go – an' we can still go to London.

NASH: Phil, d'y'not understand me?

PHIL: Yeah, the ship yards is closing. Nita's in business. We don't need to be there. We could send a card.

BASH: That's big of us.

PHIL: Yeah, okay, Nash, it's bad news. It's a shame. It's not the end of the world.

NASH: Isn't it?

PHIL: There must be other jobs goin'.

NASH *looks at her for a moment, then screws up the letter.*

NASH: I'll see yer sometime, Phil. (*He walks off.*)

PHIL *jumps up to follow him, then realises it's futile and slowly walks off the other way.*

Two dustbins outside ALICE *and* KEVIN's *house.*
   NITA *and* BETH *are hiding behind them, watching for* ALICE *and* KEVIN *to*

come home. The stage is dark and the following conversation is conducted just above a whisper.

NITA: Keep still —

BETH: Me leg's gone dead —

NITA: They'll be here in a minute —

BETH: Nita, I bin thinking —

NITA: What? —

BETH: Just suppose we see something?

NITA: *See* something?

BETH: Bit of . . . y'know . . . aggro?

NITA: What aggro?

BETH: 'Case he's still hitting her.

NITA: I've told yer, haven't I? They've talked. Alice says it's all sorted out.

BETH: What we sat here for, then?

NITA: Be on the safe side.

BETH: Couldn't we just kill him?

NITA: Listen, if he looks quiet . . . an' Alice is okay . . . wait five minutes, then . . .

BETH: Piss off.

NITA: Exactly.

BETH: I wish they'd bloody move it. I'm gasping f'r'a wee.

NITA: They won't be long.

BETH: Neither will I . . . it's all that tea . . . oh God, nobody mention tea . . . nobody mention running water . . .

NITA: Sssshhh, who's this?

BETH: Oh God, that's done it —

NITA: What? —

BETH: I'll have to go —

NITA: Beth . . . Beth, what y'doing? — Beth, pull them up *now* . . . Beth, it's them . . . they're here . . .

BETH: I'm doing it as fast as I can.

NITA: Ugh . . . Beth . . .

BETH: Now what?

NITA: It's gone in me shoe . . .

BETH: Ssssssshhh . . .

NITA: Ssssssshhh . . .

Dead silence. ALICE *and* KEVIN *walk in, wrapped in each others arms.* ALICE *looks deliriously happy.* KEVIN *gives her the key to the house and she goes in.* KEVIN *staggers over to where* NITA *and* BETH *are hiding, leans over the bushes and vomits. He goes back towards the house.*

NITA *emerges, close to tears with disgust.* BETH *stalks out after her.*

BETH: Satisfied?

NITA: Perfectly.

They both stalk off, NITA *hopping on one foot and carrying her shoe.*

A pub in Salford. During the black-out, over the loudspeakers: 'This is Manchester, Piccadilly. The 16.58 from Bristol Temple Meads has now arrived at platform nine.'
PHIL walks on. As she does so the lights come up on the pub, with juke box music playing in the background. PHIL comes in and looks round, looks at her watch and is about to leave again when the door bursts open and in march BETH *dressed as a gorilla,* ALICE *dressed in trench coat, beret and dark glasses, and* NITA *and* JANINE *also in fancy dress.*

PHIL (*amused despite herself*): I don't believe this.

BETH: Where'y'been? Yer late. Y'got two hours serious supping to catch up. (*Looking at her clothes.*) So what've *you* come as, then?

PHIL: I didn't have time to dress up.

BETH: No, I can see that.

NITA: How are yer, Phil?

PHIL: Oh . . . okay . . . y'know?

BETH: Well don't overwhelm her, will yer. (*To* NITA:) Well *I* think y'done dead well anyway. *I* think it's a very nice shop.

ALICE (*with her arm round* NITA): Yeah, Nita (*Singing:*) Congratulations ... Right, I'll get the drinks in. C'mon Jan ... (ALICE *goes off with* JANINE, *still singing.*)

PHIL: What's *she* got to be cheerful about?

BETH: End of Round One.

PHIL: Y'what?

NITA: All sorted out with Kev.

PHIL: Oh yeah, as if.

NITA: Phil, y'should see it. Clothes she's got, presents he buys her. Y'go round, get asked in — all smiles, the place is spotless ...

BETH: Oh yeah, big difference. No bloodstains on the carpet — not a finger out of place ...

NITA: And she got her rings back.

PHIL: That's good of him.

NITA: Honest, Phil, y'won't believe it. It's like ...

BETH: A goal in the last seconds of the Cup Final.

PHIL: For which side?

PHIL *goes off and sits down at a table.*

BETH: Are we meant to be celebrating something?

NITA: Welcome home, Phil.

ALICE *and* JANINE *come back with the drinks and join* PHIL.

BETH: Hey, don't leave Alice on her own with Phil.

NITA: What d'y'mean?

They immediately go over to where PHIL *is in conversation with* ALICE.

PHIL: Flash Gordon? Flash Gordon isn't Art. It's crap. It hasn't even got a cult following.

ALICE: Well *I* liked it.

PHIL: When't the last time you went to the theatre?

ALICE: I don't go to the theatre. We got a colour telly.

PHIL: Y'never read, y'don't broaden yer mind ...

ALICE: I read *Jaws* last week.

PHIL: *Jaws* isn't literature.

ALICE: It's a book.

PHIL (*getting carried away with her own enthusiasm*): Know what *I* done this year? Learnt book binding. Started hang gliding. I go to the cinema, the theatre, I play squash, I speak Italian ... This summer where'm I goin'? Greece. The Greek Islands ...

BETH: Shoulda learnt Greek, then.

PHIL (*ignoring her*): This year what've *you* done?

ALICE: Got married?

PHIL: Nothing. Y'done nothing. C'mon, *do* something, Al.

ALICE: Like what, Phil?

PHIL: I dunno ... anything ... start parachuting.

There is a general outburst of derision.

(*Genuinely surprised by their response.*) Look, it's easy — it's dead easy. *I* did it. Go to night school — learn a language — travel ...

ALICE: Oh yeah, what on, Phil? Fresh air?

PHIL: Oh, typical. Any excuse.

NITA: I wish I had a tape recorder, Phil. I wish you could hear yerself sometimes.

PHIL: Okay, why don't you creep off back to your cosy little job and your cosy little world, Nita.

NITA: I'm sorry that offends you, Phil. I'm sorry *work* is such a dirty word. Earning a living's so boring, isn't it? Spouting crap, living in a daydream — that's 'where it's at' is it, Phil?

PHIL: Her — have y'seen the state? (*Pointing at* ALICE.) She's like a zombie. She might as well be six feet under.

ALICE: No, Phil — I'm still here. I do exist.

PHIL: Okay, okay — forget it — nothing changes.

ALICE: Oh, things change, Phil. Y'bin off . . . what? . . . six months? Bin dead exciting round here, Phil. Bin all sorts goin' on.

PHIL: I bet.

ALICE: Oh yeah, like . . . four factories shut down . . . four thousand jobs gone missing . . .

PHIL: Yeah, I read the papers, Al.

ALICE: Read about me dad, Phil? Yeah, y'know me dad, Phil — soft with his money? Buy y'a drink? Get yerself a new coat?

PHIL: So what?

ALICE: Got laid off, gone soft up here? Read about me mam, then? Give up work, stop home all day, stop me dad from slitting his wrists? Nothing changes, Phil? Well some things do.

PHIL: If you let them.

ALICE: Oh yeah, an' Phil got away, didn't she? Well done Phil. Well Phil had the means, didn't she? Phil had it up here. The rest of us, we stop here, and we make the best.

PHIL: Make the best? No, Alice. There *is* no best round here. It doesn't exist.

ALICE: Dead easy for you, Phil. Come home, handing out advice. Start this, do that, dump Kevin . . . (NITA *is about to intervene but sees that* ALICE *is determined to fight it out for herself.*) Well don't tell me to dump Kevin. Kevin is all there is.

PHIL: And Kevin kicks your head in three times a week.

ALICE: He does not.

PHIL: And Kevin was *always* gonna kick your head in three times a week. And anyone with half a grain between the ears could see that coming two years ago.

ALICE: Oh, I'm pleased for you, Phil. Got proved right, did yer? Well now yer about to get proved wrong. Sorry, Phil. I'm really sad I can't oblige yer any further.

PHIL: Oh, is that right, Alice?

NITA: Leave her alone, Phil.

PHIL (*turning on her*): *You*? Are you runnin' a business, Nita? Are you tryna make a living?

NITA: Y'what?

PHIL: Y'gonna get shopped down the sink, Nita. Why? 'Cos she just sold you the biggest pile of shit goin' — an' you bought the lot.

ALICE: I'm not stopping here listening to this.

ALICE *gets up to go.* PHIL *jumps up and blocks her exit.*

PHIL: C'mon, Al, let's hear it again. Life's a dream, is it? Marriage is bliss?

ALICE: Yes. As a matter of fact. It is.

PHIL: Despite we have a cupboard stashed full of ripped-off stereos?

ALICE: Kevin's not involved in that anymore, Phil. As a matter of fact, Kevin has left the gang.

PHIL: Oh no, Kevin has left the gang? An' I bet you — as a matter of fact — that Kevin keeps his fists away, does he?

ALICE: Dead right, Phil.

PHIL: Dead right, Alice? It's dark outside, Al.

ALICE: So?

PHIL: So can't y'take the truth, Al? Is it so bright it hurts yer eyes? (*She grabs* ALICE's *sunglasses and reveals her badly-bruised eyes beneath.*) I'm sorry, Alice . . .

ALICE *stands still and stares at her.*

Oh God, I'm sorry, Al . . . I wanted yer to see . . . that's all.

ALICE *snatches the sunglasses, puts them on and walks out.* BETH, NITA *and* JANINE *walk out leaving* PHIL.

ALICE *and* KEVIN's *house.*
The phone is ringing. ALICE *comes running on and grabs the phone. The lights come up on the figure of a* GIRL, *in shadow, as if standing in a phone box.*

ALICE: Hello? . . . hello? . . . who's there? . . . hello?

VOICE: Who's that?

ALICE: Hello, who is it, please?

VOICE: Is Kevin there?

ALICE: No, he's . . . gone out.

VOICE: Time's he back?

ALICE: Well, I'm not sure . . . who is that?

VOICE: Tell him it's Carly.

ALICE: Right . . .

VOICE: S'he mentioned me?

ALICE: Er . . . not that I know of . . .

VOICE: No . . . well he wouldn't. Y'give him a message?

ALICE: Yes . . .

VOICE: Just say . . . the kid. It's better. It's coming home tomorrow.

ALICE: Right. The kid's okay . . . and . . .

VOICE: Coming home tomorrow.

ALICE: I'll tell him.

VOICE: You his wife?

ALICE: Yes . . .

VOICE: Alice?

ALICE: That's right . . . I'm sorry . . . do I know you?

VOICE: Doubt it, love. I know you, though.

ALICE: Me?

VOICE: I know all about you.

ALICE: Who is this? . . . Hello? . . . Who is it? . . . Hello . . .

The phone goes dead. ALICE *hears the door open and the voices of* KEVIN *and* JOEY *in the hall. She quickly replaces the receiver.*

JOEY (*off*): Gi's the key, will yer?

KEVIN (*off*): Yeah, hang about . . .

JOEY (*off*): Who's been at this lock? — Where is she, Kevin?

KEVIN (*off*): She's out, I told yer. She's goin' out.

ALICE (*with trepidation*): Kevin . . .?

KEVIN (*tearing into the room in panic*): What you doin' here?

ALICE: I got back.

KEVIN: I told yer, didn't I? Don't be here, I said.

ALICE: I got fed up. I came home.

KEVIN: When? How long?

ALICE: Just now.

KEVIN: Shit. You stop here now.

ALICE: What's he round here for? What's happening?

KEVIN: Look, you in't supposed to be here. Go to bed, Al. (*He heads for the door.*)

ALICE: What's under the stairs?

KEVIN (*stopped in his tracks*): What?

ALICE: There's boxes under the stairs.

KEVIN: Is there?

ALICE: You put them there.

KEVIN: No, don't get me narked, Alice, please . . .

ALICE: You promised, Kevin . . .

KEVIN: Al, please — there is no boxes an' you in't seen them — okay?

ALICE: You told me it was finished.

KEVIN: Al, I'll talk t'yer after, okay?

Please, Al — it's a special job — it's been down for months — I can't get out of it.

JOEY *comes in.*

JOEY: What's she doin' here?

ALICE: I live here.

JOEY (*to* KEVIN): You givin' us a lift or what?

They are about to go out.

ALICE: I wanna know what's under the stairs.

JOEY: Kev, will y'just smack her one an' start moving it?

KEVIN (*to* ALICE): Listen you — don't start, okay? — just don't.

ALICE: Is it knocked off? Is it from Cross Lane Warehouse? *Is it*?

JOEY: Jesus Christ, I warned you, Kevin — (ALICE *rushes over to the phone.*) What the fuck's she doing?

ALICE: I'm calling the police . . .

JOEY *suddenly leaps across the room, pulls out a knife and holds it to* ALICE's *throat. She recoils in terror and drops the phone.*

KEVIN: Joey — Joey, what y'doin'?

JOEY: Get her away from that phone. (*He kicks the phone away.*)

KEVIN: F'fuck's sake, Joey, put it away, will yer —

JOEY (*throwing* ALICE *onto the floor*): That is a fuckin' time-bomb, that is, Kevin.

KEVIN: Leave her —

JOEY: She's gonna shop you. Y'goin' soft up here? Y'gonna come home one day, find the place crawling with scuffers.

KEVIN: She in't gonna say nothing.

JOEY: She wants locking up, she does.

KEVIN: I'll see to her.

JOEY (*to* ALICE): You — y'think yer bloody special, don't yer? Think yer

above the rest of us? I'm tellin' yer, Kevin, y'shoulda stopped with . . .

KEVIN: No. (JOEY *glances at him.*) Don't Joey.

JOEY: What?

KEVIN: Enough.

JOEY (*to* ALICE): Gonna be sorry, you are

KEVIN: Load the van, Joey — (*He throws him a key.*)

There is a moment when it looks as if JOEY *might assert himself. The moment passes and he backs down. He heads for the door.*

JOEY: Move it, Kevin.

KEVIN: I'm coming.

JOEY: Now.

KEVIN: You go near that phone, girl — I'll break every bone in your body.

KEVIN *and* JOEY *go out.* ALICE *edges over to the phone, makes an attempt to dial, stops, terrified. She sits down, shaking visibly. Noises continue from outside. Finally* KEVIN *returns.* ALICE *looks at him in terror.*

KEVIN: You . . . made me look a real tit there. What d'y'wanna do that for? Y'wanna get hold of yerself a bit — get y'self some tablets. You start pulling that trick too often, we've had it. (*She doesn't reply.*) C'mon, Al, what is it? It's a bit of cash on the side. What'm I supposed to do? Are we meant to manage on what the dole gives us? (*No response.*) Look, I'm gonna forget what just happened, okay? All right. Y'gonna be a good girl now an' run me bath? (*He comes over to her, puts his arms round her.*) . . . while I see how much I got for yer this week . . . see if I can't squeeze yer a bit extra for goin' into town an' getting something new . . . (*He is about to kiss the back of her neck.*)

ALICE: Who's Carly?

KEVIN (*recoiling*): What?

ALICE: I said, who's Carly?

KEVIN (*disengaging himself*): Okay, what happened? Who's bin opening their bleedin' great trap? I'll have their fuckin' necks for that.

ALICE: She did.

KEVIN: What?

ALICE: What is goin' on, Kevin?

KEVIN: Has she been round?

ALICE: She phoned.

KEVIN: Oh Christ, the stupid bitch.

ALICE: What kid, Kevin?

KEVIN (*suddenly desperate*): What's she say, Al — don't mess about. What's she say about the kid?

ALICE: It's okay. It's coming home tomorrow.

KEVIN (*almost weeping with relief*): Thank Christ for that . . . Oh Jesus God Almighty . . .

ALICE (*starting to panic*): What kid, Kevin? Whose is the kid?

KEVIN: Mine.

ALICE: What?

KEVIN: My kid. Mine and Carly's.

ALICE (*unable to speak for a while, then —*): How old . . . ?

KEVIN: Three . . . four . . . nearly four . . .

ALICE: An' coming home tomorrow?

KEVIN: From hospital. Pneumonia.

ALICE: Where's home? (*He doesn't reply.*) Round here?

KEVIN: Round about.

ALICE: Where?

KEVIN: Don't, Alice —

ALICE: Where?

KEVIN: Thirty-three.

ALICE: Thirty-three? Across the street?

KEVIN: Yes —

ALICE: Across the street from *our house*?

KEVIN: Alice, listen . . .

ALICE: Since when?

KEVIN: I dunno . . . seventeen . . . eighteen months . . . I didn't count —

ALICE: An' . . . you moved in here . . . knowing . . . deliberately . . .

KEVIN: Y'don't understand, Alice —

ALICE: Who else knows, Kevin? Joey? Nidge? Half of Salford? (*Suddenly.*) Blond hair. Bleached. That's her, isn't it?

KEVIN: Yes.

ALICE: An' the kid — it screams, doesn't it? It's always screaming.

KEVIN: Katy.

ALICE: Katy? (*She suddenly turns and smashes him in the face.*) You bastard.

KEVIN (*suddenly, in tears*): I thought she was gonna die.

ALICE (*in terror*): Kevin . . .

KEVIN: I thought she was dying. I thought she'd be dead.

ALICE (*gathering him to her, to comfort him*): She's not. She's better. She's coming home.

KEVIN: I love that kid. I'd give anything for that kid. (*He cries again.*)

ALICE: No, don't Kevin, please . . . it's okay . . . it's okay . . .

KEVIN: You hit me.

ALICE: I'm sorry.

KEVIN: We said no hitting anymore.

ALICE: I'm sorry.

KEVIN: It's all right, Alice. I won't see her. It'll just be me an' you . . . okay? Just us two.

ALICE: Yes, Kevin. Just us two.

KEVIN: I love you, Al — I do, honest.

ALICE: Sssssshhh . . . it's okay now . . .

KEVIN: We'll be all right, Al — just you
see now. I got jobs lined up — I can
give yer money. Y'don't ever need to
step outside here again. An' we could
have a kid, couldn't we? Me an' you?
Be all right if we had a kid — no
arguin', no fights — we'd be all right,
then, wouldn't we, Al?

ALICE: Yes, Kevin — we would. We'd be
all right.

The lights fade on ALICE *holding*
KEVIN *in her arms.*

When they come up again KEVIN *has
gone to bed and* ALICE *is sitting by
the phone, biting her nails. She has
been crying.*

(*To herself*:) It's all right now. It's
okay. It's all right . . .

*Suddenly she picks up the phone and
dials. After a long pause, during which
she almost hangs up again, someone
answers.*

ALICE: Nita? . . . I'll be at the corner of
Cross Lane in fifteen minutes.

The lights fade.

A piece of waste land in Salford.
    ALICE *stands as if in the light of a
street lamp.* NITA *stands apart in the
shadow.*
    *A church clock in the distance chimes
three times.*

ALICE: What'm I doin' here, Nita? I
must be mad. Three in the morning?
Kevin sleeping — an' you an' me stood
here. I want locking up.

(*After a pause*:) Kevin's not a Flora
man. He says it's junk. He chucked it
for the birds. Seven butter dishes . . .
That melamine, y'know — it *is*
unbreakable. One day it was flying
through the air an' I was in the way. It
just bounced off. That was lucky
really. He might've used the Pyrex one
an' then we'd be down to six.
Nita, what can I do? All them
presents — y'can't just up an' leave

them — y'can't break up yer home like
that. I bet Phil laughed herself sick.
Kevin loves me, y'know. Oh he does.
In a way.
I can go back there, Nita. I could. Oh
yeah, get hit, maybe. End up on
valium. Look at me, I'm smoking
again. But it's home. It's where I live.
An' I *could* stand it. I think.
I just thought it might be different.
I thought it might change — but how
can he change? What else can he be?
He thinks he has to hit to get what he
wants. His dad knocked holes out of
his mother if he wanted something.
Kevin wants things, then I get battered
for it. Why can't he just ask? I like
to do things for him. But Kevin
dun't know how to ask. Kev thinks
what y'don't steal, what y'don't
kick for in't worth having. It's what he
was taught. It's what he is.
Soft thing is, I shoulda known. I
joined the game but didn't read the
rules. Daft girl, Alice.

NITA: Alice, d'y'want to come home?

ALICE: Where's that? My home's with
Kevin.
Outside that house is the clothes on
me back, an' in me pocket a door-key
an' two cigarettes. Kevin's got things.
He doesn't need me. He's got kids, he
doesn't need mine.
But I could live with that. I could live
with Carly — meet her in the shops,
ask her what he likes for his tea. I
could have Joey round every night.
I can compromise, Nita. People do
compromise. People put up with all
sorts of things. If I left — what could I
do? What could I be if I wasn't
Kevin's?

NITA *is silent.*

Could I scream, Nita?

NITA: What?

ALICE: Could I? I feel like screaming.

NITA: Well scream, then.

With great glee, ALICE *lets out a scream.*

I bin dying to do that. For years.

NITA (*holding out her hand*): Alice? . . . come home with me?

ALICE: Look over there, Nita . . . look at the lights. I used to live there, y'know . . . (*Shouting.*) But I don't anymore.

ALICE *grabs* NITA's *hands. Both laughing, they let out an enormous scream.*

> *Blackout.*

ACT TWO

June-September 1981

NITA's *salon.*
    NITA *is at her desk going through some invoices.* ALICE *is on the phone.*

ALICE: Yes . . . yeh . . . yeh . . . er . . . yeh . . . er . . . (*Loud:*) Nita . . . (*To the phone:*) Would y'like to hold the line a sec? (*To* NITA:) Nita, can we do Mohicans?

NITA (*without looking up*): What?

ALICE: Can we do black an' orange stripes on a Mohican? (*To the phone:*) Sorry? Like a tiger? With . . . (*As if repeating:*) a tail hanging down the back, beaded and plaited . . . like a tiger. (*To* NITA:) Nita, it's another one wanting a Bo Derek. What shall I say?

NITA: Bo Derek should be shot.

ALICE (*to the phone*): Hello? . . . yes, that'll be fine . . . 10 o'clock tomorrow? And the name is? . . . Yates . . . Gary . . . thank you Mr Yates . . . bye . . . (*She puts the phone down.*) Guess who. (NITA *doesn't appear to be interested.*) One of Beth's one-night jobs behind Tesco's trolley check-out.

NITA: That doesn't exactly narrow it down, Alice.

ALICE (*to herself*): I wouldn't give *him* a 10.

NITA: Alice, aren't you meant to be neutralising?

ALICE (*in horror*): Oh God, I am an' all . . . (*She rushes off, calling:*) Mrs Wilson? Would y'like to come through, please . . .

The phone rings. NITA *answers it.*

NITA: Hello — Nita's Headlines . . . Mother, this *is* Nita . . . Fine . . . an' how's me dad? . . . He's *what*? . . . oh, an' who is it this time? . . . Because every time I come round for tea me dad serves up a new fiancé. Faisel

Latif . . . fine . . . an' where's he dug this one up from? . . . oh, a dentist? . . . do us a favour, mother, I've got perfect teeth . . . no, mother, I'm not laughing . . . I wish I *was* . . . Mother, just say *yes* . . . Nita says thanks, Nita will be there . . . and Nita is *not,* Mother, looking to get married . . . Bye. (*She puts the phone down.*)

ALICE *comes rushing in looking panic-stricken.*

NITA (*calmly*): It's fallen out, has it?

ALICE (*horrified*): What?

NITA: Mrs Wilson's hair.

ALICE: Oh no, it's come up really nice . . . but Nita . . . (*In panic again.*) . . . we've run out of that Sonata conditioner.

NITA: So?

ALICE: Mrs Wilson wants a couple to take home.

NITA: Yeah? What's the panic, Alice? We got a stack of empty bottles through there. Fill a couple up from the big jar out the back.

ALICE: Yeah, but that's the cheapo conditioner . . .

NITA: Yes?

ALICE (*horrified*): Y'mean . . . fill up the bottles with the cheapo conditioner and . . .

NITA: Sell it as Sonata . . . yes, Alice — she won't know any different — it's what we been flogging her for the past six months.

ALICE: Yeah, but that's . . .

NITA: Called 'good business', Alice.

PHIL *and* NASH's *flat in Bristol.*
NASH *is sitting at a table listening to music through a Walkman headset and marking exam papers.*
PHIL *bursts in.*

PHIL: I don't believe this. (*She throws down a folder of papers.* NASH *doesn't take off the headset.*) I don't believe it. Five jobs, five interviews, five sorry-can't help, sorry-it's gone, sorry-yer-not-what-we're-after. 'D'you know what hard work is, dear? Y'ever scrubbed floors?' (*Reeling off a list.*) . . . loaded vans . . . carted spuds . . . But the minute y'mention student . . . what, student? . . . university? Oh no, can't have students — can't stick — bone idle. Besides, yer depriving the ordinary working person of a job. Oh yeah? Well they're not exactly queuing round the block to clean up piss and sluice out bedpans . . . (*Noticing* NASH *hasn't heard a word of this, she takes his headset off.*) It's pathetic. All I want is a job.

NASH: D'y'not read the papers, Phil?

PHIL: Nash, am I a good worker or what? Do I skive? I'm not like Beth — I got exams, I'm not stupid. Sorry no jobs. There must be. There must be *one job.*

NASH *goes on marking the papers.*

I wanna go on holiday. How can I go on holiday with no money? I only need two hundred quid. (*After a pause.*) Nash . . .

NASH (*without looking up.*) What?

PHIL: I don't suppose . . .

NASH: Y'suppose right.

PHIL: I haven't even asked yer yet.

NASH: Y'wanna borrow two hundred quid to go on holiday. Right?

PHIL: Well, I just thought . . . if you *had* two hundred quid.

NASH: I don't. (PHIL *sits looking miserable.*) Last term you had off me . . . four days in Paris . . . two tennis racquets . . . a pair of gold earrings . . . the Bob Wilson Book of Football Facts . . . and two tickets to see *Nicholas Nickleby.* You've had yer two hundred quid, Phil.

PHIL: Oh, thanks a lot, Nash.

NASH: Phil, c'mon — *if* I had it — an' thought y'deserved it — I'd give it yer, wouldn't I? But as it happens, I haven't. An' I don't.

PHIL grabs her coat and heads for the door.

Now where y'going?

PHIL: Look for a job.

NASH: I shouldn't be too hasty, Phil — y'might be doin' resits, yet. (*Indicating the exam papers.*)

PHIL: Sod off, Nash.

NITA's salon.

ALICE comes in with a clipboard ready to start stock taking.

BETH comes in dressed in a blouse and skirt (her interview outfit) brandishing a sheaf of papers.

BETH (*cheerfully*): No . . . sorry . . . hard luck . . . forget it . . . sod off . . . (*Referring to each piece of paper.*) C'mere, Alice. Clock this. Is it me face? Is me armpits off? I know what — y've seen the last of me soddin' Peter Pan costume. (*Tugging at her blouse and skirt.*) Yes, dear? Can y'speak Urdu, type with yer teeth, work a word processor stood on yer head taking two hundred words a minute dictation? No? Sorry dear. Filing clerk? We *were* really looking for a Ph.D. with fluent Swahili. An' I see you haven't worked for two years, Miss Harrison. Why *is* that?

ALICE: Y'didn't get it.

BETH: Them. Five. Not to mention twenty-quid, sixty-hour week Youth Opportunities for gettin' flogged to death on less than yer dole and coming out six months older and sod-all wiser.

ALICE: Oh Beth . . .

BETH (*leafing through the papers*): Too young, too old, too much, not enough,

no chance . . . (*She tosses them into the air.*)

NITA (*off*): Alice . . .

BETH: I'm off.

ALICE: Come round tonight?

BETH: I can't. I have to referee.

ALICE: What?

BETH: Me mam an' dad.

ALICE: Who's winning?

BETH: Not me. (*She goes out.*)

ALICE starts collecting up the papers. NITA comes in.

ALICE: She didn't get it.

NITA: She doesn't try.

NASH and PHIL's house.

PHIL (*running on, out of breath*): I did it! I did it — I got me exams. Y'won't believe this — Lindy failed three papers — God, she's goin' up the wall! An' Jay screwed up American Lit. He did! An' all that crap about 'I've got *Moby Dick* sussed' . . . an' as for his *Hiawatha* — well, apparently he just . . . Nash, where are yer?

NASH (*coming in*): Is there a fire?

PHIL: Jay failed two — Lindy failed three — And I passed!

NASH: Shit.

PHIL: What?

NASH: Now I have to coach those two pillocks through resits.

PHIL: Oh, thanks a lot, Nash. (*She heads for the door.*)

NASH: Hey, Phil —

PHIL: What?

NASH: Y'done well, kidder.

NITA's salon.

NITA stands behind a client who is sitting in a chair having a consultation.

NITA: Oh dear, we *are* in a mess, aren't we? (*Tugging at hair.*) I'm afraid we've been in a real carve-up here. Oh yes . . . well if you look at the parting down this side . . . y'can see now, can't you? — it doesn't seem to know *where* it's going . . . Who usually does it for you? . . . Really? Well, to be honest, now — the complaints we get about them — you've no idea . . . the nerve! — they call this hairdressing? Well, let's let's face it — we've seen better layers on a shag-pile carpet. (*Grimacing with distaste.*) Oh yes, I think we can do something with it. 'Course, under normal circumstances, I would suggest the Magiwave — which is one of our 'budget' perms . . . but as things stand . . . No, I think I'll have to recommend the Dulcia . . . which is in fact our most expensive perm . . . but there again, we do want to do the job properly this time, don't we? Yes . . . well you're quite right, Mrs Wilson . . . you do get what you pay for . . . Can I get you a coffee while you're waiting?

(*Showing her out:*) Alice . . . (ALICE *comes in.*) . . . one Magiwave — and make sure it's in a Dulcia bottle . . . and use up the rest of that crap conditioner, okay?

ALICE: Nita, we haven't, have we?

NITA: What?

ALICE: Had complaints about Vidal Sassoons?

NITA: Not to my knowledge.

ALICE: Yeah, but you just said . . .

NITA: I know what I just said. It's called being 'competitive' — an' it's how I pay your wages. All right?

ALICE *goes out looking rather hurt.* NITA *is busy at the desk when* BETH *saunters in.*

BETH: Seen your feller just now. Pretty fit.

NITA: I beg your pardon.

BETH: Danny Boy, yeah? — down the off-licence — stacking up on the shorts? Pretty snazz stuff he got in that shop of his. Y'been in? Really fancy that four-poster with the leopard-skin curtains . . . oh, an' that aquarium that folds out into a cocktail cabinet . . . magic . . .

NITA (*trying to silence her*): Beth . . .

BETH: Tell him he can fit me a bedroom anytime . . .

NITA (*indicating* MRS WILSON *who is looking shocked*): D'y'mind, Beth? . . .

BETH: Y'goin' out with him, are yer?

NITA: No.

BETH: Y'seen him four times this week.

NITA: Have I?

BETH: Well y'must be goin' somewhere.

NITA (*apologetic*): 'Scuse me, Mrs Wilson . . .

BETH (*oblivious*): Says he's thinking about doin' a green fluorescent waterbed with built-in bidet, wine-rack an' toasted sandwich maker . . .

NITA: Beth, will you just *go* . . .

BETH (*on her way out*): Hey, he give us his card an' all . . . (BETH *gets out a card and reads it.*) 'Danny Haslam — Bedroom Specialist' . . . Is he?

BETH *going out bumps straight into* DANNY *coming in.*

BETH (*unabashed*): Oh hello, Danny . . . business as usual?

DANNY *is slightly taken aback.* BETH *freezes out.* NITA *is furious.*

NITA (*annoyed*): Alice, d'y'think y'could please shampoo? (*She storms out.*)

DANNY *looks immediately at home.* ALICE *comes in looking fraught.*

ALICE: Oh, hello Danny . . .

DANNY: Alice, be a good girl, book us a cut with the boss, will yer? I need me ends doing.

ALICE: Er . . . four o'clock tomorrow?

DANNY: Magic. Y'doin' anything tonight, Alice?

ALICE: Sorry?

DANNY: Nah, forget it. I'll see yer tomorrow. (DANNY *goes out.*)

ALICE (*still slightly puzzled*): Er . . . Mrs Wilson, would y'like to come through to the backwash . . .

An expensive nightclub in Manchester. DANNY *and* NITA *are drinking cocktails with* REUBEN *and* CARMEN.

REUBEN (*eyeing* NITA *up*): I'm impressed. I'm very impressed . . . so, tell me, Nita . . . where did he find *you*?

NITA: He bought the business next door to my salon.

REUBEN: Salon? — Oh, hairdresser? — Oh you're the hairdresser-lady, are yer? Lot of money in hairdressing . . . Cheers. (*He takes a swig of his cocktail.*) So . . . so who is it y'work for . . . er . . . Nita?

NITA: I work for myself.

REUBEN: Oh well, we're all out for Number One, aren't we? Right Danny? (*He roars with laughter.*) . . . No . . . what I mean, love, is — who *owns* the place?

NITA: I do.

REUBEN (*taken aback*): Oh . . . I see.

DANNY: Well don't look at me.

REUBEN: Very impressive. Oh yeah. You . . . er . . . doin' anything special tomorrow night?

NITA: Sorry?

REUBEN: Fancy goin' for a drive somewhere? — pick up a bit to eat later maybe . . .

DANNY: Reuben, what y'doing?

REUBEN: Chatting up your bird.

DANNY: Don't.

REUBEN: Oh . . . I see . . . the old hands-off, is it? (*Nudging and winking to* CARMEN.)

(*To* NITA:) Lovely tan. Been anywhere nice?

CARMEN (*suddenly*): Oh, *you're* the one.

NITA: What?

CARMEN: Next door to Danny.

NITA: That's right.

REUBEN: That's handy for him, hey Nita?

NITA: Pardon?

REUBEN: In case he fancies a quick haircut . . .

CARMEN: Or something —

REUBEN: Cheers.

DANNY: C'mon Nita, we're going.

NITA: Are we?

DANNY: Bird in here I could do with not seeing.

REUBEN: Which one? (DANNY *indicates.*) Oh, the gorgeous Dolores? (*Winking at* DANNY.) Heard she's after a word with you . . . (*He falls about laughing.*)

DANNY: That is why we're not stopping.

REUBEN: Nita . . . it's been a pleasure . . . (*He takes* NITA's *hand and slobbers kisses onto it.*)

DANNY *escorts* NITA *out.*

REUBEN: Have fun, Danny . . .

A street in Salford. BETH *comes in reading a newspaper.*

BETH (*reading*): 'Situations Vacant'. (*Looking through.*) Sod-all, as usual. (*She turns to the front pages and reports of Moss Side riots.*) Oh aye, the lads get a mention, do they? 'Police Vehicle Set On Fire'. Nice work, boys.

(*Folding the paper away.*) Me cousin lives across there. Our Sandy? Get told not to speak to her — her feller's a bit . . . y'know . . . *'Not all white'*? But *I* do. Oh, *I* speak. Gets right up me dad's nose.

Her feller Paul — well, he should know, he says — he's got it back-to-back — her Paul says, gonna be bother soon. They gettin' bored playing silly buggers. Joy's gone out of mugging, robbing houses — where's the fun? Gettin' met by the muzzle of a bleedin' great bull terrier guarding empty cupboards full of dog food? Sad state, innit?

Paul got the push down the soap factory. Wrong colour. (*She grins.*) Dun't look clean enough. Says, six months' time, be all dead quiet on the streets — all gone an' flogged the ghetto blasters, stop home an' booze theirselves to sleep. Get nasty round here, our Paul reckons. You watch, he says. Round here gonna go up soon. 'You lot', he says.

'Y'mean *me*?', I says.

'How come they let *you* unwind? Build yer health clubs, saunas, leisure centres, three hundred quid members only Hard day's graft? — In the car — smash it out on court — down the golf course — prune the peonies — chammy the Porsche.'

'Don't look at *me*,' I says.

'See us?' he says. 'Get home, hard day's hammer, no joy down the Job Centre — nobody lets *us* unwind.'

'Fresh air,' I says. 'What more d'y'want?'

'Good enough f'r'us,' he says, 'the waste tips, rubbish dumps, demolition sites. You lot,' he says, 'get narked, screw up, blow yer bottle? — that's legitimate. Show them yer fists? — They give yer a squash racquet. Us lot? — open hands — say please — go begging. No goals — so pick up the bricks.'

It's called 'Sport For All'.

(*Shouting:*) Ta-ra, Al — goin' visitin' . . . (*As she goes:*) Me cousins in Moss Side.

As the lights come down, the sound of rioting.

The lights come up again on BETH *in a police cell sitting on a chair. A* POLICEMAN *stands next to her.*

BETH: I never did nothing.

POLICEMAN: You never did nothing.

BETH: Look, I was just there.

POLICEMAN: Just there?

BETH: Stood there.

POLICEMAN: What for?

BETH: Watching.

POLICEMAN: Your address is 29 Elm Court, Worsley.

BETH: Yeah?

POLICEMAN: What y'doing in Moss Side?

BETH: Passing through.

POLICEMAN: At least three witnesses seen you pick up a brick an' throw it.

BETH: I bet they didn't.

POLICEMAN: Y'was using abusive language.

BETH: Y'what? Me? I don't know any.

POLICEMAN: Y'were heard to say 'Let's go an' kick their fuckin' heads in.' Does that sound familiar?

BETH: No.

POLICEMAN: I could have you strip-searched.

BETH: What for?

POLICEMAN: No reason.

BETH: I don't do bricks.

POLICEMAN: Yer mates have already told us — y'threw a brick.

BETH: What mates?

POLICEMAN: Two friends.

BETH: I was on me own.

POLICEMAN: That's just where yer wrong. Two friends — next door this very minute — two friends who were with you.

BETH: I come on me own. I was there on me own. Listen, if I wanna start a riot, I don't need any assistance.

POLICEMAN: Oh, so yer admitting y'started a riot, are yer?

BETH: If I felt like it, I'd make a better bloody job than your lot did.

The POLICEMAN *goes out leaving* BETH *alone in the cell.*

Me? Chucking bricks? Oh yeah, can see that, can't yer? Good school, nice house — me?
Give us this bottle. Y'know, milk bottle — rags stuffed in with paraffin. Oh yeah, I did chuck a bottle. Bastards got us for a brick.
Sandy, where are yer? Selfish get's gone out . . . — Paul's drunk himself under the bed. It's dead early — I can't go home — me ma'll still be on her first bottle. Hang about — s'getting dark — the alleys start to move — massing, like a rally, like a football crowd.
Phil, y'shoulda been here. It's like Wembley. It's like losing the Cup. We're off now — givin' us the nod, the nudge — doors slamming, locks on — me in me doc's — (*Showing her fists.*) Where are yer? Where are yer? (*Dancing on tip-toe like a boxer.*) I says, 'Where we going?'
This lad next to us . . . Shit scared he is. Not me. I've been here before. I've stood on the Kop an' shouted Matt Busby.
This bottle's in me hand. 'Chuck this,' he says. An' I'm chucking it. Then I'm running — an' he's running. Mind yer head, watch the fires — combing the bricks out me hair.
He says, 'Come back with us, let's watch it. Let's stand on the wall — y'get a better view.' We did an' all. We had a seat in the stands.
I'm stood there, an' it's like bein' down the fair watching the waltzers. Goin' — here's me, time of me life, an' any minute now this voice is gonna come at me — this voice goin', get down Beth, have some sense, Beth, don't y'think y'should know better, Beth?
Know better? I know what. Tonight I gotta go back, tomorrow stand in line, beg for money, get told nothing today, come back tomorrow, come back next week.
An' I got hold this bottle, an' I thought, piss on tomorrow. Piss on next week, next month, an' all the next weeks that never come, an' never come, an' when they come they come here empty-handed.
I'm walking home. This lad — Denny, his name is — 'Will I see yer again?' he says 'I'm gettin' out,' I says. 'I'm gonna make them build us a squash court. They can make a start with this.'
'It's a brick,' he says. 'I'll have that — some alsation f'r'its teeth.' Nice lad. 'Bang goes your leisure centre,' I says. Then he walks us to the bus. An' when I gets round the corner, this copper jumps us. 'What's yer name, girl? I seen you chucking bricks.' An' *I* says, 'Y'must be kidding. Chucking bricks? Me?'

The POLICEMAN *returns.*

POLICEMAN: Get out.

BETH: Y'what?

POLICEMAN: We're letting yer go.

BETH: Y'got nothing on me.

POLICEMAN: We could have — if we felt like it.

BETH: Well y'couldn't, see — 'cos what y'said I done, I haven't done.

POLICEMAN: What difference d'y'think that makes?

BETH: I'll have you for this.

POLICEMAN: Get out an' go home.

BETH: Where's that?

Outside NITA*'s salon.*
  Sounds of banging and hammering.
NITA *stands as if supervising some work.*
ALICE *comes on looking terrified.*

ALICE: What's happening?

NITA: I'm getting boards put up.

ALICE: What for?

NITA: Don't you watch the news, Al?

ALICE: It's quiet round here.

NITA: I'm not taking any chances. Shops gettin' smashed up — stuff gettin' ripped off . . .

ALICE: Nita, what they gonna rob from here? Sack of perm rods? Half a ton of blow-wave lotion? Christ, Nita — even the prices *you* charge no one's gonna bother rifling the stock.

NITA: Twelve months took me gettin' this on its feet. No way I'm goin' back to square one 'cos a bunch of bone-idle cretins got nothing better to do than kick bricks around. I'm just here, tryna make a decent living. Why pick on shopkeepers? What've *we* done?

ALICE: Got shops?

NITA: It's pathetic. It's irresponsible. Look at that, Alice — (*Showing her the newspaper.*) There's no excuse for that sort of behaviour.

  ALICE *goes out.*
  BETH *swaggers on and looks over* NITA*'s shoulder as she reads.*

BETH (*casually*): I was there.

NITA: You were where? No, I don't believe this.

BETH: Told yer I was going.

NITA: Y'want lookin' into, you do.

BETH: Was a good night out.

NITA: Yer pathetic, Beth.

BETH: And what else is down f'r'us round here?

NITA: Get up off your arse and get a job.

BETH: Show us one, Nita.

NITA: If you tried. If you really looked . . .

BETH (*grabbing the paper*): Ooooh look . . . Inverness, Milton Keynes . . . oil-rig drillers, deep-sea divers . . . Heard the one about the ostrich, Nita? Head in the sand, got grit in its eye? *You* know where all the jobs is hiding? Tell me.

NITA: You wanna job? I'll find work for yer. I'll show yer a job.

BETH' I'll lay yer a fiver on it, Nita. (*She goes out.*)

  NITA *walks out to where* DANNY *is lounging across his desk, in his office.*

DANNY (*on the phone*): I'll hold . . . yeah, thanks a lot, babe . . . (*He blows* NITA *a kiss.*) Give us two minutes.

NITA: Where's Tracy?

DANNY: Got the elbow. (*Seeing her look of surprise.*) Not up to scratch, was she? (*To the phone:*) What? . . . Lou . . . how y'doin', mate? Yeah . . . got it right here. Do yer . . . er . . . third off, all right? The pink, is it? — Or the teak with gold beading? — Great stuff, Lou — that'll be . . . call it a round fifteen hundred, okay? Buckshee ottoman thrown in? Red flock, carved feet? It's on its way. Hey, listen Lou — can y'get us a couple of season tickets sussed? Yeah . . . yeah, magic, Lou — I owe yer one . . . give yer a ring next week, mate. (*He puts the phone down.*) Macari.

NITA: Never.

DANNY (*sidling over to her*): Y'know, I never think of you as a Stretford Ender. I see you more in yer fur coat — exec suite — sipping yer brandy an' babycham at half time. Hey, d'y'fancy goin' again next season? Seat in the stands?

NITA: Danny, I need a favour . . .

DANNY: Nita, my love, you name it . . .

NITA: Y'need a new PA, don't you?

DANNY: Got any ideas?

NITA: I do yeah, but . . .

DANNY (*encouraging*): Yeah? But?

NITA: It's a favour, Danny. Don't forget. An' I can't be held responsible if y'go out of business.

DANNY: Friend of yours, is it?

NITA: Sort of . . .

DANNY: I tell yer what — talk about it after dinner tonight — fair enough?

NITA: All right then.

DANNY: Eight o'clock? Hey, y'know what? — Maybe time I took yer home to see me mother.

NITA: What?

DANNY: Nah, maybe not — she gets weird ideas. I'll see yer later, babe.

NITA *goes out.* CANDY, DANNY'*s sales assistant, appears.*

CANDY: Cracked it yet?

DANNY: Oh, it's a tough nut, Candy. Much tougher than you were.

CANDY: Piss off, Danny.

DANNY: Listen you — we got four quotes to get done between now and six — so y'better shift yer arse now, or y'might find yerself without that lovely Capri you worked so hard for.

CANDY: It *was* hard work an' all.

DANNY: No, Candy. At the time you thought it was the easiest five grand you ever made.

CANDY: What happened to Tracy?

DANNY: Jealous?

CANDY: That slag?

DANNY: Shame about that one. Onto a

winner there. Then what happens? Soft get sees off the tail-end of that vodka, goes home, tells that fiancé why she's working late three nights a week. We never had this bother with you, did we? You couldn't keep away.

CANDY: You make me sick.

DANNY: So . . . looks like y'can hang on a bit longer, sweetheart.

CANDY: I'm looking for another job.

DANNY: Nah, I shouldn't bother, Candice. I should try to hang on to the one you got. (CANDY *is about to leave.*) Hey, Candy — get on the phone an' order us ten quid's worth of roses, will yer? (CANDY *picks up the phone.*) For Nita.

BETH *walks on and meets* NITA.

NITA: You owe us a fiver.

BETH: What for? Hey, hang on, Nita — I paid yer for them cans at the Cup Final — it was two years ago.

NITA: I got yer a job.

BETH: A what?

NITA: Yer starting Monday.

BETH: Hey Nita, now hang about — I don't have to wear tights, do I?

NITA *walks off.*
BETH *finds her way to . . .*

DANNY'*s office.*
BETH *is now installed at the desk as receptionist, feet up and lounging back in her chair with two phones in front of her.*

BETH (*into one phone*): Oh yeah, so I says to him, 'Hey, listen you, if you're so bleedin' suave, how come we have to do it in the back of your motor?' Yeah, 'cos anyone can get their foot stuck in the steering wheel . . . (*The other phone rings.*) Yeah, hang on a minute . . . (*To the second phone, an attempt at a posh voice.*)

Hello, Ladylux Fitted Bedrooms . . .
no, I'm afraid he's not here at the
moment . . . no, sorry, I can't help
you there . . . no, I'm afraid I've got
no idea . . . sorry . . . (*She puts down
the second phone.*)
(*To the first phone:*) So he says to us,
'Well, you're the first, darlin'?' An' I
says, 'Oh yeah, what y'been laying the
rest of the time, bloody midgets?'
(*The second phone rings again:*) Hello,
Ladylux? . . . no, he's not . . . no, he
won't . . . no, I don't . . . bye . . .
(*She puts the phone down. To the first
phone.*) So he stops the car an' he
says, 'Get out.' Yeah. I says, 'Get
what? — what d'y'think this is? Yer
not the 68 bus, love. We happen to be
Junction 10 on the M62 an' I'm still
missing at least two items of
underwear . . .' (*The second phone
rings.* BETH, *fiercely:*) Yeah, Ladylux
. . . oh, hello Danny . . . nah, nothing
. . . nobody . . . nah, s'all been dead
quiet . . .

DANNY *walks in.*

DANNY: Except for your voice.

BETH: What d'y'mean, my voice?

DANNY: Stood under that window with
two women from Knutsford, tryna
get them to part with two thousand
quid on new bedrooms — all we can
hear is stories of how you got laid
in the back of the bus on the way
home from Goodison Park.

BETH: Well? Did they buy it?

DANNY: What?

BETH: Did they buy the bedrooms?

DANNY: Yeah, they did . . .

BETH: Well there yer are, then — you
owe us commission. (*The phone rings.*)
Hello, Ladylux . . .

NASH *and* PHIL's *flat.*
    PHIL *walks in (having just returned
from the library).* NASH *can be heard*
*outside saying goodbye to some of his
students.*

NASH (*off*): Yeah . . . an' don't waste
yer time on Browning — most of it's
dross. I'll see yer tomorrow . . . (*He
comes in.*)

PHIL: I'm sick of this.

NASH: What?

PHIL: I'm sick of it. I come home — I
can't move for bloody students.
Breakfast, dinner, three in the
morning — Sorry to wake you, can I
speak to Nash? — Is Ibsen realism or
naturalism? Christ, Nash — you must
give some bloody awful tutorials.

NASH: If you appeared at them a bit
more often, you might find out what
sort of tutorials I give.

PHIL: *I* passed me exams. *I* don't need to
come to class to discuss Symbolism
In D.H. Lawrence. I can do that stood
on me head at home.

NASH: Don't kid yerself. (*Settling down
to do some work.*)

PHIL (*seeing he's not listening to her*):
Or if you prefer — in its natural
habitat? — face down in a field of rape
with a mouth full of red
chrysanthemums.

NASH: What I *would* prefer, Phil, is that
next term half the university wasn't
aware that you take up three-quarters
of the bed, two-thirds of me grant, and
that once in a while you would
condescend to hand me in an essay on
time.

PHIL: Hey, yer not me proper tutor,
y'know — yer only a bloody Ph.D.
student. And why do you get the job
of dragging a load of stupid dickheads
into their third year?

NASH: Some of those stupid dickheads
are your friends.

PHIL: Well, *I* . . . have just bought half
a pound of stewing steak . . . an' I
am about to make Beef Strogonoff for
supper . . . an' if I have to share it

with *anyone*, Nash . . . I'm gonna chop their bloody fingers off!

NASH: Shut up, Phil! (*She does.*) You *will* . . . now that you mention it . . . be sharing your dinner with somebody . . . With Lindy and Jay to be precise — who are coming round here to discuss 'Flower Imagery in *The Winter's Tale.*' And if I see you so much as *glance* at a carving knife . . . I shall bring up the subject . . . of dried privet leaves.

PHIL: Don't you dare.

NASH: I do dare. (*They suddenly burst out laughing. After a pause.*) D'y'wanna come home with me?

PHIL: What? — Y'mean World's End?

NASH — I know — y'wanted three weeks on Crete. I'm offering ten days' chronic frostbite on the Tyne. But come if y'want to.

PHIL: But . . . yer mam an' dad . . . they'll all be there.

NASH: Yeah, I know, Phil — and you swear, and talk with yer mouth full — but I dare say they'll make allowances.

PHIL: Y'mean . . . come home to meet yer mam and dad?

NASH: I mean . . . come to Wallsend with me.

The ladies room at an expensive Manchester nightclub.
  CARMEN *teeters in on high heels, sinks down with relief in front of a mirror and starts redoing her make-up.*

CARMEN: Di, I'm lending yer mascara, all right? Hey don't be all night in there, will yer? (*She spits on the mascara and applies it liberally.*) She's in again, y'know. That Nita. Tarted up to the eyebrows an' honestly, Di, I'm not bein' catty but it's getting a bit much her an' Danny — y'can't get a word in edgeways. Mind, I was just saying to Reuben now

— talk about set up? I mean, when y'think she's only . . . what? . . . 20? . . . an' walkin' in here like she's something special? I tell yer what, Di, she's not exactly . . . now hang on, Di, 'cos y'know me — what am I like? Talk to anyone, me. But let's face it, Di — considering she's half . . . y'know . . . paki? . . . well she in't half done well f'r'herself.
  She'll be hanging on there if she's got any sense. 'Cos apparently, y'know, he set it up, Danny did — that business of hers? Oh yeah, apparently. Course, she lets on it's hers, dun't she? Must think y'was born yesterday.
  An' he's dumped that Dolores. Oh God, yeah. *And* that Karen whatsername . . . the one that does the foot powder ads?
  Reuben reckons she's a stunner in the sack. Well, she'd have to be, wouldn't she? Y'don't hang about that long for what she's got between the ears. 'Course, how long she'll last is anybody's guess. D'y'reckon?

NITA (*coming out of toilet*): Oh, anybody's . . .

She smiles at CARMEN *and walks out.*

DANNY's *bedroom.*
  BETH *comes sneaking in on tip-toe, dragging* ALICE *behind her.*

BETH: Sssssshhh . . . sssssshhh . . . s'all right, he's out . . . here y'are (*She does a fanfare.*) . . . this is it, this is the sacrificial stone . . .

ALICE (*looking round in amazement*): Oh God . . .

BETH (*nudging* ALICE): Hey Al — fancy gettin' laid on genuine fake tiger fur . . . (*Pointing to the ceiling.*) in 3-D cinemascope.

ALICE (*in horror*): Wall-to-wall mirrors? Oh no . . .

BETH: Press that button. Go on — press it.

ALICE (*pressing gingerly, then springing back in shock*): Oh my God — what is it?

BETH: It's a pop-up cocktail dispenser, dickhead. Hey, hang on a minute . . . wait there . . .

BETH *rushes just offstage.*
At the flick of a switch, exotic lighting comes on and the strains of Ravel's Bolero *are heard.* ALICE *stands amazed.*

ALICE (*noticing something on the wall*): What's all these?

BETH: Oh, them? Charts from all the big model agencies — an' you'll notice that most of the photos got little scribbles next to them.

ALICE (*looking closer*): 'B-plus — pretty fair', 'Straight C — could do better', D-minus — not even trying' . . . D'y'mean . . . oh God, Beth, I know her — she comes in to have her roots done . . . 'E-minus — in-growing toe-nails'? . . . oh Beth . . .

BETH: Hey Al — has Nita . . . y'know . . .

ALICE: What?

BETH: Been in the bullring yet? (*She mimes a bullfighter and joins in the* 'Bolero'.)

ALICE: I've no idea.

BETH: Hey, y'should get her in there, Al — I've heard he's shit-hot, y'know.

ALICE: Only 'heard'?

BETH: Yeah, worse luck — but I'm working on it.

DANNY (*in the doorway*): Don't work too hard, will yer, Beth? (*Coming in.*) Not much danger of that, though, is there? (*He switches off the special effects.*)

BETH (*under her breath*): Shit.

DANNY: There *is* a small charge for guided tours, Alice. As it's you, we'll call it quits . . . (ALICE *rushes out in*

embarrassment.) Beth, I don't pay you to run an art gallery. (*Putting his arm round her.*) Fact is, I don't know *why* I pay yer. I think y'best come out with me tonight, Beth — see if we can't have a little chat about your prospects? Now get in there before I kick yer arse in for yer.

BETH *heads out, scowling at* DANNY.

BETH (*over her shoulder*): I see y'got a photo missing, Danny.

DANNY: What photo?

BETH: Nita's.

DANNY's *bedroom.*
DANNY *is on the phone to* REUBEN.

DANNY: Yeah, I'll see yer in there about nine — yeah, don't worry — I'm bringing me own tonight — y'what? — oh no, Nita's all right — that's all chasing the inevitable — nah, this is a new one . . . fit? . . . no, that's not quite the word . . . but entertaining . . .

A Manchester nightclub.
DANNY, NITA *and* BETH *are just arriving.* CARMEN *and* REUBEN *pass by.*

REUBEN: All right Danny? Nita? How's business?

DANNY: Making a living.

REUBEN: Macari likes his suite . . . (*Eyeing* BETH.) Yeah, I see what yer mean . . . I'll get them in . . . (*He heads to the bar with* CARMEN *in tow.*)

BETH *suddenly clutches hold of* DANNY *so tight that he spills his drink.*

BETH: Look who it is —

DANNY: Beth, d'y'mind? — I had a shower before I come out.

BETH (*in ecstasy*): It's Joe Jordan . . .

DANNY (*looking across*): All right, Joe?

BETH (*tugging at* NITA, *much to her*

embarrassment): He said hello.

DANNY: He's a mate of mine.

BETH (*diving into his pocket*): Bit of paper . . .

DANNY: What for?

BETH: Get his autograph. (*Flinging off attempts to stop her.*) Hey Joe, can y'put 'To Beth — with everlasting love an' devotion' . . .

NITA: I knew this was a bad idea.

Newcastle, the Tyne Bridge.
Night time, PHIL *and* NASH *stand on the bridge looking down the river.* PHIL *is in a state of excitement.*

PHIL: Nash, I'm a Geordie.

NASH: Yer a what?

PHIL: I am. I been here before. I know this bridge.

NASH: When?

PHIL: Oh, years ago. I stopped with me uncle. Me Uncle Geordie.

NASH: Oh, give over, Phil.

PHIL: I did, honest. (*Pointing.*) That's the Tyne Bridge, right?

NASH: No, Phil — this is the Tyne Bridge.

PHIL: Me Uncle Geordie. I've stood on this bridge — an' he says — Phil, look there. The Five Bridges. (*Running to look at the other side.*) I'm back. I can't believe it. No . . . hang on . . . where is it? . . . (*Pointing vaguely in one direction.*) . . . steel works, up the hill . . . Worked in the furnace — used to — 'fore he kicked the bucket — me cousins an' all — kept the place going, our lot. God what a scream. They'd laugh at anything. Y'could rob the roof from over their head — they'd still see the joke. S'right what they say about up here, in't it? Always see the funny side.
(*Suddenly remembering.*) Hey, d'y'still race whippets up here? D'y'still grow leeks?

PHIL: Oh yeah, we still do that.

PHIL: Oh, I love them places. Working solid, head down, just get on with it . . . They never change, do they? D'y'ever think that?

NASH: Think what?

PHIL: *I* do. Some nights, sat there, tryna write an essay, tryna understand your lecture notes. I don't know what I'm doin' half the time. But I can't go home, can I? Me mam like a siren stood on the doorstep — oh, yer gran's just died, yer school's burnt down, our street's not there, yer dad's laid off. I go back — an' everywhere another bit's got chiselled off. It's not the same. But up here's the same. Your house is the same. Y'could live up here an' feel safe. Don't y'think that's nice? That some things never change?
(*Trying to remember.*) . . . steel works . . . Cosley . . . Conway . . . oh, where is it, Nash?

NASH: Y'mean Consett.

PHIL (*delighted*): Consett. That's what I mean.

NASH: I'll take yer to Consett.

PHIL: Will yer? Oh, will yer? Can we go tomorrow? Could we? Hey, it'll be like sight-seeing. God, I feel dead nostalgic. Where is it? Shall I look it up in the book?

NASH: It'll not be in the guide book, Phil. It's not exactly a tourist attraction. But it's a sight.

DANNY's *flat.*
Sunday morning. NITA, *just dressed, in last night's clothes, comes in.*
She starts to do her hair in front of a mirror.

DANNY (*off*): Nita . . . (*She doesn't reply.*) . . . Nita . . .

NITA: In here.

DANNY (*coming in, in a dressing-gown*):
Nita, what y'doing? — it's Sunday
morning.

NITA: Do I get to be on the chart?

DANNY: The what?

NITA (*musing to herself*): What would I
get? B? C? Good effort? Try again?

DANNY: D'y'want some breakfast?

NITA: Do I want breakfast?

DANNY: Nita . . . are you . . . all right?

NITA: All right?

DANNY: What's the matter?

NITA (*studying him*): Award yerself a
six.

DANNY: Pardon?

NITA: High on charm — low on
originality. Oh, I see y'don't have a
photo of yerself up there. Why's that?

DANNY: Nita —

NITA: Scared of unfavourable marks?

DANNY: What've I done?

NITA (*calmly*): Added me to the list?

Consett.
    PHIL *and* NASH *have just got out of
the car.* PHIL *looks puzzled.*

PHIL: Where are we? Why've we stopped
here?

NASH: What d'y'think of it?

PHIL: What is it?

NASH: Why don't y'look?

PHIL: What at? It's derelict.

NASH: I know.

PHIL: You said we're goin' sight-seeing.

NASH: We are.

PHIL: This isn't a sight.

NASH: Why not, Phil? Is it not pretty
enough for yer?

PHIL: Oh, give over, Nash — we come all
this way to see rails gone rusted an'
windows boarded up? There's nothing
here. That — falling to pieces — what's
that supposed to be?

NASH: It's supposed to be a steel works.

PHIL: I don't wanna see steel works.

NASH: What d'y'wanna see, Phil? Picture
postcards? Picturesque countryside?
Round here isn't pretty, Phil — it
isn't picturesque.

PHIL: I can see that.

NASH: Is it the same, Phil? Is it what you
thought? Five bridges, cloth caps an'
whippet racing? — where d'y'learn
that, Phil? *When the Boat Comes In*?

PHIL: I been here. I seen it.

NASH: What else d'y'wanna see, Phil?
Brand new shopping centre they built
for us? Nice place. Always packed.
Not with money, not with people
buying — with people keeping warm,
dossed in corners — wondering where
the redundancy pay went to, what a
decent day's work feels like.
Nice to see the funny side, though,
Phil. Good to know y'can still laugh
at it.

PHIL: It's what I remembered.

NASH: Romantic.

PHIL: It was.

NASH: It's not romantic, Phil.
Shut-down is not romantic.
Redundant is not romantic.

PHIL: Did I say it was?

NASH: D'y'wanna go to Consett?

PHIL: Can we?

NASH: Here y'are, then.

PHIL: This isn't Consett.

NASH: Oh yes it is.

PHIL: No, it can't be. This isn't the place.
There must be another.

NASH: There's only one, Phil. Now
there isn't any.

PHIL: You knew, didn't yer?

NASH: 'Course I knew. *I* don't walk round with me eyes shut.

PHIL: You did this on purpose.

NASH: An' of course, people who live in ivory towers shouldn't climb down.

PHIL: Do *I* live in an ivory tower?

NASH: You? – y'got the penthouse suite.

PHIL (*after a pause*): Nash . . . would you say I was dead ignorant?

NASH: Sometimes.

NITA'*s flat.*
  NITA *sits writing a letter.*

NITA: Phil, I could really do without this. Jealous. *Me.* Jealous of Beth. Why couldn't *I* get laid at the age of twelve, drunk on shandy, behind the bike-sheds, like any *normal* person. Instead of which . . . twenty, fully-conscious, should-know-better. Okay, Phil, say 'I told yer so'. Beth says 'be cool'. Beth's idea of *cool* is wait five minutes then go f'r'is zip. Phil, *I'm* cool. I could turn out ice cubes. So laid back, I'm falling over.
  Totally unimpressed. But he's not. He's fascinated. He's truly taken in. Phil, now what? What do I do? What d'y'say?
  Oh, where are yer when yer needed, Phil?

She screws up the letter and starts again.

Dear Phil . . . Things are pretty much the same as usual round here . . .

ALICE *comes in with some sheafs of paper and a hairdressing colour chart.*

ALICE: Nita? . . . what d'y'think of Bronzed Beech and Truffle?

NITA: For what?

ALICE: As a combination.

NITA: Revolting.

ALICE: No . . . well . . . p'raps yer right . . .

NITA: What y'doing, Alice?

ALICE: It's me design for the competition.

NITA: The competition? This year's Colour Trophy? Y'not thinking of entering, are you?

ALICE: Well, I thought I might . . .

NITA: Alice, have you any idea what you'll be up against?

ALICE: Well *you're* entering.

NITA: Alice, I'm a trained stylist.

ALICE: I thought I'd have a go.

NITA (*slightly taken aback*): Oh well . . . if y'fancy yer chances . . . by all means . . . but Bronzed Beech and Truffle, Alice . . . it's not a very promising start.

ALICE *looks suddenly despondent.*
NITA *realises she's been a little harsh.*

Of course, if y'wanted to get a better idea . . . (*She gets out her own design.* ALICE *is visibly impressed.*) Y'see . . . these bits come round like this . . . all Burgundy underneath, with a section here . . . Blond and Rust . . . this piece is sort of Copper-Coral . . . and the front section has Raisin and Plum tapering into Apricot Gold . . .

Towards the end of this conversation, DANNY *saunters in. No one takes any notice of him and he is finally obliged to interrupt.*

DANNY: Nita? (*Trying to kiss her.*)

NITA: Mmmmmmmm?

DANNY: What y'talking about?

NITA: The competition . . . (*He tries to put his arms round her.*) Danny, yer in the way . . . (*To* ALICE, *indicating the design.*) See what I mean? . . .

DANNY (*trying a new approach*): What competition, Alice?

ALICE: Oh, what Nita's gonna win this year. Didn't she tell you?

DANNY: No.

ALICE: Then next year – if I work dead hard – I might come in the Top Ten.

DANNY: Oh.

ALICE: The Top Ten get to the Finals in London.

DANNY: I see . . . (*Trying again.*) What competition, Nita?

NITA: I'm gonna win it. Didn't I tell you?

DANNY: No. (*He continues to be ignored, so picks up the leaflet and reads out:*) 'The biggest and most prestigious hairdressing competition of its kind in the world.' That's right, Nita – don't be too modest.

NITA: Danny, presumably you have nothing better to do at the moment than make a nuisance of yourself?

DANNY (*to* ALICE, *trying to joke*): She's gonna win it.

NITA: Possibly not the Final – hopefully the Manchester heat.

DANNY (*slightly taken aback*): Well don't let *me* stop you.

NITA: I won't.

NASH *and* PHIL*'s flat.*
Late night. PHIL *sits at a table with a portable typewriter.* NASH*'s books are piled up at the other end of the table.* NASH *comes in.*

PHIL: Who's on the phone?

NASH: Me mother.

PHIL: Gone midnight?

NASH: She couldn't sleep. (*Leaning over her shoulder.*) No 'i' in 'desecrate'. (*Before she can turn he goes and sits down at the other end of the table.*) Goin' a bit senile.

PHIL: Y'what?

NASH: Says to come again. *Liked* yer. Poor soul.

PHIL (*pleased*): Did she?

NASH: What y'doin'?

PHIL: Writing.

NASH: What for?

PHIL: I dunno . . . just me, prob'ly. 'Case I forget.

NASH: What?

PHIL: Yer dad.

NASH: Me dad?

PHIL: It's not 'the same', is it?

NASH: He's all right.

PHIL: He's not, though, is he?

NASH: No.

PHIL: Sat in that chair. Counting the hours. Waiting while the giro drops.

NASH: Had a good run f'r'is money.

PHIL: I never thought.

NASH: What?

PHIL: It could get like that.

NASH: Well now y'know.

Without warning he takes the page from the typewriter.
PHIL *jumps up.*

PHIL (*as he reads it*): Oh no . . . I know . . . it's crap . . . no, look, I know it's crap . . . it's okay, I'm gonna rip it up . . .

NASH (*having read it*): *I* wouldn't. (*He hands it back.*)

PHIL *is delighted and glances through the page again.* NASH *goes on with his work.* PHIL *watches him for awhile, then puts the page down and wanders round to stand behind his chair.*

PHIL: Nash . . . (*He doesn't look up. She daren't come any closer.*) Y'gonna be up all night?

NASH: I have to finish this chapter.

PHIL (*temporarily at a loss, then suddenly, grabbing the book*): D'y'wanna bet!

NASH: Phil . . .

PHIL *runs off round the other side of the table and starts to read from the chapter he's up to.*

PHIL (*reading*): 'What is the play of *Hamlet* about? It is of course about many things . . .'

NASH: Don't mess about, Phil . . .

PHIL, *now eager to pursue this, turns to a postcard NASH has been using for a bookmark. She starts to read it aloud.*

PHIL (*reading*): 'Mykonos is full of loud Americans wearing Sony Walkmans and very little else.'

NASH: Don't, Phil. (*He puts out his hand for the book and card.*)

PHIL (*playfully defiant, continues to read*): 'Nicky left today. I've had enough. Home in August. What about a cottage on Skye?' (*Suddenly less playful.*) Who's Rebecca?

NASH: A friend.

PHIL: When did this come?

NASH: Last week.

PHIL: Why not to our house?

NASH: She writes to Wallsend.

PHIL *tries to look unconcerned. She reads the postcard again.*

PHIL: 'What about a cottage on Skye.' What cottage on Skye?

NASH: Somewhere she used to want to live.

PHIL: Used to want? Who is she, Nash?

NASH: A girl in my year.

PHIL: I mean, who is she to you?

NASH (*trying to sound casual*): I . . . used to live with her.

PHIL: What?

NASH: Before you. I used to live with her. (*Pause.*) I lived with her for two years.

PHIL: You never told me.

NASH: You never asked.

PHIL (*totally thrown*): What?

NASH: We had an agreement, Phil.

PHIL: What 'agreement'?

NASH: I never asked. Did I ask? What you did is yer own affair.

PHIL: What *I* did?

NASH: You. Before. Other blokes. All the passionate affairs. Don't tell me. I don't wanna know.

PHIL: Other blokes? Oh, brilliant. What 'other blokes'? What 'passionate affairs'? I'm not Beth – I *can* say 'no'. Oh yeah, affairs, passion – up here. Love at two hundred paces – Man United, me an' sixty thousand others? You lived with her for two years? Why aren't y'*still* living with her? What'm I doin' stood here when I could be doin' something useful like stick a bullet in yer? Why is she on Mykonos fending off loud, naked Americans?

NASH: She left.

PHIL: Left.

NASH: To have a baby.

PHIL: Oh no, I don't believe this – I don't believe it –

NASH: Try not to wake the street up, Phil.

PHIL: Let me in, Alice – let me join the club.

NASH: Don't be stupid, Phil . . .

PHIL: Congratulations, Phil – you have just won one artistic ex-girlfriend, plus child, living on Mykonos . . .

NASH: Not mine.

PHIL: What?

NASH: Not mine.

PHIL: She lives with you for two years – an' has someone else's kid?

NASH: She said it was mine. I knew it wasn't.

PHIL: How could you know?

NASH: I knew whose it was.

PHIL: When?

NASH: Just before I met you.

PHIL: Oh, it gets better. Then *I* get involved. Well done, Phil. Why drag *me* in?

NASH: For spite?

PHIL: For what?

NASH: To spite her.

PHIL: Why pick on *me*?

NASH: I dunno. Like Everest, Phil. Because you were there. (*After a long pause.*) I thought you'd be okay.

PHIL: Thanks a lot.

NASH: I thought you'd be a laugh.

PHIL: Like Rebecca?

NASH: No. Not like Rebecca.

PHIL: But of course you took her home, an' of course yer mother loved *her* an' all.

NASH: Of course.

PHIL (*daring herself to say it*): Did *you*?

NASH: What?

PHIL: Love her.

NASH *shrugs.*

PHIL: What's that supposed to mean?

NASH: Who knows?

PHIL: *Don't* you?

NASH: Do *you*?

PHIL *hasn't the courage to say 'yes', so after a pause . . .*

PHIL: Will she come back? (*He shrugs.*) Here?

NASH: I don't know.

PHIL: Are you going?

NASH: Where?

PHIL: To Skye.

NASH: Phil, I work here.

PHIL: So I have to go.

NASH: Go where?

PHIL: Move out.

NASH: You live here.

PHIL: I do now.

NASH: Jesus, Phil, what y'talking about? Y'live here. It's your house.

PHIL: It's *your* house.

NASH: Y'live with *me,* don't yer?

PHIL: I did, yeah.

NASH: Christ, Phil, stop acting so fuckin' stupid. I lived with her. She writes me letters. She has a kid who looks nothing like me an' the dead spit of me best mate. I lived with her an' now I live with you. Does that not suggest something to yer?

PHIL: Why d'y'live with me?

NASH: Why d'y'think?

PHIL: For spite?

NASH: For two years? That's a fair share of spite, Phil.

PHIL: Y'went with me for spite. To spite Rebecca.

NASH: I did, yeah. I stay with you for something else.

PHIL: For what, Nash?

NASH (*after a pause*): Not for spite, Phil. (*After a pause he sits down at the table again.*) Y'got a nine o'clock tomorrow. Go to bed.

PHIL: Now?

NASH: Go on. I'll see yer later.

PHIL: Talk to me?

NASH: I've said it all. (*More gently:*) Go on, Phil – go to bed.

PHIL *hesitates but finally goes.* NASH *opens his book, then closes it again, unable to work.*

A Manchester nightclub.
    BETH *stands, as if at a wash basin,*

trying to make herself sick. NITA
looks on.

BETH: Nita . . . what is it the Romans
do?

NITA: They fall on their swords, Beth.
Try this. (*She hands her a nail file.*)

BETH: Oh God, I don't know what
happened – I've only had four glasses
. . . five . . . an' a bit . . . an' that
champagne . . .

Enter CARMEN.

CARMEN (*cheerfully to* BETH): Oh
hello, y'suffering a bit, are yer? (*Groan
from* BETH.) Oh me, I'm just the
same – don't enjoy meself unless I've
had a drink. Hey, aren't they awful,
them two, givin' us treble vodkas in
them cocktails. Y'not drinking, Nita?
Beth, this feller fancies you – I knew
he did – next table down eating
shrimp-in-a-basket? (BETH *groans.*)
Saudi or something – an' apparently,
he puts his teeth in the safe every
night, 'cos there's ten thousand quid's
worth of gold bullion in his fillings . . .

NITA *storms out in disgust.* BETH *is
still trying to make herself sick.*

What's up with her? Hey, did I tell
yer? – met this bloke last week – said
I should be on the front cover of
Vogue . . .

*During this speech, they both move
into the main nightclub area where*
DANNY *is trying to talk to* NITA
and REUBEN *is reclining on a bar
stool.*
As BETH *emerges she is pounced on
by the* SHEIK *and dragged off into a
recess out of sight.* CARMEN,
oblivious, continues chatting.

Fantastic taste . . . says I should be
modelling swimsuits . . . I don't know
where he got that idea . . .

DANNY (*annoyed at having his
conversation with* NITA *spoiled*): Ask
him next time, will yer?

CARMEN: Next time what?

DANNY: Next time he gets his leg over.

CARMEN (*shrieking*): Danny! Nita, he's
so disgusting, isn't he? (*She falls in
convulsions of laughter and goes to
join* REUBEN.)

NITA (*ignoring them*): Danny, how can
you let her make exhibitions of
herself? (*Looking over to where* BETH
disappeared.)

DANNY: Hey, hang on, hang on – she's
past the age of consent, y'know. Hey,
c'mon Nita – I been tryna talk to yer
all night.

NITA: Of course, *you* don't give a toss
how cheap she looks –

CARMEN: Cheap? What d'y'mean? He's
just give her fifty quid.

REUBEN (*leaning over*): Hey Danny,
better than a porno movie or what?

DANNY: Nita, can we go somewhere
quieter?

NITA: Oh yeah, run away – pretend it's
not your responsibility.

REUBEN: Hey, hang on – he never
introduced her – she fell into his
ice bucket. (CARMEN *shrieks with
laughter.* DANNY *is looking very ill
at ease.*) Have to say it, Danny –
y'certainly know how to bring yer
own entertainment along.

NITA (*seething*): Entertainment?

DANNY: Reuben, give it a rest.

REUBEN (*to* CARMEN): Beats a video
any time.

NITA: Is that what she is? Is that what
you call her?

DANNY: Nita, he's been drinking since
lunch time . . .

NITA: Oh, so Danny knows how to bring
his own entertainment, does he?
Danny likes a good laugh? Is that what
I am, Danny? Entertaining?

DANNY: Nita, shut up, will yer? – I
wanna talk to yer . . . (*She gets up.*)
Where y'going?

NITA: Home. (*She heads out. He catches up with her at the door.*)

DANNY: Nita, hang on, will yer —

NITA: What for?

DANNY: I wanted to ask if y'felt like . . .

NITA: What?

DANNY: Moving in with me —

NITA: What?

DANNY: Would yer?

NITA: Y'what? — move in with *you*?

DANNY: Will yer?

NITA: If you think I could possibly live with someone who shares his bedroom with 50 square feet of tinted glass and three acres of brushed nylon tiger fur . . .

DANNY (*embarrassed*): Sssshhh, Nita . . .

NITA: If you think the idea of living with a self-seeking, irresponsible, immoral piss artist is remotely tempting . . . (DANNY *realises he's blown it.*) . . . yer very sadly mistaken. And y'can have *that* (*A swipe across the face.*) to round off yer evening's entertainment.

NITA's *salon.*
Same night. Noises of crashing and banging from next door. ALICE *comes in almost screaming.* NITA *has just arrived back from the nightclub.*

ALICE: Nita . . . Nita, come quick . . . oh God, Nita, something's happening . . . there's terrible noises coming from Danny's . . .

NITA (*coming in*): Now what's the matter?

ALICE: He's ripping his flat to pieces . . . (*She rushes outside again.*) Nita, all that glass, them mirrors . . . it's being shifted out . . . (*She rushes outside then back again carrying the tiger-skin bedspread.*) Nita, look what Danny just give us — I can use it to make cushions for the cat . . . Nita, y'won't

believe this . . . he's chucked out that cocktail cabinet with the goldfish in it . . . (*She rushes out.*)

DANNY *appears in the doorway.*

DANNY: Does that make a difference?

NITA (*coolly*): Well, it's certainly an improvement.

She walks past him and goes out. DANNY *looks after her, bewildered, then runs after her.* ALICE *is left holding the tiger skin.*

A street in Salford.
KEVIN *walks on. He looks around as if waiting for someone. Finally* ALICE *appears.*

KEVIN: I thought y'wouldn't come.

ALICE: Why wouldn't I come? (*He shrugs.*) How y'doing?

KEVIN: Oh, okay — y'know . . . always skint.

ALICE: Still with Joey?

KEVIN: On an' off. It keeps us going. In't just got meself to think of now.

ALICE: I heard.

KEVIN: 'Bout Carly?

ALICE: Movin' in?

KEVIN: Get used to sharing, don't yer?

ALICE: I'm with Nita.

KEVIN: Doin' dead well.

ALICE: We are. We're doin' great. I can do things. Me. Can y'believe it? Good at something?

KEVIN: Think about yer sometimes, Al.

ALICE: Do you?

KEVIN: I suppose we couldn't ever . . . y'know . . . get back?

ALICE: Kevin . . .

KEVIN: No . . . I didn't think so.

ALICE: Kevin, I have to go now. I got this competition. I have to practise.

KEVIN: I hope y'do dead well, Alice.

ALICE: I'll let yer know. If I win, I'll take you out.

KEVIN: Promise?

ALICE: I'll see yer, Kevin . . . (*About to go.*)

KEVIN: Alice . . .

ALICE: What?

KEVIN: I loved you.

ALICE: I know.

NITA's *flat.*
   2 a.m. NITA *is sitting up working on her design.* DANNY, *obviously just wakened, comes in.*

DANNY: Nita, what y'doin'? — it's two o'clock.

NITA: Is it?

DANNY: Y'gettin' obsessed with this competition. (*He tries to kiss her.*)

NITA: Danny, if y'must stay the night, can't you do it quietly?

DANNY: Nita, c'mon, what is it? A competition. Y'so pushed for prize money? Here, Y'can have a cheque now.

NITA: Danny, it's not the money.

DANNY: Okay, whatever. What d'y'want? Attention, publicity — I'll get yer publicity. I know people. I'll get yer Macari in a kilt lit up an' hanging in yer window. I'll sort yer out.

NITA: Danny, I can't.

DANNY: Can't what?

NITA: Take hand-outs from you.

DANNY: Why not?

NITA: Danny, you help people out, right? People help you out. That's business. Well people help me out an' all. People been helping me out since I'm in teething rings. An' I'm getting bored, Danny. I've had it

up to here.

DANNY: Like me, y'mean.

NITA: Like you, like Phil — me dad, me brothers . . . the bank manager, for God's sake. I go in, I want a loan — he's falling off his desk pushing money at me. Ten, twelve, what about a car? What about new clothes. What about a drink sometime? Danny, I coulda walked away with half the assets of that bank. I always do that. 'I want' — an' ten seconds later — I get.

DANNY: That's an achievement.

NITA: That's not an achievement.

DANNY (*trying to put his arm round her*): Nita, you make me laugh sometimes.

NITA: Danny, I'm not a doll. (*Shrugging him off.*) . . . Wind her up, press the button, make her say please and thank you.

DANNY: Is that what you think?

NITA: Danny, I'm this high, I'm in me pram. Me mum, she can't keep hold of me. Hordes of people, prodding, poking — what a lovely child, what a pretty face. Can I buy her a lolly? — can I take her on the swings? You, y'wanna take me on the swings an' all, don't yer? Pat me, dress me up an' wheel me out for all yer mates.

DANNY: That isn't what I want.

NITA: Well just for once I'm gettin' out the pram. Just f'r a change the lovely child dun't need carrying up the slide. I'm gonna win it, Danny. All right? So sod off back to bed and stop giving me earache about eight hours kip and Lou Macari's kilt. (DANNY *hesitates.*) All right?

DANNY *realises she won't be moved. He admits defeat and goes to bed.*

NASH *and* PHIL's *house.*
   NASH *is immersed in work.* PHIL *walks on carrying a hold-all.*

NASH (*looking up*): Y'goin'?

PHIL: Me train's at five past.

NASH: Tell Nita good luck f'r'us.

PHIL: I will.

> NASH *deliberately goes on with his work.* PHIL, *defeated, heads for the door.*

NASH (*suddenly*): Hang on . . .

PHIL: What?

NASH: I'll walk yer.

PHIL: What for?

NASH: I feel like it.

PHIL: When's she coming, then?

NASH: Who?

PHIL: Rebecca.

NASH: Y'what?

PHIL: She phoned you last night.

NASH: Yeah?

PHIL: Asking to come here?

NASH: Of course.

PHIL: And?

NASH: I told her she couldn't. I'll just get me coat. (*He goes off.*)

> PHIL, *unable to believe it, jumps into the air and screams. As she lands on the floor,* NASH *comes in again. To cover up, she pretends to be searching for something.*

NASH: What've you found?

PHIL: Guess.

> *She holds out both hands, closed, to him. He touches the first: empty. He touches the second: also empty. He grabs both her hands and pulls her up to face him.*

NASH: D'y'wanna miss the train, kidder?

> *He picks up her hold-all and walks out.* PHIL *runs after him.*

NITA*'s salon.*
> *The night of the competition.* ALICE *is ready to leave,* NITA *still tidying up.*

ALICE (*checking through a list*): Combs, spray, dryers, tongs, pins, brushes, make-up . . . anything else?

NITA: Ticket to South America?

ALICE: Nita, how d'y'feel?

NITA: How d'*you* feel?

ALICE: Sick.

NITA: Look, I'll see yer down there — just gotta clean up here first.

ALICE: Okay . . . (*She starts to go.*)

NITA: Alice . . .

ALICE: What?

> NITA *grabs* ALICE *and gives her a hug.*

NITA: Good luck.

> ALICE *goes out.* NITA *tidies round, makes final checks and turns out the lights so the salon is in darkness and the only light comes from the doorway. Suddenly a shadow appears in the door.* NITA *jumps, then realises who it is.*

NITA: Alice isn't here.

JOEY: I don't want Alice. I want you, Nita.

NITA: I'm just leaving.

JOEY: No, I don't think so.

NITA: Get out of my way, Joey.

JOEY (*strolling round the room*): Doin' dead well for yerself, Nita. Hear yer making a packet.

NITA: Yeah, I'm doin' all right, thank you.

JOEY: I never had me hair cut, Nita.

NITA: I'm busy, Joey.

JOEY: I can see yer not in a friendly mood, Nita. Let's get it over with now, shall we. (*He takes hold of her. She pushes him away.*) Nah, don't be like that, Nita. (*As if it's just occurred to him.*) How's the boyfriend?

NITA: You wait.

JOEY: Oh, I don't think he'll have much to say. Me an' Danny Boy done business couple of years ago. I'll just have to watch me back, that's all.

NITA: D'you want me to call the police.

JOEY: I wouldn't bother, Nita. Me an' the scuffers, we have this special arrangement. They don't come looking for me − but I'll come looking for you if I so much as see a panda cross the end of our street.

NITA: Get out.

JOEY: I been watching you, Nita. Y'be surprised how much I know about you. I could write a book on it. (*Circling round her.*) Y'like things yer own way, don't yer? Yer like me. I like me own way an' all. An' I can be dead persuasive, Nita.

NITA *backs off*. JOEY *continues to circle her. Finally he corners her. She is too terrified to move.*

C'mon, Nita, what's it to be? I can stay here all night. I can find things to do. Don't think you'd like them very much but y'certainly wouldn't get bored. Now shall we get heavy . . . or are yer gonna be a good girl an' open that till for me.

NITA: What?

JOEY: Are yer disappointed? D'yer think I wanted something else? I could have both.

NITA: Joey, I need that money.

JOEY: But I need it an' all, Nita. Now which of us needs it most? (*Finding a key in her pocket.*) Be a good girl, hey Nita?

He gives her the key. NITA *takes it, goes off, comes back with a bag full of money ready for banking.* JOEY *has a quick look inside.*

Yer doin' better than I thought. Now

that wasn't dead hard, was it?

NITA: Will you please go?

JOEY: I'm off now, Nita. I'll have me hair done another time. Hey listen, if I think yer getting too cocky, I might have to bring yer down the odd peg . . . I'll be seein' yer, Nita . . . (*He blows her a kiss and leaves.*)

NITA *is shaking with rage and fright.*

NITA: Bastard . . . you bastard. (*She suddenly grabs her things and runs out.*)

The Ritz Ballroom in Manchester.
The night of the competition. BETH *is sitting at a table laden with drinks.* ALICE *is pacing up and down being comforted by* PHIL. *In the background, music and the sound of people talking and drinking.*

ALICE: Where is she?

PHIL: She'll be here.

ALICE: What is she doing? (*Refusing to be calmed.*) She's gonna miss it − she is − I could kill her . . .

PHIL: Alice, calm down . . .

Enter CARMEN *(with a ridiculously flamboyant hairstyle) accompanied by* REUBEN.

CARMEN (*as she comes in*): Course, *I* coulda been a model − I was asked − I got perfect hair − but y'don't like to draw attention t'yerself, do yer?

REUBEN: Evening all . . . Danny Boy not in yet?

BETH: He's on his way.

REUBEN: C'mon, park yerself, Carmen − yer making the place look untidy. (CARMEN *sits down.*) Right, I'll get them in . . . (*He goes off to get some drinks.*)

ALICE (*still pacing about*): I'll be sick. I will. I'll blow it all wrong. I'll be disqualified . . . oh God, where is she, Phil? . . .

PHIL: Alice, just sit down . . .

Suddenly NITA *rushes in, looking as if she's about to collapse.*

ALICE (*springing up, almost screaming*): Where y'been? Y'nearly missed it.

CARMEN: We thought y'wasn't coming — y'nearly give us heart failure.

PHIL: Nita, are you all right?

NITA: I'm okay . . . I just feel a bit . . .

PHIL: Nita, sit down — d'y'wanna drink? (*To* BETH:) Can y'get her a drink?

NITA: No, I don't want a drink.

ALICE: Is it nerves?

CARMEN: Oh, it's nerves.

NITA (*snapping*): It's not nerves.

REUBEN (*coming in with drinks*): Here y'are then . . . oh, don't tell me — pissed before it's even started.

BETH: Have y'took anything?

NITA: I don't want anything.

CARMEN: Y'should — oh, y'should, Nita . . .

NITA: Where's Danny? He's s'posed to be here.

ALICE: He's coming.

REUBEN: Tied up in the shop, is he? (*Nudging* CARMEN.)

BETH: C'mon Nita, have this . . . (*She gives her some water.*)

Over the loudspeaker comes the announcement 'Will all competitors please report to their places?'

ALICE: Nita, it's starting . . .

BETH: C'mon, Nita, get yer skates on.

NITA *tries to compose herself.*

NITA (*getting up*): I'm all right . . . (*Then nearly collapses.*) I can't . . . I can't stand up . . . Phil, I'm gonna pass out . . . (*She sits with her head between her knees, shaking.*)

DANNY *runs on, at first not realising what's happening.*

DANNY: Nita, I'm sorry — I couldn't park . . . Nita? . . .

PHIL: She's not well.

DANNY: Nita, y'all right, babe?

CARMEN: *I* don't think she should go on. (BETH *glares at her.*) That's what *I* think, anyway.

DANNY: What's the matter with her?

CARMEN: Nerves.

ALICE (*snapping*): It's not nerves.

CARMEN: Well *I* think she'd be better off in bed.

REUBEN: Too right.

ALICE: Phil, what we gonna do?

REUBEN: Hey Danny — should have a word with the judges. How much cash y'got on yer?

CARMEN: Best get her home. *I* would. D'y'want some valium?

PHIL: No.

DANNY: What?

PHIL: She's not goin' home.

DANNY: Oh, I dunno, Phil . . .

PHIL: She's not copping out that easy —

DANNY: Look at the state of her, Phil.

PHIL: I seen the state on her, Danny.

DANNY (*getting annoyed*): You taking charge now, Phil?

BETH (*eagerly stepping in*): Tell him, Phil.

DANNY (*turning on her*): You keep yer nose out, you.

BETH: Up yours, Danny.

PHIL (*ignoring them all*): Get up, Nita.

DANNY: Leave her, Phil.

PHIL: Get up, Nita.

NITA: I can't, Phil —

PHIL: You can — get up — stop acting soft —

ALICE (*looking worried*): We'll have to

go — they're ready to start . . .

PHIL *picks up a glass of water from the table.*

PHIL: Nita . . . (*Louder:*) Nita . . .

NITA *looks up.* PHIL *throws the water in her face. There is a rush to protect* NITA *and fend* PHIL *off, but* PHIL *pushes them away.*

Get off her — leave her alone . . . (*Very softly.*) Nita, c'mon, get up . . .

NITA: I can't, Phil —

PHIL: Yes . . . you can, Nita . . . (*Suddenly losing her temper, dragging her up.*) Get up, Nita . . .

DANNY: What d'y'think yer doing, Phil.

PHIL: Gettin' me own back.

DANNY: What for?

PHIL: That earache *I* copped two years ago.

NITA: What earache?

PHIL: Don't come that with me. Two years ago — go on, Phil, get out, Phil — go to college, *do* something. Rings a bell, Nita? *I* was looking for quiet life an' all.

NITA: I'm not looking for a quiet life.

PHIL: Y'not gonna get one. (*She pulls her up.*) *I* didn't.

Now with NITA *on her feet,* PHIL *is roughly cleaning up her face.*

An' this is my way of saying thank you.

Grabbing her arm.

Get up on that stage, Nita . . . get hold of her, Alice . . . (ALICE *hesitates.*) — do as I say, Alice . . . grab her arm . . . right, now move . . .

One on either side, they both drag NITA *off.* DANNY, CARMEN *and* REUBEN *are amazed.*
In the background the loudspeaker is heard 'Ladies and Gentlemen, the Manchester heat of this year's Colour

Trophy Competition is now about to begin.

BETH: Right then — we gettin' a few bevvies in while it get's going?

A corridor outside the main room.
PHIL *is walking up and down trying to keep calm.* DANNY, *with* REUBEN *in attendance, is pacing about the opposite side of the corridor.*

PHIL: I wish I smoked. I might have some nails left.

DANNY (*pacing up and down*): Christ, I feel like she's givin' birth out there.

REUBEN: Oh, that's a good one, hey Danny? (*Laughing to himself.*)

DANNY (*coming over to* PHIL): She's blown it. She has, Phil. She won't even get placed.

PHIL: An' where would she be if *you'd* had yer own way?

DANNY: Me?

PHIL: Dosed to the eyeballs in bed, feeling sorry for herself? Perfect cop out.

DANNY: Phil, you saw the state on her. She was ill.

PHIL: She was not ill. (*Pause.*) She was terrified.

DANNY: What of?

PHIL: Not winning.

REUBEN: Christ, he could really do with being halfway up the M1 when the scores get read out.

PHIL: Fat lot of use he'll be there.

REUBEN: *She's* terrified? He's fuckin' petrified. You tried bein' around when she's not getting her own way?

PHIL: Two years I've not been around — precisely *because* she got her own way.

DANNY: I shoulda took her home. (*No one replies.*) Oh Christ, what'm I gonna say to her? If she dun't get placed, I'd rather she had an excuse.

PHIL: Danny, she shouldn't *have* an excuse.

REUBEN (*to* PHIL): You, y'love arguments, don't yer?

PHIL (*to* DANNY): Well, she'll just have to learn to be a gracious loser, won't she?

There is a moment of sympathy between them, broken by REUBEN.

REUBEN: Oh yeah, an' Stockport County might win the Cup next season.

Back inside the main ballroom. Round the table CARMEN *is lounging about trying to look glamorous while* BETH *is waiting for* PHIL *to come back.* REUBEN *and* DANNY *come in, followed by* PHIL. *The* COMPERE *can be heard announcing the finalists. His commentary runs under and simultaneously with the dialogue between* DANNY, BETH, PHIL, REUBEN, CARMEN, NITA *and* ALICE.

COMPERE (*off*): Ladies and gentlemen, the judges have now made up their minds . . . and I know you'll agree that the standard this year has been exceptionally high – I think I can say our highest ever – and that definitely goes for the turn-out – an amazing two hundred and sixteen entries, all vying for those top ten places and the Grand Final in London . . . well, I certainly don't envy the judge their work tonight, do you? . . .

BETH: Christ, *he* loves the sound of his own voice, doesn't he?

DANNY (*irritated*): Beth . . .

BETH: I'm not out with you now.

COMPERE (*off*): And I'd just like you to give a big hand to all the judges . . . and to our special guests . . . Simon Le Bon . . . (*Sounds of screams in the background.*) And world-famous football personality . . . Bobby Charlton! . . .

BETH *joins in the screams.*

Bobby Charlton? What does *he* know about hair?

COMPERE (*off*): So . . . before we go on to the results, I'd just like to tell you what's in store for this year's winner . . . (*He continues in the background.*)

PHIL (*suddenly*): What's she doin'? She's meant to stop onstage.

REUBEN: Blown it. Definitely.

CARMEN: Oh God, she looks terrible . . .

Well of course *all* the top ten finalists receive a diploma *and* a sash . . . that goes for the boys too! . . . The winner of the Grand Final will receive a cheque for two hundred and fifty

NITA *comes in as if from the stage.*
ALICE, *looking anxious, has followed*
her.

NITA: I blew it.

DANNY: Nita, you all right, babe?

NITA: I really cocked it up.

BETH: Looks all right from here.

NITA: It's not. It's a shambles.

DANNY: It doesn't matter, Nita.

NITA: It matters to *me*.

CARMEN: Next year, Nita . . .

NITA: I don't want it next year. I
want it *now*.

ALICE: Nita, *I* saw what you did. It
was good. It was really good.

NITA: No, it wasn't, Alice.

ALICE: It was. There was no
difference.

NITA: I was pathetic. I had about as
much skill as a carthorse.

DANNY: Nita, c'mere . . . (*He puts*
his arm round her.) You'll get it
next year.

REUBEN: If we have to bribe all the
judges and ship the rest of the
competition to Siberia.

NITA (*suddenly*): I'll have a drink.

ALICE: You sure?

NITA (*picking up a drink*): To next year.

DANNY (*glad of the diversion*): To next
year . . .

BETH: How d'you get on, Alice?

ALICE: Oh, okay, y'know – I was
pleased with it.

NITA (*suddenly remembering* ALICE):
You looked great, Alice. Y'looked
really good.

pounds . . . yes that's *two hundred and*
fifty pounds . . . a magnificent silver
trophy *and* . . . the opportunity to
represent England as part of the World
Cup team who will be travelling to
Mexico for the World Hairdressing
Finals next year!. . . And as you look
around you, ladies and gentlemen,
at this truly inspirational display of
hairdressing expertise you see before
you . . . just remember, this is where
you saw them first – the styles, the
fashions . . . whether you like it or
not . . . *these* are the styles you will
be wearing *next year!* . . . Yes, that's
right . . . *truly inspirational* . . .
And meanwhile . . . what about a big
hand for all those *truly marvellous*
girls – *and* boys . . . mustn't forget
those boys, must we? . . . – all those
boys and girls who have taken part in
this year's competition . . . *as*
models . . .
There is a sound of applause.

The COMPERE *continues in the*
background ad lib, until:

Ladies and gentlemen! . . . I've just
been handed a slip of paper . . . that
magic piece of paper . . . which
contains the names of this year's
top ten winners . . .

Sounds of applause.

So without further ado . . . here . . .
in ascending order . . . are the results
of the Manchester heat of the 1981
Colour Trophy . . .

In tenth position . . . Are you all ready
out there? . . .

In tenth position . . . Ladies and
gentlemen . . . From Stockport . . .

Table Number 62 . . . Philip
Yates . . .

Sounds of applause.

ALICE: I think it's the best I've done —
I mean, for *me* it was the best —
(*Raising her glass.*) This is to next
year, Nita . . .

They half-catch the mention of
ALICE's *name.*

NITA: What? —

ALICE: *Me*? —

BETH: *You*? —

PHIL: Al, it's *you* — it *is*!

ALICE (*in hysterics*): It's me! It's me!

BETH (*grabbing hold of her*): Go on,
go on . . . it's *you* . . . get up there . . .

ALICE *rushes off amid general
applause.*

BETH (*dancing about*): Nice one, Al!

NITA: She deserved that . . . she worked
dead hard. I'm dead pleased for
her . . . (*She bursts into tears.*)

DANNY (*out of his depth*): Nita? . . .
c'mon, Nita . . . (*Putting his arm
round her.*)

NITA: I'm dead proud of her.

PHIL: She did well, Nita. Next year
you'll do it.

BETH (*doing a football salute*): Yeah,
dead right! No messing.

NITA: I think I'm gonna go . . .

BETH: Nah, y'can't go . . .

DANNY (*at a loss*): D'you want me to
come with you?

NITA: No, it's okay . . . I'm all right . . .

She is about to go.

BETH: Nita, I'm not kidding, if that
thing up there with red an' black
stripes wins, I'm gonna lynch that
Simon Le Bon.

NITA (*to* PHIL): Tell Alice I'm dead
pleased for her . . .

She goes out.
BETH *watches her go.*

BETH (*to* DANNY): Go with yer, y'dick.

In ninth position . . . and
remember . . . *all* the top ten go to the
Grand Final in London . . . from
Salford . . . Table Number 75 . . .
Alice Gilmore

Sounds of applause.

In eighth position . . . from Cheadle
Hulme . . . Table Number 116 . . .
Joseph Heywood . . .

Applause.

In seventh position . . . from
Stretford . . . Table Number
52 . . . Helen Foxdecker . . .

Applause.

In sixth position . . . from Irlam . . .
Table Number 178 . . . Michael
Dobson . . .

Applause.

In fifth place . . . from Eccles . . .
Table Number 202 . . . Gina Dinsdale-
Fewkes

Applause.

In fourth place . . . from Whalley
Range . . . Table Number 98 . . . Flora
Mackintosh . . .

Applause.

In 3rd place . . . ladies and gentlemen
. . . from Old Trafford . . . Table
Number 7 . . . Ronnie Atkinson . . .

Applause.

And the runner-up in this year's heat
. . . from Altringham . . . Table
Number 17 . . . Marcus Wright . . .

Applause.

And in First Place . . . the winner of

DANNY: I can't. What can I say?

BETH: Danny, yer a wanker, you are.

DANNY (*getting annoyed*): Hey, you'll
be out if you don't watch it.

BETH: Y'what? Me job? Working f'r'a
wanker like *you*? You know where
y'can stuff it, Danny . . .

DANNY: Yer askin' for something, you
are . . . (*He is about to grab* BETH.)

*Everyone is momentarily stunned,
then suddenly it sinks in.*

BETH: Nita! —

PHIL: She did it! —

BETH: The daft get — where is she?
(*Shouting to make herself heard above
the cheers.*) Nita, where are yer?

NITA *suddenly appears in the
doorway.*

NITA (*almost a whisper*): I won it.
(*Screams.*) I won it!

Everyone rushes to congratulate her.

PHIL (*rushing her forward*): Nita, get up
there and take it.

NITA *goes off onto the stage. The
applause is now deafening.* CARMEN
prepares to take photographs.
REUBEN *rushes on with champagne.*

NITA *and* ALICE *come back with
their sashes and awards. Photos are
taken, streamers thrown. Everyone
joins in the congratulations.*

PHIL *is standing apart from the rest,
watching.* NITA *sees her, goes up to
her and puts the trophy into her hand.*

NITA: One-all, Phil.

*Suddenly the sound stops dead. The
lights are out except on* PHIL *who
now comes forward.*

the 1981 Manchester heat . . .
Ladies and gentlemen . . .

From Salford . . .
Table Number 74 . . .

Nita Sharman!
Prolonged Applause.

PHIL: One-all? Is it? Did you just
equalise, Nita?
Look at yer now. Name on the sheet.
Alice an' all. That's a turn-up for the
book.
Me an' Beth — we're a joke. What've
we been doing? Twin strikers, never
got past the halfway line. While you
two stuffy gets come sneaking up the
wing an' lob one in from forty yards.
Man of the Match. Both of yer.
Now what? Change tack? Swap sides?
Beth just pulled her shirt on by the
looks of it. No more sitting with the
subs for Beth. Watch yer backs out
there — she'll break yer neck. And me?
Oh, the boss is saying, too speculative,
too much time-wasting. Get yer sleeves
rolled up, Phil. Y'got another half to
play — y'could score a hat-trick. This
lot's shown yer how it's done. So get
out there . . . and break the net!

Blackout.

COMMAND OR PROMISE

Command or Promise was first performed at the Liverpool Playhouse on 17 November 1983, with the following cast:

ALICE *(21)*/BETH'S MOTHER	Sally-Anne Jackson
NITA *(21)*	Tara Shaw
PHIL *(21)*	Julia North
BETH *(21)*	Angela Catherall
NASH *(25)*	Martin Wenner
DANNY *(36)*/JOEY *(27)*/AMBULANCEMAN	Roger Hyams
BETH'S FATHER/POLICEMAN/AMBULANCEMAN/	
REUBEN *(37)*/KAZ *(23)*	John Wild
CARMEN *(27)*/LINDY *(22)*/MISS MARKS/NURSE/	
REBECCA *(28)*	Kate Lynn-Evans

Directed by Richard Brandon
Designed by John Stokes
Lighting by Steve Drummon
Sound by Jimmy Simmons

The play was subsequently seen at the Cottesloe Theatre from 24 November 1985, with the following cast:

ALICE	Sally-Anne Jackson
NITA	Tara Shaw
PHIL	Stella Gonet
BETH	Lesley Sharp
NASH/BETH'S FATHER	David Fielder
DANNY	David Cardy
JOEY	Stephen Petcher
REUBEN/AMBULANCEMAN	Roderick Smith
KAZ	Adam Kotz
CARMEN/NURSE/BETH'S MOTHER	Cheryl Prime
LINDY/POLICEWOMAN	Katrin Cartlidge
MISS MARKS/REBECCA	Caroline Goodall

Directed by John Burgess
Designed by Alison Chitty
Lighting by Stephen Wentworth
Sound by Nic Jones

The play is set in Manchester, Salford and Bristol in 1982 and 1983. Characters' ages given above are for 1982.

ACT ONE

May-September 1982

NITA's *flat.*
    NITA, ALICE *and* BETH *are in the middle of the floor at an advanced stage of the Jane Fonda workout.* NITA *is flinging herself into it,* ALICE *just about coping and* BETH *on the verge of collapse.*

BETH: I can't do it. (*She is ignored.*) I can't.

ALICE (*ignoring* BETH, *to* NITA): What's in this morning?

NITA: Two perms, four highlights an' a demi-wave at twelve. Can I leave you to neutralise?

ALICE: Who is it? Oh, not that Wilson woman? She goes mad if *I* do her.

NITA: Just tell her . . . (*Now enthusiastically exercising.*) . . . you're my second-in-command . . . an' I have every confidence in you . . . (*Redoubles her efforts.*)

ALICE (*after consideration*): But I *am* your second-in-command.

NITA: I'm aware of that, Alice.

BETH: I can't do it.

NITA (*irritated*): What?

BETH: My leg's gone dead.

NITA: Beth, it's easy – watch me . . .

BETH: Watch me, watch me . . . built like a bleedin' toy poodle, yeah it *is* easy . . . Christ, if Phil could see us now . . .

NITA: What?

BETH: She'd piss herself, that's what. (*Half-collapsing, then getting up again.*) I'm on me round at ten. Rate I'm goin', be too knackered to shift the ladder, never mind get up top of it.

ALICE: Danny wants his grey bits doin' an' all.

NITA: Not again.

ALICE: Well he's pushing 35, Nita – if y'will go out with geriatrics . . .

BETH *suddenly collapses shrieking and holding her leg.*

BETH: Sod this, Nita. There must be easier ways of keeping fit. (*She collects her things.*) *My* problem is, they all piss off after the first night . . . (*She hobbles out.*)

NITA: Typical . . . no staying power.

ALICE: Nita, I'm getting cramp . . .

NITA: Oh, not you an' all.

ALICE: Well, I wouldn't mind, Nita – it says 'once through' – not carry on till y'conk out.

NITA (*scathingly*): Don't you want to be fit and active?

ALICE: How can y'be fit an' active if y'spend the rest of the day on yer back?

ALICE *also collapses and howls with pain.*

Bristol. PHIL *and* NASH's *house.*
    The howls of pain are taken up as PHIL *sits on the floor howling in agony as* NASH *tries to give her a shoulder massage.*

PHIL: Aaah . . . ow . . . not there, y'daft get . . . here . . . further down . . . further do-ow-n . . . there . . . *there* . . .

NASH: Phil, if y'kept still an' didn't give yer mouth such a workout, we might get a chance . . . (*Digging into her shoulders.*) . . . to locate the pain.

PHIL: Ow . . . aaaagh . . . I've pulled something . . . I have, Nash . . .

NASH: You carried *one* crate of books up the path.

PHIL: Don't ask us to move house again. Just don't.

NASH: Phil, what more d'y'want? I get us a nice view of the Avon Gorge. When you blow yer Finals, you'll be nicely placed to jump off the Suspension Bridge.

PHIL: We can't all get Firsts.

NASH: Well we could . . . if we give it more work an' less jaw.

PHIL: Y'read me Wordsworth paper yet?

NASH: Yeah.

PHIL: And?

NASH: Bit derivative.

PHIL: Of what?

NASH: My lecture notes.

PHIL: Y'what? –

NASH: But other than that – sensational. (*Seeing she's looking pleased*.) As in 'over the top'.

PHIL: Yeah, all right – yer only doin' a PhD, Nash – that doesn't put yer second in line to T.S. Eliot. Is it a 2-1?

NASH: Phil, if y'don't shift yerself, it won't even be a Third.

PHIL: Did I want me head testing? Did I ever think I'd *enjoy* living with *you*?

NASH: We all make mistakes, Phil.

PHIL: I bet Rebecca never had to carry books.

NASH: Rebecca never carried anything. (*He digs into her shoulders again*.)

PHIL (*howling with pain*): Ow . . . what y'tryna do? – break me bloody neck?

NASH: Chance'd be a fine thing.

Manchester. REUBEN's *studio*.
   Again the gasps of pain are taken up as DANNY *stands in shorts and boxing gloves carrying* CARMEN, *who is wearing a bikini and a hat which bears the inscription 'Stop Me And Buy One'*. REUBEN *is taking photographs*.

REUBEN: Hold it . . . lovely . . . smile . . . tits out a bit, love . . . hold it there . . . smashing . . . knock-out . . .

DANNY (*groaning*): Reuben, can I drop her now? – she's a bloody ton weight.

REUBEN: Right, get yer clothes on, slag. (CARMEN *is unceremoniously dumped*.)

DANNY (*to* REUBEN): Okay, look, I need the contacts tomorrow – promotion starts Monday.

CARMEN: Danny? – don't y'think we shoulda been in bed together?

DANNY: Y'what?

CARMEN: Well that's what y'selling, in't it? . . . fitted bedrooms? . . . y'know, 'Danny Haslam – Bedroom Specialist' . . .

DANNY: Carmen, remind me – what is it you do?

CARMEN: I'm a model.

DANNY: Just remember that an' keep yer mouth shut, eh?

REUBEN: Yer out tonight, Danny?

DANNY: Yeah, 'bout nine. Nita's topped thousand this week, so she's buying.

REUBEN: Got her well trained, hey? Mind, so y'should – after all this time. (*Slapping* CARMEN *on the backside*.) C'mon, miss – if yer lucky, I might give yer a peek at me exposures . . . (*He falls into fits of laughter*.)

DANNY: Cheers, mate.

REUBEN *and* CARMEN *go off together*. DANNY *exits prancing about like a boxer and practising punches*.

NITA's *salon*.
   The phone rings. NITA *comes on and picks it up*.

NITA: Hello . . . Nita's Headlines . . . (*Resigned*.) . . . Yes, hello mother, it's me . . . Tuesday? No . . . got weight training Tuesday . . . Wednesday's workout, Thursday's yoga . . . Friday . . . no, in town with Danny, Friday, Sat'day . . . Sunday I *could* . . . no, hang on, we're off to London that weekend . . . tell yer what . . . I could do yer . . . (*Looking through book.*) a fortnight on Thursday after nine o'clock . . . all right? . . . Oh, an' listen, mother, I'm on a *diet* . . . so I'll send you round a list of things I can't eat . . . oh, by the way, how are you . . ?

ALICE *comes in nervously.*

ALICE: Nita . . . y'know when me an' Kev split up . . . an' you said come an' work for yer . . .

NITA (*to the phone*): Mmmmmmm? . . .

ALICE: An' you said, if I ever want anything, just ask . . .

NITA (*to the phone*): Yes . . .

ALICE: Well I do.

NITA (*to the phone*): Really? . . .

ALICE: See . . . last week, I took nearly three hundred quid . . . well, that's quite a lot . . . an' *you're* takin' at least that − prob'ly more . . . an' I reckon we must be doin' pretty well . . . so . . . (*Bracing herself.*) I think I ought to have more money.

NITA (*to phone*): Yes, mother . . . I'll see yer, mother . . . (*As she puts the phone down, she hands* ALICE *a wage packet.*)

ALICE: What's this?

NITA: Yer wages.

ALICE: Y'give us too much.

NITA: Y'bin promoted. Make sure yer worth it.

ALICE (*hugely apologetic*): Oh God, Nita, are yer sure? Can y'afford it?

NITA: If I couldn't afford it, y'wouldn't be getting it, would yer? (ALICE *delightedly looks through her wages.*) And talking of Kevin . . . (ALICE *looks up.*) Isn't it about time y'did something about a *divorce*?

ALICE: I s'pose it *is*, really . . .

NITA: Well it's two years since you left him, Alice. What exactly are you waiting for?

ALICE: I dunno, really. Get used to bein' married, don't yer? Y'know, like . . . belonging to someone? D'y'think that's daft?

NITA: Frankly, yes. Y'wanna start bein' a bit more independent. (*The phone rings.*) Hello . . . Nita's Headlines . . .

The lights come up on JOEY, *on the phone.*

JOEY: Guess who, Nita's Headlines.

NITA: Alice . . . (*She motions her out of the room. To the phone.*) Joey, I paid you last month.

JOEY: Y'did.

NITA: I don't owe till September.

JOEY: Well that's correct, Nita . . . but, see inflation . . .

NITA: Don't you dare come in here asking for more.

JOEY: Aaah, be fair, Nita. Haven't I stuck hard to me four per cent like a good lad? I'm only tryna make a decent living . . .

NITA: We had an agreement, Joey.

JOEY: Hey, them Turners next door − know what happened last week? Fire in the stockroom an' the silly get wasn't insured. Now *we* don't wanna go up in smoke, do we? Not on the money *we're* making. Them hands of yours . . .

NITA: What?

JOEY: Very pretty hands y'got, Nita. Must be worth a bit extra, wouldn't yer say? Couple of hundred a month? Go on, yer rakin' it − y'won't even notice. Y'll just have to work a bit harder . . . (*He nonchalantly lights a match and watches it burn.*) I'll be round later . . . (NITA *is about to slam the phone down.*) Aaaah, don't be like that, Nita. It's nothing personal, honest . . .

Manchester. The street.

BETH *comes on in a pair of overalls and a T-shirt that says 'British and proud of it', carrying a bucket and window-cleaning equipment.*

BETH: Yer a dirty lot of sods round here. Where's yer pride? State of them winders — y'never heard of daylight? Two quid? It's hardly gonna bankrupt yer. Downstairs, then? Or just the front?
Hey, I'll do yer greenhouse. Yer milk bottles? anything? . . .
Stingy gets. Know what I made this week? Seventeen quid. Up an' down ladders like a bleedin' yo-yo for half the price of a black market Cup Final ticket. Me mam, she drinks that in an afternoon.
Enterprise? Meant to applaud that, aren't yer? Three months solid graft — me own round, clientele. Selfish gets all got laid off, didn't they? Sorry love, no money now for splashing out on clean winders.

Well sod yer, then.

She starts to compose a letter.

Kaz Johnson, HMS Galahad, The Forklands. Friday.
Dear Kaz . . .
Nah, I'm not missing yer. What d'y'think I am?
Yer a stuffy sod, aren't yer? Take it easy, then — *I* would. Ships rations, kipping out on deck. Hey, d'you think they might take us now I got muscles? Round by us they're all signing up. Aaaaah Kaz, I wish I could be where you are . . .
Alice . . . y'won't believe this . . . Alice says . . .

ALICE (*in a spot*): I don't think they shoulda gone.

BETH: Yeah. (*She indicates* ALICE *disdainfully.*) I says to her — 'Alice, suppose some get strolls in an' walks off with yer favourite Police album — what d'y'do? Stand there, goin' "no, please, do help yerself to my Regatta

De Blanc". Or d'y'make a dive for the bread-board an' hammer the bastards into the carpet? I mean, people should be taught good manners, right?'

ALICE: Yeah . . .

BETH: She says . . .

ALICE: But just suppose it's yer Manilow Magic y'been tryna get shot of since God knows when . . .

BETH: I says, 'Y'what? — y'goin' daft, Al? It's not the Manilows, is it? It's the principle.' We wanna get out there an' show them what this means . . . (*She points to her T-shirt.*) Right Kaz?

ALICE *goes off.* BETH *remains onstage.*
Two figures (BETH's PARENTS) *appear in shadow on either side of the stage.*

FATHER: Let me finish —

MOTHER: Let him finish —

FATHER: You'll have gathered by now —

MOTHER: That your father and I —

FATHER: Haven't exactly —

MOTHER: Been hitting it off —

FATHER: So it might be better —

MOTHER: For all of us —

FATHER: But mostly you —

MOTHER: To make a clean break —

FATHER: And call it a day.

BETH: Oh.

FATHER: What with your mother's affair with the gin bottle —

MOTHER: Your father's obsession for the welfare of his typists —

FATHER: I decided —

MOTHER: Oh, *you* decided? —

FATHER: Your mother and I —

MOTHER: Thank you —

FATHER: To go our separate ways.

MOTHER: Thank God —

FATHER: So all that remains —

MOTHER: Is who gets the house —

FATHER: Is who gets you —

MOTHER: Your father thinks you'd be better off with him —

FATHER: Your mother thinks you'd prefer to stay with her —

MOTHER: But if I were you —

FATHER: I'd stay with your mother —

MOTHER: I'd go with your father —

FATHER: The choice is yours —

BETH: Well thanks a lot.

> BETH *remains on stage.*
> PHIL *(in Bristol) comes on carrying some books.*

PHIL: I hate the Histories. I'm bored rigid. *Henry IV Part One*? I wish I was doin' *The Empire Strikes Back*.

BETH: Gotcha! — y've had it now. You'll be sorry. Y'can't just take, y'know. Y'can't just rob what dun't belong. Get in there, Kaz. S'a question of honour. Yer pride's at stake. (*Pointing to her T-shirt.*)

PHIL (*reading from* Henry IV Part One): 'Can honour set to a leg? no: or an arm? no: or take away the grief of wound? no. Honour hath no skill in surgery, then?'

BETH: Y'wanna blow their fuckin' heads off. See how they like that.

PHIL (*reading*): 'What is honour? a word. What is in that word honour? what is that honour? Air . . . Who hath it? he that died o' Wednesday. Doth he feel it? no. Doth he hear it? no. 'Tis insensible, then? yea, to the dead. But will it not live with the living?'

BETH: I wanna see you back here — dripping with medals.

PHIL (*reading*): 'No. Why? Detraction will not suffer it. Therefore I'll none of it. Honour is a mere scutcheon . . .'

BETH: Get yer banners out — put the flags up. 'Rule Britannia, Britannia rules the waves.'

PHIL: Nash? — y'know this speech of Falstaff's? D'y'think it's relevant, or can I leave it out?

ALICE (*coming in from the salon, obviously upset*): Honest, Nita, there's other ways of bein' in charge than stamping on people.

BETH (*to* ALICE): Heard Danny's one about the Belgrano?

ALICE: No. What?

BETH: Spielberg bought the film rights — *Voyage To the Bottom Of The Sea.* (*She goes off sniggering to herself.*)

NITA (*coming in looking annoyed*): Alice, if you don't get in here an' blow-wave this head, it'll be *you* that's fighting a losing battle.

The dole office.
BETH *sits down to be interviewed by* MISS MARKS.

MISS MARKS: Experience?

BETH: Y'what?

MISS MARKS (*without looking up*): Experience?

BETH: An' where d'y'get experience if they won't give yer a job? —

MISS MARKS (*writing*): No experience . . .

BETH: One. One job. Winder cleaning.

MISS MARKS (*writing*): Window cleaning . . .

BETH: Freelance craftsman to the better side of Salford.

MISS MARKS (*writing*): Self-employed . . .

BETH: Problem: the better side of Salford tell yer to piss off, no experience, yer a girl, they don't like the look of yer chammy . . .

MISS MARKS (*writing*): Not successful . . .

BETH: Other side of Salford — new problem. They an't got many winders left down there. Ergo, no demand. Ergo, no money. Ergo, I'm signin' on again.

MISS MARKS (*writing*): Fresh claim . . .

BETH: Fresh claim, yeah.

MISS MARKS (*reading automatically from the form*): Have you worked since you last signed on? (BETH *puts her head in her hands in despair.*) Not worked since last claim . . . Are you registered with the Job Centre?

BETH: Registered? I'm a bloody Life Member.

MISS MARKS (*writing*): Yes . . . well I doubt if we'll get anything this week . . .

BETH: What y'meant to live on?

MISS MARKS: Well we'll just have to manage, won't we?

BETH: What's this about cutting me dole.

MISS MARKS (*writing*): That's all, Miss Harrison . . .

BETH: Incentive to get us a job, is it?

MISS MARKS (*without looking up*): Good morning, Miss Harrison . . .

BETH (*getting up*): Incentive all right —

MISS MARKS (*calling out*): Next please?

BETH: Stick me foot through the Job Centre winder.

NITA*'s garden.*
    NITA *and* DANNY *sit in deckchairs drinking wine.* ALICE *sits apart, reading.*

DANNY: No idea.

NITA: Not a clue.

DANNY: Doesn't try.

NITA: Doesn't really.

DANNY: Can't believe it — Can yer?

NITA (*shaking her head*): No . . .

DANNY: One single solitary job she's capable of finding?

NITA: Pathetic really . . .

DANNY: Chances she's had —

NITA: If people had the gumption —

DANNY: Took the trouble —

NITA: That's it — trouble —

DANNY: You an' me? Now where would we be? If we sat on our backsides all day, teeth awash . . . (*He takes a sip of wine.*)

NITA: Exactly. Where?

DANNY: Work at it. Y'gotta be prepared . . .

NITA: To work. Exactly.

ALICE: Perhaps she wants to work.

NITA (*shaking her head*): No . . .

DANNY: Not really . . .

NITA: No . . .

DANNY: Common sense . . .

NITA: Bit of graft . . .

DANNY: All it needs . . .

NITA: Anyone . . .

ALICE: Not anyone.

DANNY: Of course . . .

ALICE: Everyone isn't like that. Everyone doesn't have the knack.

NITA: The nerve, more like.

ALICE: Some people don't get lucky —

NITA: Lucky?

DANNY: Skivers —

ALICE: No —

DANNY: Alice, I tell yer — I go out, I've earned a drink — the pubs are crawling, Alice. Dossers swilling dole money down their throat. Now don't tell me a bloke is hard-up an' puts away six or seven pints a night. State handouts, see. There's the problem.

NITA: Oh yes, definitely —

DANNY: No incentive.

ALICE: I don't believe this —

DANNY: More wine, Nita? (*He pours some more and offers some to* ALICE. *She declines.*)

NITA: Look, Alice, I would like to be sympathetic — I would love to sympathise . . .

DANNY: Of course.

NITA: But let's face it, Alice . . .

ALICE: What?

NITA: Nobody gets fed laid in bed till three in the afternoon.

ALICE: Perhaps some people can't stand to be awake.

NITA: We *all* start off with nothing, Alice. Look at me — what did *I* have?

ALICE: You? You've *never* had nothing, Nita. You don't know what the word means.

She throws her book down and walks out.

DANNY (*ignoring this*): Cheers . . . not bad, eh? (*He sips his wine.*) So where is she today — the Artful Dodger?

NITA (*as if it's a joke*): Gone for a job?

DANNY: Not again? Well we all know where that'll end up, don't we?

BETH *walks onstage.* DANNY *and* NITA *are unaware of her.*

BETH (*tearing up a piece of paper*): Sod it then. The lot of yer. What's the point seein' us if the job went yesterday? Give us hope? Give us encouragement?
'Y'see pet, it's an endangered species, but not yet extinct. If only y'd come yesterday . . . last week . . . last year . . .'
It doesn't give us hope. It gives us a pain back here. Oh, but y'get used to it pet. Free milk, free valium. Number of times I been kicked in the teeth, should be on me third set of dentures. Oh, on the National Health. One of the privileges of being unemployed. There's hope for us yet.

NASH *and* PHIL's *house.*
PHIL *sits on the floor with a portable typewriter composing an article.*

PHIL: My mate Carol's twenty. (*She types.*) Till last week. Till she's found dead at the foot of Walter Greenwood Court high-rise flats in Salford. (*After a pause.*) Last six months . . . glue-sniffing's gone epidemic . . . valium chewed like . . . dolly mixtures? (*She crosses it out.*) . . . licorice all-sorts . . . And a new craze has sprung up . . . (*She types.*) . . . for jumping into the fast lane on the M62. (PHIL *contemplates her work with satisfaction.*)
Last Friday, my mate Carol celebrated three years on the dole by walking off the roof into thin air. (*To herself.*) Very nice. (*She types.*) Sister, Lesley — *also unemployed* — says . . . 'We don't know what come over her — she's *never* had a job — we thought she'd got used to it.'
Question: (*She types.*) Did she jump or was she pushed?

PHIL *is looking pleased with her article.*
NASH *comes in carrying a shirt. He has two fingers bandaged together, which is not evident till the end of the scene.*

NASH: Phil, can y'do us a button?

PHIL (*outraged*): A what?

NASH: Sew us a button on this shirt.

PHIL: I got a deadline for this tomorrow.

NASH: An' a Shakespeare paper the day after.

PHIL: I hate sewing.

NASH: Yeah, like I hate scrubbing cookers, cleaning up spiders, Saturday nights when Man. United lose an' you can't keep a civil tongue in yer head. We all have to compromise, Phil. It's called 'give and take'.

PHIL: Oh, typical. Y'think y'can just stroll in here — 'do us a button, Phil' — an' I jump to it — don't yer?

NASH (*patiently*): No, Phil — as a favour, I say, please do us a button. Because last night playing monopoly you stood on my hand and fractured a finger.

PHIL (*grins and takes the shirt*): If you hadn't been in such a rush to grab my hotels y'wouldn't've got trod on.

NASH: If you weren't such a bad loser, we wouldn't have to resort to physical violence every time I pass Go.

The street, Salford. Night time.
BETH comes in, obviously half-drunk, trailing a bottle of wine. Figures start to emerge from the dark, never seen, just voices, surrounding her.

Hey, Beth —
Hey, Beth —
What y'doin'? —
Where y'goin'? —
Got no home to go to? —
Where did all yer mates go? —
Fancy a drink, Beth? —
Fancied gettin' bevvied? —
Got much money? —
Need new shoes, Beth —
Time y'got a job, Beth —
Get up off yer arse, Beth —
Anyone can work, Beth —
Must be doin' something wrong —
Sure yer really trying? —
Got a rise last week —
Doin' dead well now —
Rocky III last week —
Seen it on the video —
Y'an't got a video? —
Where does all yer money go? —
Seen this new one, sitting in the window? —
Not a lot down for you —
'Cept yer UB40 —
See yer, Beth —
Ta-ra, Beth —
Maybe see yer sometime —
What y'gettin' next week? —
New car —
New coat —
New dress —
New job —

BETH: Fuck-all.

She throws the bottle. Lights out and the sound of breaking glass.

A police cell.
BETH *is sitting in a chair when a* POLICEWOMAN *enters.*

WPC: Yer mother says she won't vouch for yer.

BETH: Y'what?

WPC: Yer mother says, as far as she's concerned, she's never heard of yer.

BETH: Listen, me mother's never heard of us? Ask her if I got a birthmark shaped like a banana on me left buttock. Ask her how many vodka bottles she goes through a week.

WPC: There's someone here to see yer.

NITA *comes in.*

NITA: What the hell d'you think you're playing at?

BETH *is standing in the middle of the stage. Also onstage are* NITA, ALICE, PHIL *and* NASH.

ALICE: Oh, Beth —

PHIL: Oh, Beth — got arrested? What for?

NASH: Bottle through a shop window — Alice says.

ALICE: What's yer mam gonna say?

NITA: It's pathetic. It's inexcusable.

PHIL: But why?

NITA: Okay, she's out of work. Okay, she can't get a job. We all understand that.

ALICE: Do we?

NITA: Well obviously.

NASH: Alice says she's goin' missing up here.

BETH: One more. Just one more person tells us to get a job an' I'll swing for them.

PHIL: She's gettin' worse.

NASH: If *you* had nothing down for yer, what would *you* do?

PHIL: Me?

NITA: What would *I* do? That's a different matter.

ALICE: No it's not.

PHIL: That's different. I *need* to work.

NASH: It's *not* different.

NITA: No, it's different, Alice. *I* need to work. I have to keep busy. If *I* couldn't work . . . well . . . I'd just go mad.

ALICE: Exactly.

BETH: Exactly.

NASH *and* PHIL's *house.*
PHIL *comes in loaded with books.*

PHIL: God, what a day.

NASH (*looking at a newspaper*): See y'done it again.

PHIL (*not registering*): Y'll have to help us. Y'will. Six hours tryna suss out Gerard Manley Hopkins – an' I can't, Nash – this here – (*Picking up a book.*) this *Wreck Of The* sodding *Deutschland* . . . look, Nash, is it me? – I mean, who gives a toss if the odd nun gets washed overboard an' fed to the fishes? If you don't explain to me what is the point . . . I'm not only gonna fuck up that exam tomorrow . . . I might even . . . (*Noticing the newspaper he's holding*

out.) Done what?

NASH: Got yer face in the paper. (*Looking at it.*) What y'wearing, Phil? Y'look like a centrefold in Playboy.

PHIL: Oh, don't start that again.

NASH: An' what y'been doin' this time? Oh, slumming down the docks getting a worm's eye view of the worms. Hey, Phil, it's a cracker . . . (*Reading it out.*) 'Conclusive proof that a pretty face and brains sometimes go together.'

PHIL (*trying to snatch the paper*): Give me that.

NASH (*keeping it out of her reach, now reading facetiously*): 'In recent months, Phil, a 3rd Year Literature student and Deputy Editor of leading university newspaper . . . has written incisive articles . . .' Incisive? . . . Oh Phil, y'gonna love it '. . . incisive articles on health and education cuts . . . inner city problem areas . . . sexual harrassment on the university campus' . . . Oh, is that from personal experience, Phil?
Now circling round each other, PHIL *still trying to grab the paper.*

PHIL: Give me that paper.

NASH: Hey, Phil, how about 'Delusions of Grandeur'? – how about 'How to make a fast buck out of other people's miseries?'

PHIL: I hate you sometimes.

NASH: Not true.

PHIL (*after a pause*): Okay, okay . . . truce. (*She throws down the book she's been using as a weapon.* NASH *throws down the paper.* PHIL *immediately dives for it.* NASH *puts his foot on the paper.*)

NASH: I wouldn't advise it, Phil. (*He recaptures the paper.*)

PHIL: I'm gonna blow me exams.

NASH: Sit down.

PHIL: What for? (NASH *throws her a pen and notebook.*) What's this?

NASH: Write this down. Gerard Manley Hopkins is a great poet because: Point One . . .

NITA's *flat.*
    BETH, ALICE *and* NITA *sitting around.*

NITA: No booze.

BETH: No booze?

NITA: No ciggies.

ALICE: No ciggies?

NITA: No stopping in bed.

BETH: No what?

NITA: No sympathy.

BETH: No kidding?

NITA: Fresh air, fresh fruit, lots of exercise . . .

ALICE: Are you running a remand home, Nita?

NITA: Y'have to be cruel to be kind.

ALICE: Says who?

NITA: Look, I understand — I do — but y'gotta try, Beth — she's gotta try and make the effort.

BETH: Alice, do I make the effort? Where's me medal traipsing round the streets of Salford, tryna dig out a decent crust? I tell yer, Nita — *I'll* be working — if I an't drop dead of lookin' first.

NITA (*briskly*): Well tomorrow we are goin' into town an' get some decent clothes.

BETH: What on? Fresh air? The contents of me pig is gonna stretch enough to tie up a couple of shoe laces.

NITA: *I'll* worry about 'what on'.

BETH: No tights.

NITA: Tights, hankies, eau de cologne . . . We're gonna look like we mean business. An' then we're off down the Job Centre — an' get ourselves a job . . .

NITA *and* ALICE *go off.*

BETH: An' then we went down the Job Centre, Kaz, but there's still sod-all on offer even if yer are togged up in tights an' smelling like a rose bed. And Nita? — y'shoulda seen — her face fell like a sack of spuds. Big surprise — the shelves is empty as usual — barring two months sheep shearing in the Outer Hebrides or packing fish down Fleetwood Quay. So now who's talking through their arse the last three years? Well let's face it, Kaz, the only people onto a winner round here is the dole queue clerks.

NITA *comes on with a letter to* PHIL.

NITA: Phil, what could I say? Y'd be amazed. Okay, it's a bad week. I know that 'cos we been the same in the salon. No perms, not even a demi-wave - an' we're cracking the corks if we can con some poor soul off the street for a dry cut an' free coffee.
I think that Galtieri's got a lot to answer for. I mean, before he come planting his flag on other people's beaches, we're getting permed like nobody's business. Now they're all stopping in, watching the news. I tell yer, some day's it's not worth opening the till. An' to be honest, Phil, if I'd not started them Prince Andrew short-back-and-sides, I don't know where we'd be. An' it'll be just my luck if he gets shot down an' I'll have to discontinue the offer.

BETH: Hey, what about me?

NITA: You?

BETH: Now what?

NITA (*in frustration*): How should *I* know?

Bristol. NASH *and* PHIL's *house.*
    PHIL *is pacing the room waiting for* NASH *to come back. He comes in.*

PHIL (*terrified*): Well?

NASH: Sit down, Phil.

PHIL: Tell me.

NASH: Was a good year, Phil — y'got a good excuse. Oh, I seen Jeffries on the way in — says, don't feel too bad — tight marking all round — stingy bastards . . . oh, Lindy got a Third.

PHIL: Nash —

NASH: Jay got a 2-2. Only two Firsts all year.

PHIL: I knew it.

NASH: S'how it goes, kidder.

PHIL: I missed it, didn't I?

NASH: Y'gonna have to be a brave girl now. Y'didn't get a 2-1.

PHIL *sits with her head in her hands.*
NASH *gets out a piece of paper.*

NASH (*reading*): Philippa Joanna Taylor — Class One.

PHIL *looks up slowly in disbelief.*
NASH *throws her the paper.*

You stuffy sod.

They go off.

BETH *runs on as* ALICE *comes on from the other side.* BETH *grabs* ALICE *and kisses her.*

BETH: He's coming home.

ALICE: Who?

BETH: Kaz. He'll be home tomorrow! I seen his mam in the post office. (*Thrilled.*) He's wounded!

ALICE: Oh God, no —

BETH (*in delight*): Yes!

ALICE: Oh, Beth, but . . .

BETH: Nah, don't be soft, Al — it's not serious.

ALICE: Isn't it?

BETH: Oh, how can it be serious, Al? He's all mouth. He is. He says to me in this letter . . . he says, he doubts they'll see action. Read that, Alice . . .

ALICE (*reading as instructed*): 'I doubt we'll see action . . .'

BETH: There yer are.

ALICE (*reading stiltedly*): 'It all seems slightly unreal . . . can't quite believe we're here . . .'

BETH (*snatching the letter off her*): Not that bit, y'gawp. That's Kaz when he's pissed. Talks crap.

ALICE: But that letter's three weeks old.

BETH: Hey Al, what's he like? He only joined the navy to get a suntan. Can't fight to save his life. They won't get him off the ship.

ALICE: But Beth . . . on the news . . . it said . . .

BETH (*completely oblivious*): You wait — he'll be home, couple of scratches, bit of bruising . . . no, hang on . . . *a scar* . . . y'know, Clint Eastwood? — across here? (*She demonstrates.*) Hey, we can have a street party — 'Welcome Home Kaz Johnson — Local Hero' . . . I hope he's brought us something back — they don't do rock out there, do they? . . . Is me hair all right? . . . Hey, Al, he's a selfish get, in't he? Gets wounded, dun't even write to let us know. For all *he* knows, I could be worried.

NASH *and* PHIL's *house.*
NASH *is working.* PHIL *comes in.*

PHIL: I got it.

NASH: What?

PHIL: Accepted. For post-grad.

NASH: That's a turn-up.

PHIL: What d'y'reckon?

NASH: What about?

PHIL: Should I do it?

NASH: I can't answer that.

PHIL: It'd give us more time. Sort out what I want. Where to go.

NASH: It would.

PHIL: An' if I want to write. Or not.

NASH: True.

PHIL: Well?

NASH: Well what?

PHIL: It's another year. Here. With you.

NASH (*mock dismay*): That's a point.

PHIL: Nash . . . just for once . . .

NASH: What?

PHIL: I'm asking.

NASH: It's your decision.

PHIL: It's not just *me*.

NASH: Isn't it?

PHIL: I mean it, Nash.

NASH: Is that why yer staying?

PHIL: What if it was?

NASH: Is it?

PHIL (*pause, clearly she will get no response from him*): No . . . but the rent's cheap.

NASH: Fair enough.

PHIL: I don't believe this.

NASH: Now what's the matter?

PHIL: If you don't know . . .

NASH: Tell me.

PHIL (*giving up*): What's the point?

She goes out.

As NASH *walks out,* BETH *comes on looking stunned. She sits down on the floor with a bottle at her side.*
After a while ALICE *comes on.*

ALICE: Where y'been? We been looking for yer . . . (*Now, with trepidation:*) Beth? What happened? How is he?

BETH: What?

ALICE: Kaz. D'y'see him? How's he feeling?

BETH: No.

ALICE: No what?

BETH: I didn't see him.

ALICE: Why not?

BETH: She wouldn't let me.

ALICE: Who wouldn't?

BETH: His mam.

ALICE: Not let him out?

BETH: She says he can't. He can't come out an' he can't see me.

ALICE: Why, Beth?

BETH: Because he's blind, Alice.

NASH *and* PHIL's *house.* NASH *is talking to* LINDY *while* PHIL *sits apart, ignoring her.*

LINDY: You see, I find it really amazing . . . that those sort of places actually exist . . . I mean *exist* in the sense that . . . y'know what I mean? If people were more *aware,* y'know . . . more *conscious,* yeah? . . . then maybe they wouldn't still exist . . . in those sort of conditions.

NASH: Well they do, Lind. People do still live in houses without bathrooms.

LINDY: You see, I find that astonishing . . . I mean seriously amazing. I mean, we call ourselves civilised, right? But y'know . . . how can we say we're . . . like . . . really civilised, if people are living . . . y'know . . . where they can't have a bath twice a day?

NASH: Lindy, it's incredible, I know, but . . .

LINDY: It *is.* It seriously *is.* I mean, it can't continue. I really think people ought to be aware . . . y'know?

PHIL: They *are* 'aware', Lind. The ones with no bathrooms.

LINDY: No, no, no . . . I mean *really* aware. I mean *really conscious* of what's going on around them. No, seriously, I'm writing to my father. I really think *he* should be aware. *I* think we should have a walk.

NASH: A what?

LINDY: A sponsored walk. No, seriously. Because it all helps ... and *I* think if everybody went on a walk ... y'know ... I really think it could make all the right noises, yeah? I really think we could get the most amazing response. Don't you, Phil?

PHIL: Oh yeah – dead amazing.

LINDY (*getting up to leave. To* NASH): Can I put you down, then? Ten miles? Twenty? (*She kisses him.*)

NASH (*showing her out*): Yeah, put us down for fifty. (*To* PHIL:) One way.

PHIL (*after* LINDY's *gone*): Don't start.

NASH: Still know sod-all about manners, I see?

PHIL: Oh, *I* know sod-all? I know what *that* is. Born-again Thinking-Caring-Person an' it makes me ill.

NASH: Oh, y'think you've cornered the market in righteous indignation, do yer?

PHIL (*mimicking* LINDY): 'Oh Phil, look at me, I've changed sides. I shop at Oxfam, I don't eat meat, I hold hands round Greenham Common.' Where's she learn all that? *The Reader's Digest Guide To The Social Conscience?*

NASH: Oh, you preferred her pig-ignorant and self-centred, did yer?

PHIL: At least y'knew where you were.

NASH: Y'got a short memory, Phil.

PHIL: Meaning what?

NASH: Meaning two years back, top priority was *not* kids with no shoes an' homes with no bathtaps. It was using the right knife, meeting the right people ... oh, but I forgot, yer pretty spot-on now y'seen yer name in print a few times are yer?

PHIL: I'm a good writer.

NASH: Oh, is that right, Phil?

PHIL (*insistent*): I'm a good writer.

NASH: Good is not romantic, Phil.

PHIL: Romantic?

NASH: Y'should read yerself sometime, Phil. Y'make it all so picturesque. Here y'are, listen to this ... (*He gets a paper cutting from* PHIL's *file.*) 'Salford ... The Decay of the Inner City' ...

PHIL: Don't you dare –

NASH (*reading*): 'Salford Docks on a winter morning ... deserted quays washed with white light ... gates choked up with rose-bay-willow-herb ...' What y'writing, Phil? A holiday brochure? Christ, y'make it sound so tempting, y'could start a tourist boom.

PHIL: At least it points the finger.

NASH: At whom?

PHIL: Not this again.

NASH: The state of the country or the state of Phil Taylor?

PHIL: No chance.

NASH: That's why y'contrive to get yer name blazed across two columns every other week, is it?

PHIL: I am sick of hearing this.

NASH: I suspect your motives, Phil. I think yer whole reasoning is suspect.

PHIL: Oh, is that right, Nash?

NASH: See, I don't think yer out to draw attention to three million unemployed. I think yer out to draw attention to yerself.

PHIL: Well you think that then, Nash. You keep company with that thought all summer.

She picks up her coat and walks out.

NITA's *flat.*

ALICE: Oh God, but there must be something ...

NITA: Well don't ask *me.*

ALICE: I *am* askin' you. Why aren't you watching her?

NITA: I can't watch all day, can I? I got queues halfway to town.

ALICE: What's she had?

NITA: Coffee.

ALICE: That all?

NITA: Three Mars Bars, a Milky Way, four Yorkies and a Double Decker.

ALICE: Oh, Nita . . .

NITA: Alice, I got three words out of her yesterday: 'no', 'what?' and 'sod off'. *You* try holding a conversation with her.

ALICE: She wants looking after.

NITA: Phil.

ALICE: What?

NITA: Phil's coming home. Phil can look after her.

ALICE walks off to where BETH is lying on the floor. PHIL comes on.

PHIL: Don't look at me — *I* don't care.

NITA: Phil —

PHIL: I've had it up to here. Selfish, arrogant and totally insensitive. Well he can please himself what he does with his summer — not that *I* give a toss . . .

NITA: He might phone . . .

PHIL: He better bloody phone. Not that he will. Not that *I* care.

NITA: Don't you?

PHIL: What d'y'think I am?

The phone rings. NITA answers.

NITA: Hello? . . . Oh, hello Nash . . .

PHIL makes a dive for the phone, remembers her indifference and resumes her place.

PHIL: I'm not in.

Lights up on NASH.

NASH: I know she's not in, but ask her where she's put me passport.

NITA: I'd rather not.

NASH: Please?

NITA: Where's his passport?

PHIL (*outraged*): His what?

NITA: I did warn yer . . .

The lights come up on BETH lying in her room and ALICE standing outside the door.

ALICE: Beth? Are yer up? D'y'want anything?

PHIL: Where's he going?

NASH: Tell her I'm going to France.

ALICE: D'y'fancy seein' *Excalibur* down the Odeon? — Or round yer mam's maybe? . . .

PHIL: What for?

NASH: Three months.

PHIL: Three months!

NITA: Oh dear . . .

ALICE: Beth? C'mon . . . let me in . . . let me come in, Beth . . . d'y'fancy a Chop Suey roll down the Wing Yip?

BETH: What I *do* fancy is a bit of kip an' a chance to get rat-legged in peace.

NASH: I'll send her a postcard.

PHIL: He can stuff his postcard.

NASH: An' when she's grown up enough to act half her age, she can come home again.

ALICE: Beth? Have yer had yer tablets? Yer supposed to take them tablets. It's to make yer feel better . . .

PHIL (*grabbing the phone off* NITA): Who's gonna water the plants? Some of them plants are mine.

NASH: *One* is yours, Phil. The one I bought to remind me of you when y'went home. It doesn't need much water.

PHIL: What plant?

NASH: It's called a cactus.

He puts the phone down.

ALICE (*fiercely*): You wait. Phil's home now. She'll sort yer out.

PHIL: How can *I* sort her out? I just got rid of one kid. Now I gotta start minding another.

ALICE: Phil, it's yer best mate.

PHIL: What'm I supposed to do, Alice?

ALICE: Phil, y'better pull yer finger out. Or else . . .

PHIL: What? –

ALICE: *I* don't know . . . just 'or else'.

PHIL *goes and sits next to* BETH *who is lying on the floor and not replying. She talks to her very gently, attempting to awaken some interest, but nothing happens.*

PHIL: Beth? D'y'wanna go out? D'y'wanna talk? Hey Beth, remember that bonfire night you an' me set fire to the physics lab with a Roman Candle . . . d'y'remember that? God, what a scream . . .

ALICE (*seeing she's faltering*): Hey, what about them stick insects you tipped in the school custard an' got served up with lemon sponge . . .

PHIL: Oh Beth, what about the time . . .

BETH (*snapping*): Leave us alone, will yer? Just piss off, the lot of yer.

PHIL (*leaving* BETH's *side*): I give up. What d'y'say? Oh, don't expect wonders, Phil . . .
Been out here two weeks an' all we get is 'what d'*you* want?' – 'Gi's that bottle' – 'Get out, will yer'. What'm I supposed to do? No, y'can't have – no, I won't go? Alice, I give up.

ALICE *walks out in disgust.*

What can I do?

PHIL *goes to sit with* BETH *again. There is no response and she eventually no longer tries for one.*

Finally:

Beth? Y'all right, Beth? Listen, y'be okay if I just nip out for half an hour? Look I wouldn't, but . . . this strike's on in Trafford Park . . . I wanna see if I can get a story . . . all right? (*No reply.*) Look, I'll get me skates on, honest . . .

She leaves. BETH *doesn't move.*

PHIL *is now in Trafford Park.*

Er . . . 'scuse me . . . can I just say . . . I wonder if y'd mind telling me yer reaction to . . . (*Backing off.*) yeah . . . fine, fine . . . sorry to trouble yer . . . (*In another direction.*) Hello? – d'y'think y'could give me yer feelings about this . . . (*Backing off.*) right . . . well, yes . . . thank you very much . . . Er . . . I wonder if y'could tell me what y'think about the closure of this . . . (*Retreating rapidly.*) . . . er . . . yeah . . . well I'll just put 'no comment', shall I? Yes . . . thanks a lot . . . y've been very helpful . . .

PHIL *walks back in to* BETH's *room.*

Oh yeah, it was dead useful – very co-operative – I tell yer though, Beth – you think *you're* in a state . . . y'wanna get where I've just been . . . Hey, c'mon Beth – yer not laying around in bed all day . . . yer gettin' up now an' face it out . . . (*Going over to her:*) Hey, c'mon . . . (*She shakes her.*) Beth . . . (*Suddenly dawning.*) Oh God, Beth . . . get up . . . (*Shouting:*) Nita . . . Beth, please, don't mess about . . . get up . . . (*Screaming.*) Nita . . . *Nita* . . .

NITA *comes tearing in.*

NITA: Phil, I got clients downstairs can hear you halfway down the street . . . (*She sees* BETH.) Oh, bloody hell – I knew it. I knew it. (*Shouting.*) Alice . . . Alice . . . (ALICE *comes in.*) Get the hospital, will yer?

ALICE: What's happened?

NITA: Now, Alice . . . (*She shoves her out.*)

(*To* PHIL:) Where were *you*? Where were yer? Stood there, let her stuff herself with these?

PHIL: I was out. Oh God, I went out.

NITA: Y'did what?

PHIL: I didn't see her.

NITA: Phil, what did I tell you? Watch her, I said. Don't leave her alone.

PHIL: I was out half an hour.

NITA: Doing what?

PHIL: On a story.

NITA: Phil, are you kidding me? Your so-called best mate's dying here an' you go off tryna make a name for yerself. You want locking up, you do.

PHIL: Y'never told us, did yer? Y'never said she's gonna try topping herself.

NITA: If you weren't so full of yerself, Phil, y'would've seen that without telling.

PHIL: What we gonna do? . . . Beth, c'mon . . . wake up. Oh God, Nita . . . she won't die, will she?

NITA: Well if she does, you'll be able to do a cover story, won't you?

As the lights go out, BETH *is carried off, the sound of sirens in the distance.*

The lights come up on PHIL *asleep on a chair in a hospital waiting room.* ALICE *and* NITA *are standing round.*

NITA: There's nothing we can do.

ALICE: What? Y'mean, go? (*Looking at* PHIL.) What about . . .

NITA: Leave her . . . (*Seeing* ALICE *is reluctant to leave.*) Look, Alice . . . there's nothing we can do . . .

They go out together. After a while a NURSE *comes in and tries to wake* PHIL.

NURSE: Hello? . . . wake up, love . . . (PHIL *wakes up.*) I'm sorry pet — y'won't be able to see your friend . . .

PHIL: What?

NURSE: Till tomorrow.

PHIL: Is she . . . ?

NURSE: Very lucky. Very fortunate young lady. Another twenty minutes and you wouldn't be sitting here now. I should go home if I were you, pet.

PHIL: Oh no, it's okay . . . I'll stay . . . thank you . . .

The NURSE *goes out.* PHIL *sits with her head in her hands. She hears someone else come into the room. She looks up to see* NASH *standing there. Her delight at seeing him subsides as he looks at her impassively.*

PHIL: What you doing here?

NASH: Alice called us. (PHIL *doesn't reply.*) How is she?

PHIL: It's my fault.

NASH: How is she?

PHIL: Breathing.

NASH: Phil —

PHIL: Oh, she'll live. That's not the point, is it?

NASH: No, that isn't the point.

He sits down at the opposite side of the room.

PHIL: She could be dead. (*He doesn't reply.*) That's the point. We could be paying our respects now. An' what would *I* be paying? Care? Attention? To somebody else? For a change. (*After a pause.*) Know what I did? Did she tell yer that? Did she tell yer how Phil fucked it up? I was out. I was chasing a name. Headlines for Phil while Beth makes two lines on page ten under Births, Marriages and Deaths. Oh, y'woulda been dead proud of me, Nash. Y'wouldn't believe how sick. Have y'seen this? Have y'seen the state? (*She holds up her hands to show them shaking.*) Is it enough? Are you impressed?
(*Suddenly:*) She could be dead. Beth

could be dead. She looked for me —
an' I wasn't there. (*She begins to cry.*)
(*Suddenly realising:*) What are you
doing here? I left you. I came home.
(*He doesn't reply.*) I fucked that up
an' all, didn't I?

*She continues to cry. Without
speaking, NASH gets up, comes over
to her, and puts his arm round her.
She clings to him. He takes her out.*

NITA's *flat.*
A few days later. BETH *is out of
hospital and sits playing cards (very badly)
with* NASH. PHIL *sits apart, watching,
worried.*

NASH (*throwing his cards down*): Yours.

BETH: Is it?

NASH (*showing his hand*): Stuffy get.

BETH *grins to herself and collects
her winnings.*

NASH: Same again?

BETH: Yeah, go on, then.

DANNY *comes in carrying a bottle
of whisky.*

DANNY: How is she? How's
Manchester's answer to the Exocet?
Here y'are sweetheart — cheer yer up
a bit, eh? (*He gives her the bottle.*)
Put the roses back in her cheeks.

PHIL: Danny . . .

DANNY (*as if he's just noticed her*): All
right, Phil?

PHIL: Danny . . . she can't have alcohol.

DANNY: 'Course she can.

PHIL: No . . . she's on tablets.

DANNY: No, she's not. Not when there's
a bottle goin'. Sod the pills, eh, Beth?
Best medicine in the world. C'mon,
babe, get yer throat oiled.

PHIL: Danny . . . (DANNY *is about to
open the bottle.*) She'll have it later.
All right?

DANNY (*putting the top back on*): Well

mind, none of that's for you two. This
is for my Number One Girl in the
whole North West. (*Looking at* NASH's
hand of cards.) Rakin' a fortune, are yer?

Don't blame yer. She was bloody
useless — even before.

PHIL (*seeing him about to retaliate*):
Nash . . .

DANNY: See yer, then. (*To* BETH:)
Save us a drop, hey, sunshine?

DANNY *goes out.*

NASH (*to* BETH): D'y'wanna carry on?

BETH: D'y'think I could . . .

NASH: What?

BETH: Lie down a bit?

PHIL: Beth . . . (*She is about to
remonstrate when* NASH *signals her
to stop.*)

NASH: One condition.

BETH: What?

NASH: Give us chance to win some of
me money back. All right?

BETH (*grinning*): If yer lucky.

NASH: See yer, kidder. (BETH *goes out.*)

PHIL: Y'see. She won't. She won't speak
to me.

NASH: Well give her a chance. She's not
been out five minutes.

PHIL: She hates me. (*He doesn't reply.*)
She thinks it's my fault. She said so,
didn't she?

NASH: No.

PHIL: Why won't she talk to me?

NASH: She won't talk to Nita.

PHIL: Nita just says let her snap out of
it.

NASH: Well she will.

PHIL: She talks to *you.*

NASH: I let her win.

PHIL: I have to talk to her.

NASH: What for?

PHIL: To tell her. I have to explain.

NASH: For whose benefit?

PHIL: What d'y'mean?

NASH: Yours?

PHIL: Not mine.

NASH: She'll speak to you when she wants to . . . (*Putting the cards away.*) By which time I'll most likely to be two hundred quid in debt.

NITA's flat.
    ALICE stands doing BETH's hair.

ALICE: There y'are. What d'y'think?

BETH: Nah –

ALICE: Nah what?

BETH: No it's not me.

ALICE: It *is* you. It's dead smart.

BETH: *I'm* not dead smart.

ALICE: It suits yer.

    BETH *ruffles up the hair so it's all dishevelled.*

BETH: *Now* it suits us.

    PHIL *comes in.*

PHIL (*forced cheerfulness*): Hey, Beth – d'y'wanna go to the match?

BETH: What match?

PHIL: The Reds. First match of the season.

BETH: Oh, I dunno . . .

PHIL (*trying to be enthusiastic*): Frankie Stapleton? . . . Bryan Robson?

BETH: Nah, it's not the same –

PHIL: What isn't?

BETH: Since they let Joe Jordan go. I only went to watch him bite people. Now it'll all be dead clean an' sporting and boring.

PHIL: No, Beth, y'll love it – y'will. They got this Remi Moses now – an' he's such a dirty get – y'll love him, Beth, honest – it'll be instant rapport.

BETH: Well . . .

PHIL: Oh Beth, please . . . come with us? . . . (*She holds out her hand to BETH. She rejects it but takes the scarf that's offered.*)

BETH: I can manage, y'know. I'm not a cripple.

Sound of crowd noises and chants up loud.
    Later, walking home after the match, BETH *looks more relaxed, but still will have nothing to do with* PHIL.

PHIL (*suddenly stopping*): Beth, I need to speak to yer.

BETH: What for?

PHIL: Well . . . you know what for.

BETH: Dragging us off to see the Reds get pasted?

PHIL: No . . .

BETH: What then?

PHIL: The other . . .

BETH: Oh give over, Phil – it's hardly *your* fault Stevie Coppell missed a penalty.

PHIL (*in despair*): Oh, it's not the same, is it?

BETH: Oh, yer dead right there. Moses, the soft get – not a broken leg all match.

NITA's flat.
    Sunday morning. NITA *stands in her dressing-gown talking to* PHIL.

NITA: I can't, Phil.

PHIL: It's Sunday.

NITA: Yeah, an' that's why. I'm sticking me feet up an' taking it easy. Baby-sitting Beth is not my idea of easy.

PHIL: Nita –

NITA: Phil, last week, right? – half of Salford tramped through my salon. I done so many demi-waves me fingers are curling. You lot treat my house like an hotel. An' I'm knackered, Phil.

PHIL: Oh well, that's all right, Nita. You stop in bed all day an' count yer money. (*Realising what she's said.*) Oh God, I'm sorry, Nita . . .

NITA: What's the matter, Phil? Can't cope?

PHIL: If you came, it'd just . . . make it easier.

NITA: I said no, Phil.

PHIL: Don't you care, Nita?

NITA: *I* care, Phil. Ask yerself, not me. You're the one with all the debts. An' I wouldn't want yer to get behind with the payments. You go. You take her.

PHIL *starts to walk off.*

Look, I'm sorry, Phil.

PHIL *hesitates.*

She's hard work, Phil. I don't know what to do.

PHIL: Neither do I.

NITA: Here, have this . . . (*She takes her purse and gives PHIL £10.*)

PHIL: What for?

NITA: Take her out, get her on the swings — see she enjoys herself.

PHIL *hesitates.* NITA *takes her hand and makes her take the money.*

I'm sorry, Phil. I don't know what else to do. (*She goes out.*)

NASH *comes in.*

NASH: Are y'ready, then?

PHIL: She won't come.

NASH: Who won't?

PHIL: Nita.

NASH: Who asked for Nita? I'm over 21, Phil. I'm quite capable of taking two kids to the seaside. C'mon Beth, get yer bucket and spade.

BETH (*coming in*): Y'what? —

NASH: C'mon, I'm taking you two to Blackpool.

Blackpool beach.
    PHIL *and* NASH *are sitting on towels on the beach.* BETH, *with her trousers rolled up, is contemplating a paddle.*

BETH: There's crabs here, in't there. I'm not goin' in. I'll paddle me feet. Any crab gettin' a gobful of that wants its head testing. D'y'want some candy floss?

PHIL (*getting up*): Shall I go with yer? (NASH *pulls her down again.*) What?

NASH: Stop here an' keep us amused. Beth, get us a toffee-apple, will yer? (*He throws her his wallet.* BETH *goes off.*)

PHIL: She shouldn't be left. What if she tries something?

NASH: She won't.

PHIL: I'm supposed to keep an eye on her.

NASH: She's walking, Phil. She's not a stretcher case. Just leave her — she'll be all right.

PHIL *sits back and watches where* BETH *went out.* NASH *turns over and starts reading.*

PHIL (*after a pause*): Nash . . .

NASH (*without looking up*): What? —

PHIL: D'y'ever feel . . . yer doin' all right — dead clear cut an' no surprises . . . then one day something hits yer — smack in the mouth — knocks half yer teeth out . . . an' you suddenly see . . . that what you thought was hard and fast . . . is really only brittle.

NASH (*still reading*): Yeah, I know that feeling.

PHIL: Y'know, like . . . something shifted an' can't be put back again.

NASH (*still reading*): October 5th '79.

PHIL: Like what?

NASH (*sitting up but unable to look at*

her): Well, there's this bloke, right? An' he's pretty fuckin' smart — y'know, First Class, sewn up. An' it's Fresher's Week — the new stuff's in. The usual scene — stood round spouting crap on Yeats an' Auden, 'cos they think that's what y'do at college reading English. So he plays the game, the idle chat-up — it's looking sound — he's feeling pretty safe.

Then there's this girl, right? An' she's pretty fit — First Year — face like St Theresa an' a voice like it come up off the docks. An' she's sounding off to these lads the most unmitigated crap y've ever heard. So he thinks, okay now, I can ignore it, I can pass on this one. Or I can get in there, an' sort it out. An' the bells are goin' off — once bitten, give it a miss, kidder. But no — it's such a cinch, he can't resist. So he's in there . . . 'Er . . . 'scuse me — y'do realise y'need to be reasonably intelligent to come here? Y'don't *really* believe that Stevie Coppell is the best winger in England.' An' this girl, she turns round, an' looks at him, an' she says — 'Y'what?' So he gets in there, an' sorts her out. An' he's been paying for it ever since.

PHIL (*after a pause*): Do I know this bloke?

NASH (*still looking away from her*): Not really.

A pause. Then BETH *comes back with candy floss and a toffee-apple.*

BETH: I didn't get yer anything, Phil. I didn't know what y'wanted.

NITA'*s flat.*
    BETH *is sitting on the floor building with dominoes.* PHIL *comes in and watches her.*

PHIL: What y'doin'?

BETH: Building a house . . . (*Part of it falls down.*) . . . or a bungalow . . . (*It all falls down.*) . . . or a bomb-

site . . . (*Gathering up dominoes.*) Story of my life, hey Phil?

PHIL (*starting to cry*): Oh Beth . . .

BETH (*ignoring this*): Hey, did I tell yer? Seen me mam coming out the off licence. She says 'Hello pet, yer looking well.' — 'That's right, ma, I've just shifted half a crate of Benzedrines last week.' — 'That's nice, pet' she says — 'You keep up the good work. Get yerself a drink, love' — an' slips us half a quid in 2p bits. (*Now seeing* PHIL *is really crying.*) Yer a soft get, aren't yer? I'm dead hard, me. I am. I'm tough as old nails. Y'won't cop me turning the taps on. Know when's the last time I had a good cry? Know when? Not since me mam reversed over the gerbil an' wouldn't let us give it a Viking funeral with full military honours. Hey, talk about tears — I had the bloody street out. Not now though. Not a drop. (*She gives* PHIL *a hankie.*) Oh aye, I know *you* can. Let's have a look at yer? Yeah, them's good enough. Mind you, there's the difference — me an' you, hey? You can an' I can't.

PHIL: Can't what?

BETH: Anything.

PHIL (*suddenly getting up*): Here — get hold of this . . . (*She gives her a piece of paper and a pen.*)

BETH: Y'what?

PHIL: Go on, get hold of it.

BETH: What for?

PHIL: Sit down — an' write us a list — of everything you're good at.

BETH: Y'what?

PHIL: You heard. Everything you can do.

    BETH *after a pause takes the paper and keeping it well concealed, starts to scribble something on it. She appears to be very industrious.* PHIL *watches her. After a while she stops, folds the paper and hands it to* PHIL.

BETH: Me list, what I'm good at.

PHIL *opens it and looks surprised.*

PHIL: There's nothing on it.

BETH: Exactly.

BETH (*seeing* PHIL *about to lose her temper*): Oh, what d'y'want, Phil? All smiles?

PHIL: Listen you —

BETH: Fuck off, Phil — I'm not blaming yer, am I? I'm stating a fact. All right?

PHIL: Don't give me that crap.

BETH: Is it?

PHIL: People care for you, y'stupid get.

BETH: Oh yeah?

PHIL: Oh yeah. You wanna watch it, Beth — more earache spent on you than us three put together.

BETH: Shame.

PHIL: Is it?

BETH: *I* can do without it.

PHIL: So can I. Up half the night, wearing holes in the carpet — oh, Nita, Alice, what we gonna do? she (ALICE) can't sleep, she's (NITA) not eating. Nash . . . an' why should *he* fuckin' care? He does though, an' he's not daft. If he cares, then it's worth caring. *You* are worth caring for. Well please yerself, Beth. I've had it up to here. It's just a fuckin' joke.

BETH: Joke? Oh yeah. I'm laughing. Seen this? (*She points to her face and grins.* PHIL *turns away, unable to cope.*) Hey, Phil — (PHIL *turns back.*) — people care, do they? Oh, in't that nice? I'm touched. I'm really moved. Well Beth dun't give fuck-all what people care, does she? If I was you, Phil, I'd sod off home an' spend it somewhere else.

PHIL *is so upset she would walk out but* BETH *stands in the door.*

PHIL: Shift, will yer?

BETH (*taunting*): Care, Phil, did yer?

What's it like to waste it?

PHIL *suddenly snaps and dives on* BETH — *they fall to the floor fighting. Neither is winning, but* BETH's *howls bring* NITA *and* ALICE *running.*

NITA: Phil, what y'doing? — what y'doing?

ALICE: Phil, don't — y'll hurt her . . .

NITA *and* ALICE *separate them. They sit scowling at each other.*

NITA (*suddenly*): Right, that's it. I've had enough of this. (ALICE *looks alarmed.*) I've had enough. (*To all of them:*) Get changed.

ALICE (*alarmed*): Y'what?

NITA: Get changed. Stoppin' in, feeling sorry . . . we're all a wash-out. Well, not tonight. (*Nobody moves.*) Well, go on, then.

ALICE: Where we goin'?

NITA: Never mind. Just get ready. (*Seeing* BETH *is making no move.*) Beth? (*No response.*) Beth? (BETH *gets up.*) Phil? (PHIL *looks up.*) You an' all.

PHIL *is still sitting on the floor. She looks at* BETH. BETH *goes over to her.*

BETH: Give in?

PHIL (*after a pause, surrenders*): Give in.

Inside a Manchester nightclub. 11 p.m. and the final stage of BETH's *night out. The nightclub is plush, tastefully lit, with a pianist playing offstage.* NITA *comes on.*

NITA: I'm sorry, Alice — what could I do?

ALICE (*following her*): Get them put down?

They both sit at a table. CARMEN *strolls on after them.*

CARMEN: Oh, we couldn't, could we? Let yer just go out by yerselves? Should enjoy yerselves a bit . . .

(CARMEN *sits down*. ALICE *and*
NITA *look disgruntled*.) Beth dun't
look too happy — has something upset
her?

ALICE (*pointedly*): I expect so.

CARMEN (*draping herself into a chair*):
Anyway, I'm just saying — I gets there,
an' she's sat up in this jacuzzi, with
these tea bags over her eyes, an' I says
'I come about the job.' And she says,
'languages?'. I says, 'Y'what?
language? — what the bleedin' hell
d'y'think I am? Now listen Miss
Collins,' I says — 'let's get one thing
straight, Joan. If I did decide to take
it on as yer new Personal Assistant,
we'd be talking strictly executive.'
Then she dumps the tea bags, shoves in
the contact lenses — an' then she says
'I specifically asked them not to send
someone wildly attractive. *Why* have
they sent you?' (*Misinterpreting their
response*.) Yeah, I know — 'cos
otherwise, I'd've walked it, wouldn't
I?

DANNY *and* REUBEN *roll up,
obviously much more drunk than
everyone else*.

REUBEN: Right — I'll get them in . . .
(*He goes off*.)

DANNY (*sitting down*): Right, where is
she? — where is she? Where's the
queen of the junkies? (BETH *comes
on in conversation with* PHIL *and*
NASH. DANNY *captures* BETH *and
stations her next to him*.) Right,
you're next to me where I can keep
an eye on yer. None of this dropping
the odd bomber while I'm at the bar —
all right, babe? (*Seeing someone*.) All
right, Lou? See yer cocked it up,
Sat'day — lost yer touch a bit, have
yer? Give us a ring sometime . . .
(*Suddenly launching an attack on
PHIL:) So . . . what d'y'reckon, Phil?
Classy spot or what? Know a lot of
journalists actually — hang round here
quite a bit — y'know, get the juice
hot off the presses. Tell yer what —

I'll take yer here sometime when it's
not so crowded — show yer what's
what, hey? (*Patting* NITA's *hand*.)
Business, babe — strictly business.

NITA (*fed up with him*): Good for you,
Danny.

REUBEN *comes back in with the
drinks*.

REUBEN: Here we are, then.

DANNY: Right, let's have a toast. To
Beth . . . (*Everyone raises their
glasses*.) To Salford's All Comers
Record Champion Pill Popper . . .

NASH *puts his glass down*, PHIL *and*
ALICE *stop in mid-toast*. CARMEN
and REUBEN *are already drinking*.
BETH *sits without touching her drink*.

NITA (*hurriedly*): To Beth . . . thanks for
coming out with us.

REUBEN: I know what — if *I* was gonna
overdose, I'd make bloody sure it was
on this stuff. (*He raises his glass*.)

PHIL (*hurriedly standing up to prevent
a confrontation*): To Beth — with love
from all of us . . .

Everyone drinks the toast except
BETH, *who remains silent*.

DANNY (*banging the table*): Speech . . .
speech . . . (*loudly seconded by*
CARMEN *and* REUBEN.)

NITA: Danny . . .

DANNY (*louder*): Speech . . . speech . . .

NITA: Danny, I really don't think this is
the time . . .

DANNY: Oh, Nita doesn't really think
this is the time. Well, I tell yer what,
Beth? If y'fancy nipping back to the
shop after — you an' all Phil? — got
some new waterbeds in . . . no? . . .
some other time, eh? . . . I tell yer,
Phil, y'don't know what yer missing.

CARMEN: 'Course, *I* always think . . .
(*Spraying herself liberally with
perfume*.) . . . it's not everyone
appreciates . . . y'know . . . the finer

things in life? . . . y'know, 'cos y'get some come in here, an' it's way over their heads . . . y'know, an' wearing these (*In great distaste.*) 'off-the-peg' suits . . . an' some of them only drive Cortinas.

REUBEN: Well, yer right there, for a change, Carmen — it's a gift — it's definitely a gift.

CARMEN: Oh, definitely . . .

REUBEN: Now everybody has a gift — that's my theory. Everybody has something they're good at — know what I mean? Take Danny . . . now Danny Boy is good at making things. Am I right old son? Whereas Nita . . . well Nita is very delightful, very decorative . . .

DANNY: Oh, very decorative . . .

REUBEN: And pretty handy with the old scissors . . . as is little Alice . . . added to which our Alice doesn't talk to strange men or play with matches. (*Turning to* CARMEN.) Now Carmen . . . well now . . .

DANNY: Carmen knows which side her bread's buttered. That is Carmen's saving grace. That and an eagerness to please.

CARMEN: Oh, Danny . . . isn't he awful, Nita?

DANNY: Now Phil . . . (*Leering across at her.*) . . . well Phil has a lovely smile when she wants to use it . . . an' it's my suspicion she hasn't used it much up to now . . . but we could do something about that, hey Reuben? — given time and the right atmosphere . . .

REUBEN: Oh, too right . . .

DANNY: Now me — well I own up — see, I don't know fuck-all about yer Shakespeares an' yer Oscar Wildes an' all their mates — but what I do know is scratching out the odd crust an' enjoying meself — an' I make no bones about it.

REUBEN: Oh aye, yeah — why not? Should imagine there's plenty here be glad to swap places with yer.

CARMEN: Oh, *I* think so . . .

DANNY (*suddenly, turning on* BETH): Oh, hey, I forgot, didn't I? What's Beth good at? What can Beth do? Well, I think we better pass on that one, hey? — till someone comes up with a bit of evidence? Hey Beth, y'gone very quiet. Whatever happened to that old foghorn we used to know and love? C'mon, babe, this'll perk yer up a bit. Get yer back teeth round that. (*He gives her a drink.*)

BETH: No, I don't want any . . .

NITA: Danny . . .

DANNY: Paid good money for that, Nita — you wanna think about someone else for a change.

NITA: Danny, if she doesn't want it . . .

DANNY: Oh, that's all the thanks y'get for being generous, is it? C'mon, Beth, open wide . . . be a good girl for Danny . . . (*He tries to force* BETH *to drink.*)

NASH (*suddenly, without moving*): Get your fuckin' hands off.

DANNY (*springing up*): Oh yeah?

NASH: You heard.

DANNY (*adopting his boxing stance*): I'll fuckin' have you. (*Beneath his breath.*) I fuckin' will. I suppose yer a fuckin' pacifist an' all, are yer?

NASH: D'y'wanna find out?

CARMEN: Oh Danny, not in yer new suit — it's not worth it . . .

ALICE (*suddenly springing on* CARMEN): You stupid, tit-brain, ignorant bitch . . . (*She starts tearing at* CARMEN's *hair and dress.*)

There is a general movement to separate them. The pianist has stopped playing.

NITA: Alice . . . now calm down, Alice . . .

ALICE (*glaring at* CARMEN): She was asking for it . . .

CARMEN (*being comforted by* DANNY *and* REUBEN): Me earrings . . . who's had me earrings.

During the fight, no one has noticed BETH *get up and go to the microphone.*

PHIL (*suddenly seeing her*): Beth . . . where's she going? . . .

DANNY: What's she doing? — she can't go up there — I've signed her in. Oh Jesus Christ, people know us in here — I been seen with her . . .

NITA: Shut up, Danny . . .

DANNY: She can't do that . . .

NITA: Now, Danny . . .

DANNY *watches in horror and tries to leave as* BETH *takes the microphone.*

BETH: All right now, can we have a bit of hush, please . . .
(*Seeing* DANNY *about to make an exit.*) All right, Danny? . . . (*Before he can leave.*) Big hand for Danny Haslam there . . . stand up Danny, so we can see yer . . . oh sorry, Danny, yer *are* stood up. My mistake.
Okay, now we got a surprise for yer all tonight. Me. Now Danny Boy's got a point, right? What's Beth good at? What can Beth do? Well tonight . . . she's gonna do a turn.   .
That's right.
And she could give yer something out of her football songs repertoire — but all you ladies jangling yer jewels, an' all you lads who'd be two stone lighter without yer gold bracelets — she won't do that, in case some of yer disapprove the odd dirty word . . . y'know, like *love* . . . an' *support* . . . an' *evermore* . . .
Now I won't dedicate this — 'cos some of you arrogant sods might think it's for you. But if it *is* for you, y'won't

need telling. Okay?
Right, Sam — y'can carry on . . . (*No response.*) Yeah, pal, I'm talkin' to *you* . . .

The pianist starts to play again. BETH *starts to sing.*

DANNY (*barely audible*): Me membership . . . they'll fuckin' drop me membership.

NASH *gets up.*
The rest of the scene goes on in the background behind BETH's *song.*

I'll fuckin' have her . . .

NASH: D'y'wanna bet?

DANNY: All right, then — we'll see, shall we?

He throws a punch at NASH. NASH *punches* DANNY. PHIL *and* NITA *spring to separate them.* CARMEN *weighs in, supported by* REUBEN. ALICE *joins in to support* PHIL *and* NITA.
The battle rages in the background. BETH *finishes her song, grins at the fighting behind her, takes a bow and then exits.*

Blackout.

ACT TWO

March-May 1983

BETH *at work.* BETH *comes on dressed in overalls, wiping oil off her hands with a rag.*

BETH: Oh, hello Mr Stone. Yer Porsche, is it?
Well, I've fettled the clutch like yer asked for . . . oh yeah, an' that left indicator's on the blink, but I give it a good kick an' it's right as rain now. Hey, y'don't mind, do yer . . . I've had to trim off yer tiger fur round the dashboard. Y'wanna watch that, y'know — s'like driving a fur coat in a built-up area an' it took us half an hour to find the ignition.
Word of advice . . . y'll never pass yer MOT with all them nodding dogs blocking yer back winder — an' if y'got rid of them furry dice, y'd cut yer petrol costs by half.
All right? See yer again, Mr Stone. Y'what? Oh, the knocking sound? Some silly get left a bag of spanners in the carburettor.

NITA'*s salon and a private room adjoining.*
ALICE *comes and sits down at the desk. She is on the phone.* NITA *and* JOEY *sit in the next room drinking wine.* JOEY *is counting money.*

ALICE: Danny, she's busy. She's got someone with her.

JOEY: Eighty-five, ninety, ninety-five — an' one back for yerself, Nita — for bein' a good customer.

NITA: No, please Joey — I'd rather you kept it and bought me a little surprise.

JOEY: Well I might just take yer up on that, Nita. (*He toasts her.*) An' how's Danny Boy these days?

ALICE: Danny, I can't do that.

NITA: Why d'you ask?

JOEY: Professional interest.

NITA: What profession?

ALICE: Why don't you tell her yerself?
JOEY *rustles the money.*

NITA: Why don't you ask him yourself?

JOEY: I might just do that. (*He pours himself more wine.*) Y'know, when y'think of it, Nita, yer onto a winner.

NITA: Oh, you reckon?

ALICE: Oh really?

JOEY: Oh, I do reckon, Nita. Like, when do I let so much as a graze get across that lovely window of yours, hey? — an' next door's had theirs in three times last week. Now y'must admit, Nita — I do look after me clients.

NITA: You're not exactly cheap, Joey.

JOEY: But effective, Nita. (*She joins him in a toast.*)

ALICE: Very funny, Danny.

JOEY: Y'know what — I almost think yer getting quite fond of me.

NITA: I wouldn't go that far.

ALICE: Don't kid yerself.

JOEY: Oh, wouldn't yer? Shame, that. An' I see I didn't cop for me haircut as usual. I'm thinking of having a bit of colour put in. What d'y'reckon?

ALICE: I reckon she'll hit the roof.

NITA: I reckon it'll cost yer.

JOEY: Oh, nothing too extortionate, I should hope.
ALICE *slams the phone down.* JOEY *kisses* NITA *on the forehead and goes out in the opposite direction to the salon.* NITA *finishes the wine and goes into the salon.*

ALICE: Danny's been on.

NITA: Oh?

ALICE: He can't manage lunch. (*Pointedly.*) Again.

NITA (*glancing at appointment book*): Y'got a perm waiting, Alice.

ALICE: I don't know why y'bother.

NITA (*ignoring her*): And don't use the decent stuff — it's only Mrs Wilson. She never tips.

ALICE (*persisting*): Why *do* y'bother, Nita?

NITA (*unable to avoid a reply*): Two of a kind?

ALICE: Not yet. But the way you're going, y'very soon will be.

> ALICE *goes out.*
> NITA *goes over to the phone and dials.*

NITA: It's Nita . . . oh, is he not? . . . no. Never mind, then . . . no, no message . . .

> *As the lights fade on* NITA *with the phone in her hand, lights up on* BETH *running on in United scarves and colours, laden with cans.*
> *It is Piccadilly Station in Manchester, and* BETH *and* PHIL *have just come back from the FA Cup semi-final, where United have just got through to Wembley.*

BETH: Three years ago, she wouldn't be seen dead here.

> PHIL *comes on, dressed in United colours.*

PHIL: Three years ago, I wouldn't be seen dead here.

> *Back in the salon,* NITA *puts the phone down dejectedly and walks out.*

I'll be struck off the party list for this. I will. You wait. I'm so uncivilised. It's uncouth. It's irrational. But we're on our way to Wembley, an' it's absolutely fuckin' magic.

BETH: Education for yer.

PHIL: What d'y'mean?

BETH: Soft get. Takes her four years to go an' do the things she always done, without she wonders if or not she should.
(*Singing.*) 'One-nil down, two-one up,

now we're gonna win the Cup' . . .
(PHIL *joins in with her.*)
Stay . . . c'mon, why don't yer? Me an' Kaz'll treat yez. Go on, I'm loaded this week. I took home fifty quid. We could have a right laugh — drag Alice out — thumb a lift with Danny Boy — get right up Nita's nose — oh go on, Phil — stay.

PHIL: I can't.

BETH: Y'can.

PHIL: I've got to get back.

BETH: Phil, we won. (*Singing.*) 'We're goin' to Wem-ber-lee' . . . Oh, c'mon, he won't expect yer back till next week. He'll know y'll be spraying the town red.

> PHIL *looks as if she might be persuaded when the train announcement is heard: 'The train now standing at Platform 11 is the 19.55 to Bristol Temple Meads, calling at . . .'*

PHIL: I'll have to go. I'll see yer, kidder.

BETH: What's up? S'he got another woman? (*She rolls about laughing at the idea.*) Hey, Phil — (*Singing.*) 'One Bryan Robson . . . there's only one Bryan Robson . . .'

PHIL (*joins in with the song, and runs off to catch her train*): Football's not a matter of life and death, y'know, Beth. (*After a pause.*) It's much more important than that.
(*Seeing someone.*) Hey Kaz, y'daft get — what y'lookin' at?

KAZ: Heard there's fights goin' off in Piccadilly — thought y'might need an armed escort.

BETH (*going over to him*): Oh aye, armed with what? Yer stick?

KAZ: Nah, brought yer a bottle — on the off-chance y'was only half-cut.

BETH (*seizing the bottle*): That'll do for me. Hey, Kaz, that goal of Robbo's . . . (*Dancing round to demonstrate.*) Oh, an' Frankie

Stapleton . . . the grace of the feet . . .
the heading of the ball . . .
brilliant . . . (*Still dancing about in
ecstasy.*)

KAZ: Where's Phil?

BETH: Gone home, daft get. I'm gettin'
worried, y'know. She's goin' soft.

KAZ: Just us, then?

BETH: You'll do. Right, what's the
programme? Pissed, rat-legged or
arseholed? – an' in what order?

*BETH and KAZ march off
arm-in-arm.
ALICE walks on.*

ALICE: Oh no, y'd never catch me goin'
to see the Reds. Not now. I couldn't.

NITA walks on.

NITA: Sat'day afternoons? Busiest day of
the week? Oh no, I might chance the
odd midweek Cup Tie – assuming we
get an' invite to someone's box an' me
fur coat's not at the cleaners.

ALICE: Never been since that Sat'day
before I give Kevin the elbow. Can't
help it now. I sometimes think, when
I see Beth an' Phil doin' a sprint down
Warwick Road dressed in flags an' red
wrist-bands – hey, I wouldn't mind
goin' again. But I never do. Well it
wouldn't be the same, would it?

NITA: The terraces? Stretford End? Oh,
that'd look well, wouldn't it? Now
that I do root perms for Lou Macari
it's hardly decent for me to be
screaming meself hoarse every week.
I'm past all that sort of thing.

ALICE: Daft thing is, we know people.
We could get seats every week if we
wanted. Yeah, but y'can't, can'yer?
Gotta grow up sometime, hey? Stop
enjoying yerself.

*Train announcement: 'This is Temple
Meads, this is Bristol Temple Meads.
The 19.55 from Manchester is now
approaching platform four . . .
PHIL, taking off her scarf and putting
it away, walks across the stage as if*

she's just got off the train.

ALICE: Nita, y'll never guess what.

NITA: What?

ALICE: Y'know Joey? Y'know, Kev's
friend? I seen him talking to Danny
last night. Honest.

NITA: Really?

ALICE: Fancy them two knowing each
other.

NITA: Yes. Just fancy.

*As NITA and ALICE walk off, NASH and
REBECCA come on. The scene is now
PHIL and NASH's house in Bristol.
NASH is lying on his back on the
floor smoking a cigarette. REBECCA
sits on a cushion drinking wine.
REBECCA has a postcard in her hand.*

REBECCA (*looking at the postcard*):
July 17th 1981. God, is it that long
ago? Did I send that? (*She laughs.*)

NASH: It's your writing.

REBECCA: And Sasha's three next week.
Oh, you must see her. Such a gifted
child. Like her mother.

NASH: Or even her father.

REBECCA: Or even her father.

NASH: How is he?

REBECCA: Nicky? Don't tell me he
never got in touch.

NASH: Well he would hardly do that,
would he?

REBECCA: It didn't work.

NASH: Never.

REBECCA: Well we all have to
compromise somewhere, don't we?

NASH: Do we?

REBECCA: I've sold the villa. You'll
be glad to know I've given up
'exploiting the peasants'.

NASH: Good for you.

REBECCA (*reading from the postcard*):

'Mykonos is full of loud Americans wearing Sony Walkmans and very little else. Nicky left today. I've had enough. Home in August. What about a cottage on Skye?' You might've said yes.

NASH: No.

REBECCA: No?

NASH: I told you why.

REBECCA: Oh, you did. In no uncertain terms. And so I stayed. But ever-curious, here I am — back again. As you see. Well, come on, say something. Lovely to see you? Oh, don't tell me you didn't expect me?

NASH: I always expect you. (*Permitting himself a smile.*)

REBECCA: Do you?

NASH: Y'didn't waste much time.

REBECCA: I've been back a week.

NASH: Exactly.

REBECCA: Am I staying?

NASH: I would put money on it.

REBECCA (*looking round*): So . . . domestic bliss . . . well, this is all new . . . matching cups and saucers? . . . whatever happened to drinking out of ashtrays and eating off the carpet . . . Real flowers? — my God, the idea — and in a vase? Where did all the milk bottles go? God, this is really starting to freak me. Not even a cannibis plant?

NASH: We don't smoke.

REBECCA: 'We' don't smoke? Now that's an odd word, isn't it? — from the person with a manic aversion to using the plural? So . . . where is she, then?

NASH: Football match.

REBECCA: I'm intrigued now.

NASH: Are you?

REBECCA: Oh, just remind me — so I don't put my foot in it. What was it you told her about the dreaded

Rebecca?

NASH: That I lived with her?

REBECCA: Oh, very good.

NASH: That she took a shine to Nicky.

REBECCA: Got pregnant?

NASH: That I told her to get out — and she got out. End of story.

REBECCA: Oh, good story, Nash. Very pretty. Now what about the bits you *didn't* tell her.

PHIL (*standing in the doorway*): What 'bits you didn't tell her'?

NASH (*resigned*): Rebecca — Phil. Phil — Rebecca.

The street.
BETH *skates on.*

BETH: Pretty? I wouldn't call him pretty. I wouldn't say he's fit. But he's nice. He's a laugh. He dun't cost much.
See, I've resigned meself to Life-after-Simon-Le-Bon. An' me chance for copping with Sting seems to recede daily. But this one's all right. He's a lad. He'll do. For now.
Come on, dickhead, are we goin' or what?

She goes over and drags KAZ up. He is wearing skates, and even with the aid of his stick looks very unsteady.

KAZ: Goin' where?

BETH: The zoo, dickhead.

She drags him off.

NASH *walks on and stands looking at something. There is the sound of a tiger roaring. NASH stands and watches it.*
   REBECCA *comes on and looks at it over his shoulder.*

REBECCA: Tigers know a thing or two. Don't you think? Very together, very sensitive. This one's got it sussed.

PHIL *walks on, looking slightly bewildered.*

A real tiger makes a commitment — and doesn't spend his life playing silly games. I like a good tiger. (*She moves on to another cage.*) Oh, this is more like it — this is really lovely. (PHIL *goes over to look.*) Shame it's stuck in a cage all day with only that miserable old buzzard for company . . . Should be out there, stretching its wings . . .

She wanders off. PHIL *stands contemplating the cage.* NASH, *keenly alive to* REBECCA's *tactics, bides his time.*

REBECCA: Oh, here we are — what about this, Phil? (PHIL *goes over and looks into the cage.*) Sits round sulking, won't let anything near it. Can you imagine? — attitude like that and wondering why nobody wants to know? I always feel sorry for porcupines, don't you? (*She and* PHIL *exchange a look of recognition.*) Now where to?

NASH: In here . . .

REBECCA: Oh, what's this? The Insect House.

NASH: Yeah, I want yer to meet an old friend — the Black Widow Spider.

They all go off.
BETH *immediately skates on with* KAZ, *dragging him unsteadily behind her. From one of the cages comes the sound of wild boars squealing.*

BETH: Don't look . . . don't look . . . (*She tries to cover his ears with her hands.*) That's bloody disgusting, that is . . . go on, yer filthy little sods — an't y'got no decency? Y'got sties for that!

KAZ (*fighting her off*): Hey, watch the hair, will yer — watch the hair!

BETH: I'm takin' yer home now.

KAZ: Hey, sod off, dickhead, we've not bin here five minutes.

BETH: Not a lot doin', is there?

KAZ: Where d'y'get yer ideas from, girl? I know this place. Used to come here when we was kids. I know the sounds. (*Sniffing in distaste.*) I know the smells.

BETH: Oh yeah?

KAZ (*pointing with his stick*): Elephants . . . (*Sniffing, then pointing.*) . . . Camels . . . (*Pointing again.*) Wart-hogs . . .

BETH (*delighted*): Oh, yer a right smart-arse, you, an't yer? What this here, then? (*Putting his hands to her face.*)

KAZ (*sniffing*): Rare breed of wild pig . . . not yet fully domesticated . . . highly dangerous . . . Do Not Feed.

BETH: Y'know what, you — what I'm gonna do to yer — drive yer to the middle of Spaghetti Junction — an' dump yer there.

NITA (*coming on*): Beth, it's not on. Y'shouldn't speak to him like that.

BETH: Fend for himself, can't he?

NITA: It's not very nice, Beth.

BETH: Hey, y'can be killed with too much kindness, y'know.

KAZ: Oh yeah? Fat chance.

BETH *skates off dragging* KAZ *after her.* NITA *looks appalled.*
ALICE *walks on.*

ALICE: Nita, have you had yer dinner?

NITA: I'm not hungry.

ALICE: Nita, will you get in there an' get something ate. You've had no breakfast.

NITA: I've had two herb teas an' a multivitamin. I really can't work on a full stomach.

ALICE: If you pass out in the middle of a perm, who's going to neutralise? . . . Okay, shall you explain to Mrs Quinn why all her hair's fell out, or shall I?

NITA: I'm just going to do my work-out.

ALICE: Nita, I know Danny goes for dogs, but if yer tryna be a whippet, yer goin' about it the right way.

NITA *ignores her and walks off.*

Take over would you, Alice? Why certainly, Nita. Fifteen perms, ten blow-waves, half a dozen streaks. Give us a knock around midnight.

PHIL *and* NASH's *house.*

REBECCA *is sitting on the floor with a glass of wine, with a tarot deck in front of her.* PHIL *comes tip-toeing into the room carrying a half-empty bottle of wine. They both look at each other and burst out laughing.*

PHIL (*trying to stifle the laughter*): Sssssshhhhhhh . . .

REBECCA: Out?

PHIL: Cold. (*They both start to laugh.*)

REBECCA: Sssssshhhh . . . now sssssshhhh, Phil — we'll have the whole deck at the back of the fire if he wakes up.

PHIL: No Becky — people in that state don't wake up. They dry out.

REBECCA (*toasting*): Always confront your problems with a bottle.

PHIL *bursts out laughing again.*

REBECCA (*trying to contain herself*): Have you quite finished? Can we go on? (PHIL *tries to resume a serious face.*) Past Foundation . . .

PHIL: What's that?

REBECCA: What it says. Events in the past now effecting the present. Oh, and look who it is — can you take it Phil? — it's . . . The Fool!

PHIL: Oh, I wonder who that is!

REBECCA: Immature . . . foolish . . . irrational . . . inconsiderate . . . think, Phil — does this ring a bell?

PHIL: Well . . .

REBECCA: The odd tinkle? — the odd sonic boom?

PHIL: I'll have to think about that one.

REBECCA (*pointing to next card*): Okay, now this is . . . events now or just passing . . . and, what's this? It's the good old Page of Swords.

PHIL: Who's he?

REBECCA: Why, it's a perceptive and discerning person of course!

PHIL: Oh, of course.

REBECCA (*trying to sound significant*): It's a person adept at uncovering the unknown or less obvious . . . mmmmmm very interesting . . . (*Going on, to next card.*) Now here we have . . . Future influence . . . in other words, 'What sort of a weekend are we going to have?' . . . Oh dear, and it's falsehood and conflict and misrepresentation . . . (*Cheerfully.*) What more can I say?

PHIL: Oh, what about — dear Phil, you won't get a job — sorry Phil, y'gonna blow yer thesis . . .

REBECCA: Which is a distinct possibility . . .

PHIL: If I don't get me finger out an' start working . . . yeah, I know . . .

REBECCA: Can I ask you something?

PHIL: Go on.

REBECCA: What did you expect?

PHIL: What, *you*? Oh God, I dunno . . . not a lot to go on, is there? 'I don't wanna talk about it. I lived with her. I kicked her out. End of conversation.'

REBECCA: Oh, ran off with Nicky, did she? Ran off with his best friend? Did he tell you why? Did he mention that? No?

PHIL: Not exactly.

REBECCA: D'you know how they train dogs?

PHIL: What? —

REBECCA: How to keep a good dog: starve it, kick it, lock it up. Just imagine, once in a blue moon – the odd scrap? – the odd pat? It's on its knees eating from your hand. I know that trick. Too well.

Now Nicky . . . well Nicky is . . . rash? Nicky used some very taboo phrases – you know, like . . . 'thank you'? . . . 'please'? . . . 'that would be nice'? . . . And even . . . oh, this one day, went really wild, went right over the top. 'Rebecca,' he said . . . 'Rebecca, I really like you.' Oh God, and the shock. I'm really phased. I've forgotten what to do when people say nice things. Then it's 'Can I take you for a drink?' – 'What about this play?' – 'I bought you these flowers.' For me?

The first time – when was it? – I stayed away all night. 'Where've you been?' he said. 'Your dinner's in the bin.' – then turns over and that's that, Phil. Suddenly you get a taste for flowers again – and where we lived, we didn't have a garden.
(*Pause.*) But *Nicky* looked as if he might have green fingers. So off we went to Mykonos. (*Pause.*) And nothing grew there either.
(*Noticing* PHIL's *face.*) Well cheer up, Phil. D'you want to see what the future holds? (*She points to remaining cards.*)

PHIL: I think I've got a fair idea.

REBECCA *turns the cards over as* NASH, *looking really ill and dishevelled, comes in.*

NASH: Phil, is there any aspirin?

PHIL: Y'talking to me?

NASH: Yer name's Phil, isn't it?

PHIL: Is it? Y'never heard the word 'please'?

NASH: Phil, don't mess about. I want *one aspirin.*

PHIL (*getting up and going out*): Get it yourself.

NASH (*watching her go*): Thanks Becky.

REBECCA (*looking at the cards*): Pleasure.

ALICE *comes in.*

ALICE: This feller's asked us out. I do his ends every other week. He tips like nobody's business. I've said no, of course. Don't ask us why. Used to think it's me wedding ring gettin' in the way, but since me divorce come through I'm pushed for excuses. Sometimes I think, why not? – go out, get tanked up on Pina Coladas. But then I think, no, best not. Bit over the top. So I stop in with *Dallas,* two cans of coke an' a packet of Smarties. 'Get out,' Beth says. 'Get pissed, roll home legless, three in the morning if that's what y'feel like.'
I *do* feel like it an' all, sometimes. But I don't do it. Well y'can't let yerself go like that, can yer?

BETH *skates on and skids to a halt.*

BETH: What d'y'mean *see?* Course he's gonna see. This is 1983.
Look, he won't be long. He's on the waiting list. You ask his mother. Oh yeah, y'would've thought, wouldn't yer – can send them out, get shot to pieces fast enough – why can't they start a few more nurses, get them sewn back together again? But Kaz can wait. Kaz says he'll wait. So we're waiting. Y'what? Hey, what d'y'mean? *I* can wait.
Goin' on? No there is not. Y'got a mind like a sewer. There's nothing goin' on. We're mates, right? We're just mates. Hey, y'can have mates, y'know – lads as mates – without y'make a bee-line for his inside leg. Me an' Kaz, we're platonic – y'know, like – no hands? Right Kaz? (*Louder:*) Right Kaz?

KAZ (*gingerly edging on in roller skates*): Not if I can help it.

BETH (*skating round him*): Oh yeah, what y'gonna use? Radar?

She skates off, dragging him with her.

DANNY's *office.*
DANNY *walks in to find* NITA *waiting at the desk.*

NITA: Who's Fifi?

DANNY: What?

NITA: I said, who's Fifi?

DANNY: I don't know any Fifis.

NITA *immediately switches on the answering machine which plays back the following message:*

FIFI: Hi, babe, it's Fifi. Darling, I can make tomorrow, usual place. Don't bother to dress up. Bye . . . (*Kissing sounds.*)

NITA *switches it off.*

DANNY: Oh, *that* Fifi . . . (*Seeing* NITA *doesn't find it funny:*) Now that wasn't very nice, was it, Nita? Listening to private conversations? (*Seeing she's really annoyed.*) Oh, c'mon Nita, what d'y'think this is? Okay, okay, if y'must know, it's for Reuben.

NITA: Reuben?

DANNY: Look, don't say nothing to Carmen. S'a bit of snatch he got lined up. Very hush-hush.

NITA: Speaking of which . . . she's been on again.

DANNY: Carmen?

NITA: *Reuben* says he'll see you later.

DANNY: Good stuff.

NITA: Reuben lost his voice, has he?

DANNY: How d'y mean?

NITA: Third time this week that woman's been on with a message 'from Reuben'.

DANNY: Well, what are mates for?

NITA: I don't know, Danny. What *are* they for?

NASH *and* PHIL's *house.*
NASH *and* REBECCA *are having breakfast. The atmosphere is strained.* PHIL *comes in carrying two letters.*

PHIL (*reading*): 'Dear Miss Taylor, we are delighted to be able to invite you to join our staff as a trainee Sub-Editor, working mainly on the Arts and Entertainment section, starting in August . . .'

REBECCA (*taking the letter*): *Cosmopolitan*? Phil, that's amazing — why didn't you say? You kept that dark, didn't you? Oh, isn't she wonderful? (*She hands letter to* NASH *who is not impressed.*)

PHIL (*reading*): 'Dear Phil, Following our chat the other day, we'd very much like you to join us at the *Evening News* as a trainee reporter. When can you start?'

REBECCA: Oh, I don't believe it. You *are* in demand. Oh God, what are you going to do? Which one?

NASH: She won't be doing either if she doesn't shift herself an' get that thesis done.

PHIL: P'raps I might, given a bit of peace, an' not so many distractions. (*She screws up letter and throws it at him.*)

REBECCA (*retrieving the letter*): Oh, but it's Manchester. She can't. She has to go to London. She must.

NASH: D'you wanna tell her?

REBECCA: But she has to. Oh, but there's no contest, is there?

NASH (*abruptly, leaving the table*): No, I wouldn't've thought so.

ALICE *comes in with a letter.*

ALICE: She'll go spare. I daren't tell her. This new place opened round by me

mam's. Money's good. Manageress.
Can y'believe it? Me? S'ever since I
started doin' streaks for Frankie
Stapleton. Word gets round. Oh, I'll
have to turn it down of course. I'll
have to say no. I'm not cut out to be
a boss. Fancy me bein' asked, though.

NITA *walks in looking ill.*

NITA: Take over my column, will you
Alice. (*Is about to wander out.*)

ALICE (*as if to a client*): 'Scuse me a
minute, Mrs Yates – give us a shout if
yer ears start to burn . . . (*Dragging
NITA off.*) Where've you been?

NITA: Out.

ALICE: Nita, I've had to cancel three
appointments. Mrs Driscoll's goin' up
the wall. What y'playing at?

NITA: Go out an' enjoy meself, can't I?

ALICE: Enjoy? Getting soaked on
brandy? Fumes in here enough to get
the whole shop breathalised. What
y'tryna do?

NITA: I'll be upstairs if anyone wants
me.

ALICE: Prove y'can hang on to that
tosser when y'know he's been through
half of Manchester behind yer back?

NITA: Alice, d'you mind?

ALICE: *I* don't mind, Nita. I *do* mind
seein' you become a standing joke
among that piss-head crowd *he* hangs
about with. An' that slag's been in
again. Carmen, who else? Did you
say she could have a free manicure?

NITA: Probably.

ALICE: Oh, I wonder why, Nita? See she
keeps her claws pared down to a
decent length?

NITA: Alice, I'd prefer it if you got on
with your work.

ALICE: I tell yer what, Nita – no way
I'm shifting a muscle to serve that slag.
She wants her talons doin', *you* do it,
Nita. Y'give her just about everything
else.

NITA *goes out.* ALICE *composing
herself, goes back into the salon.*

There y'are, what did I tell yer, Mrs
Finch. Y'look the spit of Lady Di –
y'do, honest . . .

NASH *and* PHIL's *house.*
PHIL *is sitting reading glossy
magazines.* REBECCA *is sitting opposite
her reading.*

PHIL: 'How To Make The Most Of Your
Acne'! (REBECCA *glances up at her.*)
'Emasculate Your Man For Under A
Fiver'! (*In response to* REBECCA's
look of amazement.) So? It's what
people wanna read, in't it? Okay,
yeah, it's crap. I know it's crap. But
that's the point, right? (REBECCA
looks quizzical.) What I mean is, y'can
write crap an' still keep yer integrity,
can't yer? – as long as yer *know* it's
crap. (REBECCA *goes back to her
book.*) The money's good. (*Almost
to herself.*) Money's amazing. 'Course,
I could still go home from time to
time – keep in touch with it all. *'Up
north.'*
Back there, what can y'do? Yer
fighting a losing battle. Big deal,
y'write about no jobs, no money.
Nobody reads yer. Why should they?
Why read it when y'can live it first-
hand? What can *I* do? Nothing
changes.
People like a laugh, don't they? The
best way to cope is to laugh, right?
I can laugh – I can entertain – that's
just as valid, in't it? That isn't copping
out.
Look, if I go back there, what am I?
If I went to London . . . I could do
something. Oh, I could. I could change
things. But first you have to play the
game, don't yer? You can't change
the rules if y'don't join the game.
(*After a pause.*) Oh God, all I want is
a quiet life – me own place – money
coming in – an' the Reds winning the
Cup.

REBECCA: That's all?

PHIL: No, but it's a start.

REBECCA: Then come to London.

PHIL: Should I?

REBECCA: Oh Phil, if you wanted, you could have the most amazing time. Theatre, opera, films . . .

PHIL: United an' Spurs, United an' Arsenal, Wembley . . . oh no, don't Becky . . .

REBECCA: Phil, I mean it — you really could (*A sudden idea.*) And we could share a flat.

PHIL: Me an' you?

REBECCA: And Sasha.

PHIL: Oh God, it sounds . . .

REBECCA: What?

PHIL: Amazing.

REBECCA: Well then?

PHIL: When?

REBECCA: Whenever you like.

PHIL: Honest?

REBECCA: But make sure, Phil . . .

PHIL: What?

REBECCA: It's what you want.

PHIL *grabs her coat and runs out. She runs into* NASH, *about to light a cigarette. She takes it out of his mouth and snaps it. He doesn't retaliate.*

PHIL: Rebecca says I should go to London.

NASH: Does she?

PHIL: Should I?

NASH: Rebecca says so.

PHIL: Well I might.

NASH: Good for you, Phil.

PHIL: Why should I listen to you?

NASH: Why indeed.

PHIL: Okay, if y'gonna be so obnoxious . . .

NASH: Go to London, Phil. If that's what you want, just go.

PHIL: I am *trying* to be nice now. I'm asking for your opinion.

NASH: No, don't ask us, Phil. I haven't got an opinion.

PHIL: Oh God, did I ask yer to commit to something? Oh, what'm I thinking of? Mind you, I did notice a very disturbing trend yesterday. You, in the shop ask for three Cumberland sausages an' a quarter of Camembert. Wasn't that goin' a bit far? Admitting that other people actually exist? Don't you feel you might've compromised yerself a bit there?

NASH: Christ, what d'you have to give for a quiet life? Thanks Rebecca.

PHIL: Not Rebecca.

NASH: If she hadn't come back —

PHIL: You wanted her to come back.

NASH: Did I?

PHIL: Didn't you?

NASH: Curiosity.

PHIL: Satisfied?

NASH: Are you?

PHIL: Very.

NASH: Two of us.

NASH *walks off into the room where* REBECCA *is sitting.*

NASH: Listen you —

REBECCA: I'm going on Monday.

NASH: So soon? Are y'sure y'done enough damage? D'y'not fancy a crack at next door's marriage? Or maybe y'could get the rest of the street needing psychiatric treatment before yer left?

REBECCA: I feel so sorry for you.

NASH: Please don't, Rebecca.

REBECCA: I do feel sorry. I see you about to fuck this one up like you did the last. Oh just remind me . . . (*Before he can walk out.*) what was

your First in? English Lit? What a
shame you never did subsidiary in
'Other People'. Still it's just as well,
really. On your record, you wouldn't
scrape a pass.

NITA's flat.
NITA *is looking in the mirror trying
to make herself look presentable. In
reality she looks ill and drawn. DANNY
saunters in, has a quick look in the
mirror.*

DANNY: Nita, remind me to tell yer,
y'look fuckin' awful. Y'wanna get a
decent dinner inside yer. I'd take yer
meself, but I'm busy tonight . . .

NITA *walks out of the room and
meets* ALICE.

ALICE: Nita, are you gonna eat
something?

NITA: I'm not hungry.

ALICE: When's the last time you ate?
(NITA *ignores her.*) Yesterday? Day
before? Last week?

NITA: I can't remember.

ALICE: Have you been to the doctor's?

NITA: What for?

ALICE: What d'you *weigh*, Nita?

NITA: Weigh? Alice, I'm huge. I'm like
a whale. Look at all this flab. I want
to lose a good seven pounds.

ALICE: D'y'wanna close this shop?

NITA: What d'y'mean?

ALICE: Yer goin' to the doctor's
tomorrow. I'm not letting this shop get
shut up.

NITA: If I go, he won't give me anything.

ALICE: If *he* doesn't, *I* will.

NITA *goes out.*

(*Shouting after her:*) And get away
from those weights. Yer in no shape to
be keeping fit.

DANNY *comes on.*

DANNY: Alice, I think we ought to shut
the shop.

ALICE: What for?

DANNY: Nita's in no fit state to run it.

ALICE: I wonder why.

DANNY: Why is irrelevant. She can't
cope. Y'll just have to shut for a week
or so.

ALICE: Oh, will I?

DANNY: Take a holiday.

ALICE: Nita isn't the only person who
works round here.

DANNY: What? – y'mean *you*? Run it?

ALICE: I wonder what you think goes on
those afternoons she's out boozing
with you till all hours. D'y'think we
take no customers then? D'y'think we
put the locks on an' wait for Nita to
come home pissed out of her skull?
Last week I took seven hundred quid.
Yeah, Danny, work it out – that's
twice as much as Nita. Plus we think
we're lucky if she can see straight an'
doesn't shampoo with bleach or cut
and blow the back of someone's neck.
Now if y'don't mind getting from
under me feet, I do have clients
waiting.

ALICE *walks out.* DANNY *looks
amazed. He follows.*

NITA's flat. NITA *walks on.*

NITA: Bother? What bother? I'm a
success, right? I'm making a packet,
I drive a Capri. I got family,
friends . . . my boyfriend . . . is a
success. Like me.
There's no such thing as stress. Not to
me. I thrive on it. I'm not afraid of
hard graft. Chip on the shoulder?
Me? Yer joking. Mother, English.
Father . . . yeah . . . 'of foreign
extraction' – But I fit in. I'm in
control. I got nothing to prove.
Drink? Oh yeah, I like a drink. Now
and again. It helps you relax. Not

that I need to. Not that I can. Rushed off me feet most days. But I'm dead happy. Most days.

Look, I'm fine. I am. I'm where I want to be . . .

Y'what? Me? Scared? What of?

Suddenly JOEY *rushes on, panic-stricken, and grabs hold of her.*

JOEY: Nita, what's out the back?

NITA: What?

JOEY: The back — what's out there?

NITA: A yard . . .

JOEY: Wall? (*She nods.*) Then what?

NITA: The road . . . then the park . . .

JOEY: Nita, do us a favour, hey? Someone comes askin' for us, y'don't know where I am, you in't seen us for weeks. All right? (*He kisses her on the cheek and runs out.* NITA *is completely bewildered. She stands mesmerised for a few seconds. Then there is a knock at the door. She remains rooted, unable to move. The knocking continues. Finally she goes to the door.*)

NITA: Joey Russell? (*A pause in which we see her reach a resolution.*) Yeah. Two minutes ago. Through the park.

She stands still while the implications of what she's done begin to sink in. Then she turns and behaves normally.

It is now the following morning and she briskly goes about her usual business in the salon.

If I were you, Mrs Muttley, I would definitely go for the Wild Fox with Beachcomber frostings . . . it's just right for your complexion . . . (*Seeing* ALICE *wander in.*) Alice, could you just rinse Mrs Muttley while I'm seeing to this . . . (*Seeing her face.*) What on earth's the matter?

ALICE: God, it's just . . . I dunno, I used to hate him . . . I did . . . but I'd never wish that . . .

NITA: What?

ALICE: S'Joey.

NITA: Joey?

ALICE: Kev's friend.

NITA (*affecting unconcern*): What about him?

ALICE: He's dead.

NITA (*hardly able to speak with shock*): What?

ALICE: Found this morning down by the docks. Got a brick through his skull.

NITA: No . . . oh God, no . . . (*She tries to regain her calm before* ALICE.)

ALICE: I seen Kev just now. Reckons he owed somebody. Oh God, Nita — who'd wanna do a thing like that?

DANNY walks in and sees the shock on their faces.

DANNY: State of you two. Seen a ghost, have yer? C'mon, Nita — I'm taking yer out. (NITA *is still in a daze.*) Me winnings. (*He produces some notes.*)

NITA: What? —

DANNY: Made a killing last night. C'mon, babe — we're celebrating.

He puts his arm round NITA *and escorts her out.*

BETH *runs on with* KAZ *on her back, waving a stick and carrying his skates.*

KAZ: Go on, faster . . . faster . . .

BETH: Kaz, yer a ton weight, you are.

KAZ: Well put us down then, y'gawp.

BETH *dumps him.*

BETH: Right, get these on, then. (*She gives him the skates.*) I can't spend the rest of me life carting *you* round on me back.

They start pretending to punch each other like kids.

DANNY *strolls in.*

DANNY: Hey, Kaz, how y'doin' mate? (*Seeing the skates.*) Chancing yer arm a bit with *her,* aren't yer? Hey, she tells us yer about to get put right as rain again.

KAZ: Oh, did she?

DANNY: Don't feel so bad now, hey? Done a grand job, got his medal — an' now turns out he'll be none the worse off. Tell yer what, mate — y'can dine out on that the next few years — 'specially when y'can see what yer eating . . . (KAZ *joins in* DANNY's *laughter.* BETH *is silent.*) Y'not wearing it, then?

KAZ: What?

DANNY: Yer medal.

KAZ: In't got a medal.

DANNY: Beth's bin tellin's us y'had this . . .

KAZ: Yeah, I *did* have. I give it me mam.

DANNY: Nice one.

KAZ: She chucked it down the back of the fire.

DANNY: Charming.

KAZ: Dead ungrateful, me mam. Says 'What d'y'wanna do that for? What more d'y'want?'

DANNY (*beginning to feel uncomfortable*): Well . . . y'know what they're like . . . women . . .

KAZ: Got a joke f'yer, Danny. (DANNY *cheers up.*) What I'm doin' out there. Know what? She'll tell yer. Reckon this bird's gonna land us in the shit, didn't I? Two months overdue? Thought I'd rather cop for suntan an' stripes than screaming kid an' life membership down the Job Centre. Turns out the daft get can't count — there *is* no screaming kid. An' as for suntans? — shipped off to the fuckin' South Atlantic in bleak midwinter? Fuckin' scream.
Hey, she's right though, this one. They never got us off the ship. I never seen action. It seen me though. Right laugh. Copped us unawares, like the back of yer hand across me face. Brought tears to me eyes, it did. An' here's me, squinting hard, tryna look out what I'm doin', what I'm aiming at.
Like, y'think y'got it sussed. Yer meant to, aren't yer? Else, what y'doin' there? But I'm daft, me. I get confused — I can't see where I'm going. Something's up the shoot somewhere — or is it me? Did I miss something? Y'know what? Used to wear these shades at school — dead cool, me — she'll tell yer — drive the girls daft. Eight months this time round before y'could get us out the house. People get embarrassed, see. Can't look yer in the eye. Not that *I'm* embarrassed. Not about these. Embarrassed like when y'break a leg in some pissing little Cup Tie — 'gainst a bunch of cripples — for a Cup y'wouldn't shit on if y'got the bastard home. (*Looking at* DANNY.) Go on, y'can laugh now.

DANNY (*not knowing what to say*): Yeah . . . well . . . right . . . it's . . . good to see the pair of yer . . . gi's a shout sometime, when yer feeling better . . . buy yer a drink . . .

BETH: Thank you, Danny.

DANNY: Be seein' yer.

KAZ (*after a pause*): *I* won't.

BETH: What?

KAZ: Be seein' yer.

BETH: Y'what? What y'talking about?

KAZ: Fuck-all.

BETH: Fuck-all what?

KAZ: Magic wands.

BETH: Y'what?

KAZ: Oh, like the comics, Beth? Just like the films? (*She doesn't understand.*) Dead as doornails inside here. Who's gonna touch us, Beth?

BETH: I know, but we can wait.

KAZ: Can we?

BETH: We can.

KAZ: We'll have to.

BETH: What?

KAZ: An' what's the point? There's fuck-all down for this one, Beth. Me mother's talking shit. An' maybe shoulda clocked it better that night, two years back, Tesco's car park, hey? (*He touches her face.*) 'Cos that was all the look we're ever gonna get.

BETH (*slowly*): You shit. You little shit. Y'make us look a tit an' never told us?

KAZ: Oh yeah, an' then what? Leave us while me mam gets time to wheel us out for visitors? Piss off while the coast's clear an' y'threw away me stick? Oh yeah, gi's the elbow, go on. I knew yer would. Here, y'can have yer skates back an' all.

BETH: Fuck off, Kaz. (*He stops undoing his skates.*) What've I told yer? Said I'm teaching yer to skate, aren't I? Well get up off your arse . . . (*Pulling him to his feet.*) . . . and fuckin' skate. (*She drags him off.*)

NITA's *flat.*
   NITA *and* DANNY *are getting ready to go out.*

NITA: Thirty-nine quid?

DANNY: Yeah?

NITA: You turned over nearly three thousand quid last week.

DANNY: Hey, Nita, we're after a boat, aren't we?

NITA: Oh, we're after a boat, are we? While Paul's working fifty hours for thirty-nine quid.

DANNY: In his hand.

NITA: You must be very pleased with yerself Danny.

DANNY: Nita, when *I* was nineteen, know what I was on? Twenty quid a week.

NITA: That's a long time ago, Danny.

DANNY: If people don't graft a bit, how they gonna appreciate what they got?

NITA: The money you pay, there's not a lot to appreciate.

DANNY: Look babe, you don't do too badly out of it.

NITA: Me?

DANNY: Hey, you're in business. You know what it's like. Can't get sentimental an' start cutting into the profit margin. (*Seeing the look of disapproval.*) Nita, I'm doin' him a favour. He should thank Christ he's got a job at all. (NITA *walks out in disgust.*) Now what've I said?

DANNY *walks off and* ALICE *comes on.*

ALICE: Cup Final tomorrow. Danny's got a tenner on Brighton. Done that to get Beth's back up. We could go. Lou Macari's give us free seats, but Nita says we can't. We have to mind the shop. Don't see why. Tomorrow's dead after 2.30 − not a client, not one. Funny that. Must be something goin' on.

NITA *comes in.*

NITA: Alice, y'know that crap conditioner we just bought?

ALICE: Yeah?

NITA: Don't bother to unpack it.

ALICE: Why not.

NITA: It's going back.

ALICE: What for?

NITA: Because it's crap, Alice.

ALICE: Yeah . . . but *you* said . . . we're to buy the crap stuff an' sell it as posh.

NITA: I know what I said, Alice. I am *now* saying you're to send it back. And while yer at it, y'may as well get rid of those cheap perm solutions.

ALICE (*dubious*): Right . . . I'll make a start then, shall I?

NITA (*looking through the appointment book*): I see we got nothing in after two tomorrow. I s'pose y'd better go home.

ALICE (*incredulous*): Y'mean . . . don't do Sat'day afternoon?

NITA: That's what I said, Alice. If y'get bored, y'could always watch the Cup Final.

ALICE: What'll *YOU* do?

NITA: I might even watch it meself.

ALICE (*after considering*): Nita . . . what y'doin' tonight?

NITA: Nothing.

ALICE: You *are*. I'm takin' you out for dinner. All right?

NITA: Oh . . . no . . . I don't think so . . .

ALICE: All right?

NITA: No . . . really . . . I'm not very hungry . . .

ALICE: Nita . . . it'll be all right. It will. Honest.

NITA (*after a pause*): I'll try. I can't promise.

ALICE: Who asked yer to promise? Just try.

They walk off together. PHIL *walks on.*

PHIL: I can't work. I'm not gonna do it. I can't hear meself think. Next door's chuckin' plates again. The cat's brought in a dead seagull. An' them two, fighting it out, raking up the past – I'm going, I'm staying, I'm going . . . What about me? My house? Meant to be. Now I'm shoved off in the back room where y'can't move for coffee cups an' dead aspidistras an' tea chests full of books that won't get written. I'm supposed to be writing a thesis. All I wanna do is go to Wembley!

BETH *runs on.*

BETH: I got it. I got yer a ticket.

NASH *walks on.*

PHIL: She's got me a ticket.

NASH: You can't go.

PHIL: Who says I can't go?

NASH: She can't go.

BETH: What d'y'mean? Phil, it's face-value!

PHIL: I'm going.

NASH: Yer not.

PHIL: I'll do what I want.

NASH: Not this time. (*She puts her scarf round her neck. He takes it off again.*) Beth, you'll have to go on yer own. See if y'can fix her a replay.

PHIL (*outraged*): Replay? We'll stuff Brighton in the first five minutes.

BETH: Tickets? . . . d'y'wanna ticket? . . . twenty quid? . . . all right kid, d'y'want it? . . . twenty? . . . where's yer money? . . . oh, go on then, y'can have it face value. Christ, I'm getting soft in me old age. (*Seeing* KAZ *edging on.*) Over here.

KAZ *edges over and puts a scarf round her neck.*

KAZ: Behave yerself.

BETH: Y'what?

KAZ: Less of the aggro.

BETH (*fiercely*): What aggro?

KAZ: No putting the boot in.

BETH: Oh yeah, fat chance. Seen who I'm sat next to on the coach? Her next door, old Brown Owl, Salford 7th Brownie pack . . . (*Shouting.*) Hello Mrs Fudge – get the fire started . . . (*To* KAZ:) An' that old gran across the way . . . (*Shouting.*) Got yer docs on have yer, Mrs Engels? . . . (*To* KAZ:) Trust us to get in with a bunch of tee-total geriatrics. (*Shouting.*) Oh yeah . . . great . . . Tizer . . . just what I fancied. (*To* KAZ:) Magic. Four years ago, '79, I was halfway through a crate of lager by now. Hey Kaz, stick us a fiver on Brighton, will yer? Just in case? (*As he goes out*:) Look out f'r'us on the telly.

Sound of football crowd and chants and commentary on the closing minutes of the game.
NASH *and* REBECCA *sit playing chess in dead silence, hardly daring to move, and casting the odd furtive glance at* PHIL *who sits at her desk surrounded by books and listening to the cup final commentary on a head-set.*

PHIL (*hardly audible at first*): That's it, that's it . . . hang on now . . . y'got three minutes . . . y'can do it . . . y'can . . . we're gonna win it . . . we are . . . yer magic, Reds . . . yer brilliant . . .

During this speech, BETH, NITA *and* ALICE *have become visible standing at the four corners of the stage, as if following the match.*

Hey, c'mon now, get it back, Reds . . . get it back . . . have him down . . . oh no . . . oh no . . . oh fuck. (*She throws the book across room.*) Fuck it. The lot of them. I hate football. I fuckin' hate it.

She storms out of the room.

REBECCA: I presume that was the equaliser?

NITA: Not that *I* care. I mean, would I? But just for old time's sake, it might've been nice . . . if the stupid gets hadn't let that equaliser in.

She goes out.

ALICE: Daft, me – y'know what I wish? I wish we coulda bin there – the four of us – like we were before.

She goes out.

BETH: Aggro? What aggro? Not me, mate. Them two old villains next to us – old Fudge an' Engels. Mouth? Y've never heard the like. Effin' referee, effin' Melia, effin' what d'y'think yer playin' at? An' when we let them get

the equaliser? Kicked down the effin' steps with a flag-pole up me nose. Hey, I know what they say about Man. U. supporters – but there's these two hard cases behind us an' they are bloody petrified; Granny Engels gets her stick out – then Brown Owl starts on with her camp fire tricks, rubbing skinheads up the wrong way.
Hey Phil, if you'd bin there, we coulda took them on – but there's no way I'm breaking me neck with a couple of old lunatics like that – not on two Pils an' a half of Guinness.
Oh Phil, y'shoulda bin there. Shouldn't be a replay – shoulda stuffed them there an' then. But . . . oh Phil, just bein' there . . .

Later that evening. NASH *and* PHIL's *house.*
PHIL *standing in front of a mirror getting ready to go out.*

PHIL: Sod this f'r'a lark. I'm not stopping in.

NASH *comes in.*

NASH: What y'doing?

PHIL: What's it look like?

NASH: Y'not goin' out.

PHIL: D'y'wanna bet?

NASH: Yer not getting outside this door.

PHIL: Read that. (*Showing him an invitation.*) Phil. It says. Come to our party. Bring Nash. Not Nash bring Phil or Phil stop home. I'm going.

NASH: Y'got a thesis to get done. I've made yer excuse. Becky's goin' instead.

PHIL (*snatching back invitation*): Don't bank on it.

Inside the party. Disco lighting and music playing.
PHIL *comes in with a glass of wine, by this time quite drunk.*

PHIL: Oh, hi Phil. How's it going? Get
y'a drink, Phil?
Oh, talk to us now, will yer? Gi's the
time of day? What d'*you* think, Phil —
what's *your* opinion? Oh, someone
else now, is it? Worth knowing, seen
talking to? — Now she's drinking
spritzers, wearing big ideas between
the ears. Oh yeah, that's right — I'm
off to London, Out me way toe-rags.
Coffee sometime? Let me look at the
diary. Oh sorry, must dash — the
fondu's on fire, the sorbet's gone solid.
Y'must meet Rupert sometime — oh
y'know, me new live-in lover, share a
basement just off the Heath? Does
backing vocals for Gary Numan,
poetry reviews in *Time Out*.
'Course, I've give football the elbow.
It's not my scene. I'm too much into
jazz-funk and aerobics. Oh, the odd
CND demo in Hyde Park, if the
weather's nice an' we're back in time
for The South Bank Show. Or The
People's March For Jobs — final
leg, get seen on telly.
Ta-ra then. I'm getting out. I'm
moving on. I'm gonna take you
wankers at yer own game. Yeah, an'
you laugh now — you dare. Oh, 'cos
you pissed yerself, did yer? — so pig-
ignorant, was she? Beaujolais with ice,
fish with the butter knife. Well now
it's Phil that's laughing — an' I can
get back there where I belong — drive
a '76 Cortina, drink me tea off the
mantlepiece in a saucer. Or I can come
up there an' take yer all on.
So who's first then? C'mon, who
fancies a crack? Who wants the first
left hook?

*She swings round and comes face to
face with NASH.*

NASH: Phil, c'mon . . .

PHIL (*backing off*): Oh no, oh no — not
you. You cheat. You don't fight fair.

NASH: Phil, we're going.

PHIL: Who's 'we'?

NASH (*trying to take the glass off her*):

Don't have anymore.

PHIL: Oh, what are yer, me moral
guardian? Oh yeah, that's a laugh.

NASH: Either you come now, or yer
walking home on yer own. Though
God help the poor bastard who tries
to jump *you* in a blind alley.

PHIL (*allowing herself to be led out*): See
yer in Sloane Square. Y'can buy us a
drink in Peppermint Park . . .

*After the party, PHIL is walking home
looking miserable, followed at a distance
by NASH and REBECCA. A few yards
from the house, PHIL stops and waits.
NASH gives the key to REBECCA and
tells her to go in. PHIL ignores both of
them.*

NASH: Y'goin' in? (*Trying to take her
into the house.*)

PHIL: Get off me.

NASH: Phil, c'mon . . .

PHIL: Get away from me.

NASH: Call it a day, Phil. (*She ignores
him.*) Phil, it's too late to mess about
in doorways. Y'can finish it tonight.

PHIL: Oh, is that right, Nash?

NASH: Phil, I'm tired.

PHIL: Talk to me.

NASH: I can't.

PHIL: Talk to me.

NASH: When it's finished.

PHIL: If you don't talk to me — no.

NASH: Phil, don't waste it.

PHIL: Waste what?

NASH: Four years?

PHIL: What four years?

NASH: Oh, what d'y'think, Phil?

PHIL (*hopefully*): Tell me?

NASH: Four years . . . grant, what else?

PHIL (*slowly*): I hate you.

NASH: I'm sure you do.

PHIL: I fuckin' hate you.

NASH: I believe yer. So does the rest of the street. Now get inside. (*He tries to take her in.*)

PHIL: Get off me.

NASH: Get inside.

PHIL: Get stuffed.

NASH: Y'know what, Phil — I'll break your neck one of these days.

PHIL: Don't bet on it.

He drags her inside, and pushes her towards her room.

NASH: In there.

PHIL: Don't you dare.

NASH: Get in there and finish it.

He throws her into the room and locks the door.

PHIL: Open this door . . . open this door . . . Nash, if you don't open this door . . . Nash, I give yer one last chance . . .

She is looking round for something to throw. While her back is turned, NASH sneaks in and dumps her typewriter and thesis and locks the door again before she can stop him.

You've had it now . . . y'best open this door . . . right, you wait — y've seen the last of us now . . . just you wait . . .

Having thrown papers round the room and trampled on them, finally, in desperation, she sits down at the typewriter and starts to work.

ALICE *comes on dressed ready to go out.*

ALICE (*delighted*): I'm bored. I'm really bored.
I feel great.
I been bored for years. I called it content, but it wasn't content. It was copping out. (*Looking at herself in the mirror.*) Hey Al, yer a cracker, you are. Y'look dead smart. Oh, ta. Y'could be right.
Why not? Can't stop in, the rest of yer life.

Sound of a doorbell. ALICE *takes a deep breath.*

Here we go then. (*And she walks out.*)

DANNY *and* CARMEN *come sneaking on.*

CARMEN — Danny —

DANNY: Sssssssshhhhh —

CARMEN: Danny —

DANNY: Sssssssshhhhh —

CARMEN: What if —

DANNY: She won't —

CARMEN: Danny —

DANNY: Five minutes —

CARMEN: But what if —

DANNY: Carmen —

CARMEN: Danny —

DANNY: What? —

CARMEN: I think I've lost a contact lens.

DANNY: Where?

CARMEN: Here —

DANNY: Where?

CARMEN: Down here . . .

NITA *appears. She stands listening. By this time DANNY is hunting for the contact lens down the front of CARMEN's dress. NITA braces herself and walks in. CARMEN and DANNY spring guiltily apart.*

DANNY: No, Nita . . . don't jump to conclusions . . . (CARMEN *hastily rushes off.*) . . . there's a perfectly logical explanation . . .

NITA: I'm sure there is.

DANNY: Look, Nita . . . it's not what you think. She's a friend . . . Carmen's a mate. Oh, Christ, Y'don't think . . .

gi's a bit of credit, Nita . . . look, she lost her eyelash — I was helping her look for it . . . (NITA *is laughing in disbelief.*) Nita, be fair, what'm I like? It's only you, babe — it's just . . . yer never around any more . . . Listen, I been thinking . . . maybe time we got something sorted out . . . bit more definite . . . y'know, like . . . put it in writing, maybe?

NITA: Like a merger.

DANNY: If you like . . .

NITA: Like a business deal.

DANNY: Okay, like a business deal, yeah. What d'y'say?

NITA: Give me yer hand.

DANNY: Y'what?

NITA: Go on.

He gives her his hand. She gets a toothbrush out of her pocket and gives it to him.

DANNY: It's me toothbrush.

NITA: Well done, Danny.

DANNY: What for? . . . What . . . y'mean . . . Nita, y'not serious?

NITA: I'm sorry, Danny. (*She kisses him on the cheek and goes out.*)

BETH *skates on leading* KAZ, *who, with the aid of his stick, is becoming much steadier on his skates.*

BETH: Not bad. Not bad. Hey, y'could be the Stevie Wonder of the skating rink. Y'could be Robin Cousins with a stick.

KAZ: Robin Cousins is ice, dick.

BETH: I know what he is, dick.

KAZ (*holding out a small box to her*): D'you want this or not?

BETH: Sod off, Kaz. Yer a bloody ton weight. Pick on someone yer own size.

KAZ: I'm not askin' yer again.

BETH: Call that askin'? Shovin' a

bloody great solitaire up me nose an' saying gi's yer finger?

KAZ: What d'y'want us to do? On me knees? So y'can leave us there like a dick, tryna grope me way home without skates?

BETH: Yer bloody hard work, you are. D'you know that?

KAZ: Well, what d'y'want? — a bloody medal?

BETH: Gi's a look at it then. (*He gives her the ring. She bites it.*) Just testin' — don't wanna land meself a cheapskate, do I?

KAZ: Shift, before I change me mind.

A moment of real fear crosses BETH's *face. She looks at him for a second, then . . .*

BETH: Oh yeah, why not . . . Hey, on one condition . . .

KAZ: What?

BETH: Y'gotta catch us first . . .

She grabs his stick and skates away from him. At first he daren't move, then he listens to see where she is. Finally he plucks up the courage and strikes out towards her.

BETH (*allows him to catch up, then*): Right . . . now no takin' it easy . . .

She skates off. He follows.

Bristol.
PHIL *sits with a finished thesis.* NASH *comes in and offers her a cup of coffee. She hands him the thesis.*

PHIL: Satisfied?

NASH: Are *you*?

PHIL: For what?

NASH: Look, I got a meeting. I'll hand this in f'yer. (*He is about to go.*)

PHIL: I don't believe this . . .

NASH (*coming back*): What don't yer believe, Phil?

PHIL: You. Me. What passes for my head.

NASH: Look, Phil . . .

PHIL: Save it for *them*, Nash. Yer precious students. Don't waste it on *me*. Talk to *them*.

NASH (*at a loss*): I'll see yer later, Phil.

He goes out.

PHIL: Don't bet on it.

PHIL *takes a suitcase and slowly begins to pack. She puts her coat on.* REBECCA *comes in carrying a suitcase.*

PHIL *brings forward her suitcase, stands in the middle of the room and hesitates.*

REBECCA: Come on, it's not locked.

PHIL: Oh I can't just *go*, can I? – just piss off, oh see yer kidder, it's been *fun*.

REBECCA: Well, you could.

PHIL: Ta-ra, then, I owe yer one.

REBECCA: Owe what?

PHIL: Oh God, d'y'wanna see the list? Y'got half a day goin' spare? (*She opens her case.*) Right . . . this f'r'a kick-off . . . (*She gets out her degree certificate.*)

REBECCA: Your degree?

PHIL: And these . . . and these . . . and this . . . (*Newspaper cuttings.*)

REBECCA: *You* wrote those.

PHIL: I *wrote* them, yeah.

REBECCA: You can't be *taught* to write.

PHIL: You can be taught to *see*.

REBECCA: Phil, is this a joke? See what? Teach *you* what he doesn't know himself?

PHIL: He *does* know.

REBECCA: Really? You surprise me.

PHIL: Y'shoulda seen us, Becky. Come here, know sod-all . . . So what? he says. I don't go home, don't write . . .

all that smart-arse crap down here, I fall for. Give over, he says – that's not you. So what *is,* then?
An' he explains it all – what to do, what to be, what I have, what I need . . . So now I just piss off, do I? Ta for that, but I know the answers now, thank you.

REBECCA: He'll survive.

PHIL: Will he?

REBECCA: Another term, another First-Year . . . Same old story.

PHIL: Is it?

REBECCA: We should ask him.

Sound of the door opening and closing.
NASH *comes in, looks from* PHIL *to* REBECCA, *sees the suitcases waiting.*

NASH (*not looking at* PHIL): What y'doin', Rebecca?

REBECCA: So . . . you're back. You're just in time.

NASH: Do *I* get a say in this?

REBECCA (*pleasantly*): Sit down.

NASH: What?

REBECCA: Sit down. (*He does.*) Now . . . just tell me – I'm intrigued – since you've got Phil convinced she owes you at least four years solid enlightenment . . . where is it . . . that someone gets to learn about 'Values' and 'Roots' and 'Where He's Going' and 'Where He's At' if he doesn't know where the fuck he's been?

NASH: Rebecca . . .

REBECCA: Now where might he learn all that, Phil? From his 'Background'? From his 'Family'? But how d'you learn when you despise, disown for eighteen months to play at mixing it with the aristocracy?

PHIL: What d'y'mean?

REBECCA: Have you met Sandy? – favourite sister? Missed the wedding.

Why? Oh, too tied up with polo games that couldn't be missed, and drinking port, and rubbing shoulders with the landed, loaded, idle pissed. My beloved family, in fact. Impressive. Oh, it had to be. Nash said it was impressive, and Nash spent nigh-on two years in a constant state of impressionism.

PHIL (*to* NASH): You never went?

NASH: What?

PHIL: To Sandy's wedding?

REBECCA: Oh, but you *did* send her a present — a book token — from *my* mother for *your* birthday. Of course, what a shame, little Sandy's practically illiterate, but what a way to learn, hey? What a thoughtful gesture.

NASH: Becky, I warn you . . .

REBECCA: Oh no, please don't. I really wouldn't advise it. Oh, warn me to keep quiet, perhaps? You mean about the weekends getting drunk on *my* money, getting dressed on *my* credit? Oh, but you would have loved him, Phil. You could dress him up so nicely, he looked so pretty — you could take him anywhere. Oh, and the advantage being, when he opened his mouth, he could actually talk sense, and people didn't blush into their napkins or quickly leave the room. Oh yes, Nash was impressive too. Nash knew how to impress.

NASH: That is unfair, Rebecca.

REBECCA: Is it? Oh well, I wouldn't care to doubt *you*. And of course (*To* PHIL:) You know all about this already, because — of course — our boy is nothing if not *honest* — and *open* — and *totally objective*. (*To* NASH:) Correct me if I'm wrong.

NASH: Why don't you just get out, Rebecca?

REBECCA: Oh, why be so cryptic? Why not be *really* frank? (*To* PHIL:) God, I do miss those delightful guessing games. *Now* what have I said?

— Is he annoyed? — did I go too far? — did I say 'WE'? — did I accidentally *touch* him? — Will I — for that matter — ever learn to cope with that long-standing, totally absorbing love-affair he's having with *himself*? (*To* NASH:) And how does *she* rate, then? (*Meaning* PHIL.) Come on, I'm interested now. What would you give her? Upper Second? First With Honours. Another Fail? Or will you need a second opinion?

NASH: What is the object of this exercise, Becky?

REBECCA: I'm impressed.

NASH: What?

REBECCA: I really thought we had no taste — but I see we've acquired some since Rebecca got the red card — and I'm impressed. So much, I think I'll do us all a favour. I think I'll weigh in and spoil our comfy cosy Wendy House, so when it comes round to setting up the next one, we might look after it a bit better — come down off our pedestal, stop playing silly fucking charades. (*He doesn't reply.*) Oh, what is it, Nash? What's her game, eh? What's Rebecca's problem? Well, at least Rebecca knows where she's 'Coming From' — and where she's 'Going To'. And she's not really all that ashamed of it. But Nash . . . oh dear, he took a wrong turn-off somewhere — and like all good men drivers, spends the next hundred miles blaming the innocent passenger, who thought she was just along for the ride — and never dreamed she'd have to step in and start navigating.

She goes to her case, gets out a pen and writes down a number.

Here . . .

She gives it to PHIL.

Give me a call when you get to London.

She kisses PHIL *and goes out.*
PHIL *watches her leave. She looks at*
NASH. *He can't bring himself to look*
at her. PHIL *picks up her case and*
walks to the door. At the threshold
she turns back. NASH *looks up at her.*
After a pause she puts down her
suitcase, comes back, goes over to him.

PHIL (*very softly*): Well?

NASH (*also softly*): Well what?

PHIL *stands and looks round the*
room.

PHIL: Nash . . . d'you ever go home an'
think, Christ, there but for the grace
of God?

NASH: Yeah, I do go home.

PHIL: An' what d'y'think?

NASH: There but for the grace of God?

She laughs.

PHIL (*suddenly*): It's tomorrow. The
replay. Tomorrow's Wembley. (*Pause.*)
I wanna go. I wanna be there . . .
an' there won't be any tickets.

NASH: Well, cheer up, Phil — next
year y'can queue up for them.

PHIL: Where?

NASH: London. You'll be living on
the doorstep.

PHIL: Will I?

NASH: Well *you* should know.

BETH *walks on.*

BETH: Should I?

NITA *walks on.*

NITA: Well?

ALICE *walks on.*

ALICE: What d'y'reckon?

NITA: I'd have to shut the shop. An'
tomorrow's dead busy.

ALICE: I might look a right dick, though.

BETH: They'd prob'ly laugh at us . . .

NITA: I don't know . . .

BETH (*as if just noticing her*): I know

what — too bloody grand now, that
one. Y'can't talk to her. Do her a
world of good gettin' back there on
the terraces. Trod an' pissed an' spat
on by yer ordinary man-in-the-street.
'Stead of this musical chairs in private
boxes — tilt the odd glass when they
stick one in the net . . .

ALICE: An' what'm I gonna wear?

BETH: An' *her*, y'know — if she weren't
so scared gettin' her feet wet, steppin'
out of line. Know what she needs? A
good scream. A good shoulder charge
down the steps an' let her fight her
way back up again.

PHIL (*dubiously*): Well . . . it's not the
end of the world . . .

BETH (*scornfully*): D'y'believe *that*?
She wants her head seen to.

NASH *picks up* PHIL's *suitcase.*

NASH: C'mon, then.

PHIL: Where to?

NASH: Time y'got you sorted out.

They walk off together. BETH, ALICE
and NITA *come into focus.*

BETH (*contemplating her engagement*
ring): Pretty? I wouldn't call him
pretty. I wouldn't say he's fit. But
he'll do.

NITA (*suddenly*): Well, I'm going. Why
shouldn't I? (*She goes off.*)

ALICE (*suddenly*): I'll go. Why don't
I? (*She goes off.*)

BETH: I will, then. Why not? (*She goes*
off.)

As BETH *goes off,* NASH *and* PHIL
come forward.
It is now Wednesday evening, eve
of the Cup Final replay. They stand
on Trafford Bridge, Salford, looking
down the Manchester Ship Canal.

PHIL: I'm back.

NASH *stands apart, watching her.*

I'm here. I can't believe it. Trafford
Bridge.

(*Looking over the bridge.*) Down the Ship Canal from Trafford Bridge to Pomona Docks. Not in any guide book. Not a beauty spot. But it's a sight. (*Listening.*) Quiet, innit? Like Southern Cemetery. Like Consett Steel Works. (*Pause.*) That day y'took us there — good day, that — good games — come to Consett, spot the worker. Starts yer thinking, 'Hey Phil, yer a dick — where y'been the last ten years?' Come over this bridge, thirty, forty Sat'days every season. See United . . . see Old Trafford . . . Seen Trafford Park? What happened? Where've y'gone?

Gets too familiar. Like an old acquaintance. Y'never ask them how it's goin' an' one day they drop dead. Round here's been dead for years — but what's it to you? — y'got used to the smell. An' anyway, Georgie Best might stick on in this afternoon . . . or Charlton break the net . . . or Pearson, Jordan Robson . . .

Tunnel vision. That's what it is. An' what's the best? — the one place left standing in the middle of a fuckin' desert — is a fuckin' football ground.

Pause.

Magic.

Hey, we're soft up here, y'know. They can do 'owt they like to us. No sense, no feeling . . . we're just a stack of numbers — add up, cross out, subtract, divide . . .

We *are* soft, though. We're fuckin' mental. Five to three, stood there, packed out, all eyes on the tunnel. An' it's daft — it's mad — but there we are, the silly gets, *hoping* . . . that something's gonna turn out f'r'us today. Believing . . . that we are gonna win it.

Have y'seen the state? Bombed out, boarded up, bleedin' great acres of devastation — an' in the middle of all that, fifty thousand stupid pillocks think we're gonna win.

Oh, me an' all. *I'm* round the twist. I stand here, an' it makes no grain of sense, but I've still got me fingers crossed. I can't give over.

Y'see, up here, we're all fuckin' mad, but we're not dead. Something's moving. Something's still awake. Yeah, an' we might get pissed on an' shot at an' hacked to the bone — but I'm arsed if I'm gonna stick me hands up, or sell out the firing squad. I'm fucked if I'll stand around at parties, sipping spritzers, an' goin' 'Oh, up there? — oh, I used to live there meself. Tragic really, but what can y'do? If yer right ar, offends thee, cut the bastard off — an' if yer left can't earn its keep, then slit the bastard's wrists.'

Well, not this knife. Not me.

(*To* NASH, *after a pause*:) Do something f'r'us?

NASH: What?

PHIL: Post us this letter on yer way back?

NASH: What is it?

PHIL: Me letter to *Cosmo*. (*Pause.*) Ta very much . . . but no ta.

NASH: Y'gonna join the Resistance, then?

PHIL: Well?

NASH: What?

PHIL: Did she do well? Did she choose the right box?

NASH: Pass Go and Collect Two Hundred?

PHIL (*pleased for his approval*): Hey, y'know this is? The song.

NASH: What song?

PHIL: Que sera sera. Yeah, y'know . . . '77 an' the Reds are off to Wembley? Oh, an' y'know us — Stretford End — what we like?

NASH: Bloody arrogant bastards.

PHIL: We *are,* yeah. Number One, no messing. An' then we come up with this song. An' it's like . . . suddenly we've gone soft. Here we are, saying . . . off we go, we're on our

way . . . we might get leathered, but we're goin' anyway.
Que sera sera. What will be, will be.
An' here's me now — an' *I* don't know what's down f'r'us. I could get murdered back here. Know what they do? Tip yer straight in. Send yer off to cover knife fights in Moss Side. 'Hey, d'y'mind lowering yer machete while we get a picture?' 'Scuse me, but d'you enjoy signing on?'. 'Tell me, what's it like to be a battered wife?' . . .
I know what — s'like givin' a schoolboy his first big game an' playing the poor sod against Graeme Souness.
Come on, then — where are yer? Gi's me shin-pads. Let's have yer, Dalglish. (*She aims a kick.*) One-nil. (*She does a goal salute.*)

NASH: Phil, I have to go . . .

PHIL: Do you? . . . (*Suddenly trying to be calm.*) Yeah, it's late . . . y'should.

NASH: Right . . . well . . .

PHIL: Nash . . . ?

Both at a loss for words, they suddenly catch hold and hug each other very tight. After a pause, NASH releases PHIL.

NASH: S'all yours. (*He starts to go.*)

PHIL: Is it?

NASH: I'll see yer, Kidder. (*He walks away. PHIL turns away and starts to cry.*) Hey, Phil . . . (*She turns round.*) Something for yer . . . (*He throws her an envelope.*)

PHIL: What is it? (*She picks it up. When she looks up, he's gone. She opens the envelope.*) It's me door key, y'soft get . . . y've left us me door key . . .

She looks towards his direction. As she does so she gradually becomes aware of a car horn, a screech of

brakes from the opposite direction, and on a car radio, the 1983 Manchester United Wembley Song playing:

Wem-ber-lee . . . Wem-ber-lee . . .
We're the famous Man. United and
    we're going to Wem-ber-lee . . .

Suddenly ALICE, NITA and BETH run on, in full United Regalia, waving scarves, singing:

Tell me ma, me ma
To put the champagne on ice
We're goin' to Wembley twice . . .

NITA *suddenly produces a ticket.*

PHIL (*grabbing the ticket*): Y'got me one! Y'got us a ticket!

BETH *puts a scarf round PHIL's neck.*

BETH: One-nil!

ALICE: Two-one!

NITA: Three-one!

PHIL: Four-nil!

ALICE: Four-nil?

PHIL: One each.

BETH *and* PHIL (*dancing round chanting*): Four-nil, four-nil, four-nil . . .

NITA: Hey, you two — what y'gonna be when y'grow up?

BETH (*suddenly breaking away, coming forward, sings*):
When I was just a little girl
I asked me mother, what will I be?
Will I be pretty, will I be rich?
Here's what she says to me . . .

PHIL, ALICE *and* NITA (*joining in*):
Que sera sera
Whatever will be, will be
We're goin' to Wem-ber-lee
Que sera sera . . .

Sounds of football crowd singing 'Que sera sera' as the lights fade.

Methuen's Modern Plays

Jean Anouilh	*Antigone*
	Becket
	The Lark
	Ring Round the Moon
John Arden	*Serjeant Musgrave's Dance*
	The Workhouse Donkey
	Armstrong's Last Goodnight
	Pearl
John Arden and	*The Royal Pardon*
Margaretta D'Arcy	*The Hero Rises Up*
	The Island of the Mighty
	Vandaleur's Folly
Wolfgang Bauer	*Shakespeare the Sadist*
Rainer Werner	
Fassbinder	*Bremen Coffee*
Peter Handke	*My Foot My Tutor*
Frank Xaver Kroetz	*Stallerhof*
Brendan Behan	*The Quare Fellow*
	The Hostage
	Richard's Cork Leg
Edward Bond	*A-A-America!* and *Stone*
	Saved
	Narrow Road to the Deep North
	The Pope's Wedding
	Lear
	The Sea
	Bingo
	The Fool and *We Come to the River*
	Theatre Poems and Songs
	The Bundle
	The Woman
	The Worlds with *The Activists Papers*
	Restoration and *The Cat*
	Summer and *Fables*

Barrie Keeffe	*Gimme Shelter (Gem, Gotcha, Getaway)*
	Barbarians (Killing Time, Abide With Me, In the City)
	A Mad World, My Masters
Arthur Kopit	*Indians*
	Wings
John McGrath	*The Cheviot, the Stag and the Black, Black Oil*
David Mamet	*Glengarry Glen Ross*
	American Buffalo
David Mercer	*After Haggerty*
	Cousin Vladimir and *Shooting the Chandelier*
	Duck Song
	The Monster of Karlovy Vary and *Then and Now*
	No Limits To Love
Arthur Miller	*The American Clock*
	The Archbishop's Ceiling
	Two-Way Mirror
	Danger! Memory!
Percy Mtwa, Mbongeni Ngema, Barney Simon	*Woza Albert*
Peter Nichols	*Passion Play*
	Poppy
Joe Orton	*Loot*
	What the Butler Saw
	Funeral Games and *The Good and Faithful Servant*
	Entertaining Mr Sloane
	Up Against It
Louise Page	*Golden Girls*
Harold Pinter	*The Birthday Party*
	The Room and *The Dumb Waiter*
	The Caretaker
	A Slight Ache and other plays
	The Collection and *The Lover*
	The Homecoming

	Tea Party and other plays
	Landscape and *Silence*
	Old Times
	No Man's Land
	Betrayal
	The Hothouse
	Other Places (A Kind of Alaska, Victoria Station, Family Voices)
Luigi Pirandello	*Henry IV*
	Six Characters in Search of an Author
Stephen Poliakoff	*Hitting Town* and *City Sugar*
	Breaking the Silence
David Rudkin	*The Sons of Light*
	The Triumph of Death
Jean-Paul Sartre	*Crime Passionnel*
Wole Soyinka	*Madmen and Specialists*
	The Jero Plays
	Death and the King's Horseman
	A Play of Giants
C.P. Taylor	*And a Nightingale Sang . . .*
	Good
Peter Whelan	*The Accrington Pals*
Nigel Williams	*Line 'Em*
	Class Enemy
Theatre Workshop	*Oh What a Lovely War!*
Various authors	*Best Radio Plays of 1978* (Don Haworth: *Episode on a Thursday Evening:* Tom Mallin: *Halt! Who Goes There?;* Jennifer Phillips: *Daughters of Men;* Fay Weldon: *Polaris;* Jill Hyem: *Remember Me;* Richard Harris: *Is It Something I Said?*)
	Best Radio Plays of 1979 (Shirley Gee: *Typhoid Mary;* Carey Harrison: *I Never Killed My German;* Barrie Keeffe: *Heaven Scent;* John Kirkmorris: *Coxcombe;* John Peacock: *Attard in Retirement;* Olwen Wymark: *The Child*)